WOMEN,
ANIMALS, &
VEGETABLES

WOMEN, ANIMALS,& VEGETABLES

ESSAYS & STORIES

MAXINE KUMIN

ONTARIO REVIEW PRESS

PRINCETON

Copyright © 1994 by Maxine Kumin
Reprinted by arrangement with W. W. Norton & Company, Inc.
All rights reserved
Printed in the United States of America
First Ontario Review Press printing 1996

The text of this book is composed in 12/14 Bodoni Book,
with the display set in Radiant Bold Condensed.
Composition by the Maple-Vail Book Manufacturing Group.
Printed by Princeton Academic Press.
Book design and ornaments by Margaret M. Wagner.
Cover design by RJ Smith.
Cover photo by Victor Kumin.

Library of Congress Cataloging-in-Publication Data
Kumin, Maxine, 1925–
Women, animals, & vegetables : essays & stories /
Maxine Kumin.
    p.   cm.
   Originally published: New York : W. W. Norton, 1994.
   1. Farm life—New Hampshire—Fiction.   2. Farm life—New
Hampshire.   3. Authorship.   I. Title.
[PS3521.U638W66   1996]
818'.5408—dc20   95-42216

ISBN 0-86538-084-8 (pbk.)

Ontario Review Press
Distributed by George Braziller, Inc.
60 Madison Ave., New York, NY 10010

FOR MY SISTER POETS AND HORSE AMBASSADORS

Alicia, Annie C., Carole, Carolyn, Eleanor, Enid, Jana, Keyo, Robin B., Ronnie, and Wendy

ACKNOWLEDGMENTS

Some of these essays and stories have appeared
in the following journals:

The American Voice: "Beginning with Gussie."

The Atlantic: "The Word," (in a slightly different version).

The Boston Book Review: "Children of Darkness."

The Colorado Review: "The Cassandra Effect."

Country Journal: "Long Road to an Upland Farm"; "Gone to the
Dogs"; "Enough Jam for a Lifetime."

Mademoiselle: "Solstice," first printed as "Creature Comforts."

Poets and Writers: "Have Saddle, Will Travel."

Sonora Review: "Mutts."

Tri-Quarterly: "Menial Labor and the Muse."

The Hudson Review: "Flotation Devices."

The Kenyon Review: "Bummers."

The Company of Animals, edited by Michael Rosen, Doubleday, 1993,
"Jack," first printed as "Jack: A Memoir."

The Ontario Review: "The Match."

The Southern California Anthology: "Hey Dude."

"Labors of Love" was originally published, in part, as "Praise Be" in *Equus* and as "Labor of Love" in *Countryside*.

"Jicama without Expectations" was originally published, in part, in *Prairie Schooner*. Other sections appeared as "The Volunteer" in *Organic Gardening* and as "Mulching with *The Times*" in *Country Journal*.

CONTENTS

CONTENTS   12

PART I

ESSAYS

THE WORD

We ride up softly to the hidden
oval in the woods, a plateau rimmed
with wavy stands of gray birch and white pine,
my horse thinking his thoughts, happy
in the October dapple, and I thinking
mine-and-his, which is my prerogative,

both of us just in time to see a big doe
loft up over the four-foot fence, her white scut
catching the sun and then releasing it,
soundlessly clapping our reveries shut.
The pine grove shivers as she passes.
The red squirrels thrill, announcing her departure.

Come back! I want to call to her,
we who mean you no harm. Come back and show us
who stand pinned in stopped time to the track
how you can go from a standing start
up and over. We on our side, pulses racing
are synchronized with your racing heart.

I want to tell her, Watch me
mornings when I fill the cylinders
with sunflower seeds, see how the chickadees
and lesser redbreasted nuthatches crowd
onto my arm, permitting me briefly
to stand in for a tree,

and how the vixen in the bottom meadow
I ride across allows me under cover
of horse scent to observe the education
of her kits, how they dive for the burrow
on command, how they re-emerge at another
word she uses, a word I am searching for.

Its sound is o-shaped and unencumbered,
the see-through color of river,
airy as the topmost evergreen fingers
and soft as pine duff underfoot
where the doe lies down out of sight;
take me in, tell me the word.

MENIAL LABOR
AND THE MUSE

An all-day rain of the mizzly seductive sort, compounded by snow fog; twilight began this day and will mediate it until fully dark.

Before settling in at my desk I've distributed an extra bale of hay to the horses, making a quick trip from house to barn in my slicker and muck boots. The whole main floor of the barn is packed, this time of year, with last August's second cutting, a mix of timothy and brome grass, mostly without the seed heads. The bales are still green, so sweet it makes me salivate as I inhale their aroma which cries *summer!* on the winter air. I have never understood why some entrepreneur has yet to capture the scent and market it as a perfume. Doesn't everyone melt, smelling new hay? I must have been a horse in the last incarnation or had a profound love affair in some sixteenth-century hayloft.

A perspicacious student once pointed out to me that it rains or snows in a large percentage of my poems. She's right, of course, though I hadn't ever thought of the connection.

Stormy days are my best writing days. The weather relieves me of my Jewish-Calvinist urgency to do something useful

with one or another of the young stock, to longe or drive or
ride the current two-, three-, or four-year-old. Or, in season, to cut around the perimeters of the pastures, work that's
known as brushing out. Or clean out and re-bed the run-in
sheds and the central area under the barn my friend Robin
calls the motel lobby. No need to bring the vegetable garden
into this, or the sugar bush of a hundred maple trees. We
probably won't be setting any taps this March. Acid rain and
the depredations of the pear thrip that followed have so
weakened the trees that they need a rest period.

This year's wood is in, all split and stacked. Next year's
is already on the ground, split in four-foot lengths to dry. It
snowed before we could get two truckloads of manure on the
garden, though. Victor says we'll have a thaw, that there is
still time. He's still puttying and caulking as we button up
for the hard months. *Still* is the wrong word, as there is no
beginning and no apparent end. Outside water faucets are
drained and closed off, heating element installed in the
watering trough, and so on.

Writing and well-being. In the most direct, overt, and
uncomplicated way, my writing depends on the well-being
that devolves from this abbreviated list of chores undertaken
and completed.

One set of self-imposed deadlines nurtures the other:
something harshly physical each day, the reward being a
bone-tired sense of equipoise at nightfall. A daily session at
the desk even when, as Rilke warned, nothing comes. I
must keep holy even disappointment, even desertion. The
leaven of the next day's chores will redeem the failed writing, infuse it with new energy or at the very least allow me
to shred it while I await the Rilkean birth-hour of a new
clarity.

The well-being of solitude is a necessary component of

this equation. A "Good! No visitors today" mentality isn't limited to snowstorms or Monday mornings. On the contrary, this feeling of contentment in isolation pervades every good working day. My writing time needs to surround itself with empty stretches, or at least unpeopled ones, for the writing takes place in an area of suspension as in a hanging nest that is almost entirely encapsulated. I think of the oriole's graceful construction.

This is why poems may frequently begin for me in the suspended cocoon of the airplane, or even in the airport lounge during those dreary hours of layovers. There's the same anonymity, the same empty but enclosed space, paradoxical in view of the thousands of other travelers pulsing past. But I have no responsibility here. I am un-called upon and can go inward.

My best ruminations take place in the barn while my hands (and back) are busy doing something else. Again, there's the haunting appeal of enclosure, the mindless suspension of doing simple, repetitive tasks—mucking out, refilling water buckets, raking sawdust—that allows those free-associative leaps out of which a poem may occasionally come. And if not, reasons the Calvinist, a clean barn is surely a sign of the attained state of grace. Thus I am saved. And if the Muse descends, my androgynous pagan Muse, I will have the best of both worlds.

LONG ROAD TO AN UPLAND FARM

In the end, I think it was pickles that propelled us out of suburban Boston into the Mink Hills of New Hampshire. From the spring of 1963, when we bought outright a derelict 200-acre farm in Warner, until the summer of 1976 when we, with trepidation, became year-round residents, I was in charge not only of the pickles, but also of the groceries and sundries.

Virtually every Friday evening of the year we made the same heavily laden trip north with three children, dog, laundry, odds and ends of furnishings to enhance the farmhouse we were gradually rehabilitating, and cartons of food to sustain us and the various houseguests who were also converging on the property. That first hasty meal was more often than not built around hamburgers done on the grill and served with a jar of bread-and-butter pickles. Invariably I confused the contents of the two kitchen cupboards. I remember one gloomy and cold Friday night when the woodstoves sulked and were slow to catch fire, mice had gotten into the dog kibble and buried little caches of it in the sofa, red squirrels had eaten their way through from the attic into the back bedroom, and I discovered that although we had neither ketchup nor mustard, four opened jars of pickles reposed in the refrigerator just as I unpacked—triumphantly!—yet another from the supermarket.

I have not bought a pickle since 1976, the first year of our full-time tenure. Annually, I put up about thirty jars of my own. Never again will I have to juggle staples and condiments for two households. Never again will the old dog— third now in a series—in a state of high anxiety lest he be left behind, have to position himself to be stumbled over by the front door until he is allotted his corner of the station wagon. And although our nest is now empty of children and their highly variegated friends, there are equine compensations filling the barn and composing, together with the sheep, a living landscape in the pastures.

We bought our abandoned dairy farm for the same reasons that motivate most vacation-home owners. Constrained by the exigencies of a five-day workweek, hemmed in by the increasingly regimented wants and needs of three children's music lessons, sports events, and competitive social lives, we longed for a hideaway. A safe place, a retreat: How soothing it sounded. Such places usually sport signs proclaiming Bide-a-wee, or Dun Rovin. The pipe-smoking squire is down by the pond fishing. His helpmeet is on her knees in the garden contentedly tending the roses.

Luckily that was not quite our fantasy, for we could never have attained it. When we decided to look for a place in the country we had drawn a circle on a map, enclosing an area not more than two hours' drive from our suburban home. Realtors sped in front of us down paved or dirt roads, hastening us past pockets of rural poverty to desolate old homesteads with sagging outbuildings (which we could afford), or drawing us up with a flourish before Federal manses with fifteen rooms, original beehive ovens, and in-ground swimming pools (which we could not).

I sensed their exasperation; did we know what we wanted? Not exactly. What we had in mind was a vague ideal. It was less manicured, more heavily forested. Accessible, but not within eyesight or shouting distance of neighbors. Rustic, but with white plumbing. Old, but serviceable. In retrospect I now see that we were waiting to be *magicked* by a place.

As our overburdened Ford wagon shuddered along the corduroy of a dirt road that wound its sinuous way uphill and ended unceremoniously on the slant between house and barn, I felt my neck hairs rise. The approach, almost half a mile above the bottom road, was difficult enough, mysterious enough under the canopy of old trees, remote enough. We were only two miles from town but attaining this hill conveyed the sense of having landed on an island. I was ensnared, ensorceled.

What captivated us was a 200-year-old, twin-chimney Colonial, listing to one side over rotted sills, shedding clapboards and roof shingles. There were no storm windows or insulation. Woodstoves provided the only heat. But electric power had been brought up the hill just after World War II. The shallow, spring-fed well was pure, and the plumbing, though patchy, functioned. The surrounding terrain was so heavily shrubbed and wooded that the net effect suggested the castle in *Sleeping Beauty*. There was no question of lawn. To see into the windows, we had to hack away sumac and blackberry.

For six years no one had lived in the house. No livestock had inhabited the barn or grazed in the pasture. The barn, which had once sheltered forty cows, was in deplorable shape. The entire back end wobbled like a loose tooth. Built into

the side of a steep hill, the first floor of the barn still wore
wood frames for stanchions, and there were rusted bits of
machine parts, chains, and rotted work harnesses lying about.
Looking down through a trap door, we could see that the
ground level had been used as a manure pile. Sky was visible through the haymow.

It is one of those delicious ironies after the fact that we
chose, purely on the basis of impulse and instinct, such a
down-at-the-heels property. We thought we were seeking
serenity and seclusion, a Yeatsian Innisfree "where peace
comes dropping slow." Victims of the romantic fervor to get
away from it all and find harmony in nature, we did not then
know that what we secretly longed for was thirty years of
hard labor.

How many other instances of love at first sight have worked
out this well? This was no cabin, to cite Yeats again, "of
clay and wattles made."

My husband, Victor, a practical engineer, consulted with colleagues. They came up for a Sunday picnic, stood in the
cellar and dug penknives into the available timbers. They
clomped through the attic, a fearsome structure, admiring
the heft and height of the rafters. They examined the barn
and clucked over the areas where fieldstone foundations had
subsided. The back end would have to be razed.

Meanwhile, the rest of us went exploring. The outlines of
two fields were still reasonably well defined. Stone walls ran
elsewhere through the woods suggesting where others had
been established. There was a marshy area above the house
where the land flattened. One of the visitors thought it would
make a dandy pond.

The Federal Soil Conservation Service thought so, too.

That first summer of 1963, happily for us an unusually dry one, they surveyed the site, dug test holes, and mapped the perimeters. Lumberjacks swiftly tore the trees from the site. A skilled bulldozer operator followed. In eight days he had dug our pond. That fall and early winter we watched it fill, weekend by weekend noting its progress. By the next summer it had reached the margins decreed for it.

The years have been kind to our two-thirds-of-an-acre pond, accepting it as a natural part of the terrain. Pine trees shade the sandy beach we installed, shovelful by shovelful. An immense granite outcrop provides a diving platform; Ray, the bulldozer operator, thoughtfully scooped out an extra-deep hole just in front of it. Herons swoop in to take tadpoles and frogs back to the rookery. Wild ducks use the pond as a resting place during spring and fall migrations. We hadn't planned on a pond, but it has become our centerpiece.

Innocence protected us from appreciating the enormity of the restoration we were about to undertake. We were young and eager and almost totally ignorant of country ways. We had never met a black fly, or sighted a black bear in its native habitat (our farthest pasture). Porcupines and woodchucks were exotics. Skunks and raccoons, although not unknown to us in the suburbs, were hardly commonplace. A city rat was verminous; now we lived with platoons of field mice in the walls of our house. The variety of bird life was astonishing. That first summer we watched fascinated from the living room as barn swallows and phoebes nested sloppily just outside the window under the porch stringers. We had front-row seats as they swooped in and out from dawn until full dark to fill those gaping little maws. Evening and rose-breasted grosbeaks, scarlet tanagers, Baltimore orioles, and dozens of hummingbirds populated our territory.

In suburban Boston we had tended peonies and zinnias. The children grew radishes. Mostly, we painted the picket fence, mowed the lawn, and fussed over its bare spots. Now we were faced with rampant growth: nettles and thistles, poison ivy as well as wake-robin trillium, dozens of different ferns, jack-in-the-pulpit and lady slippers in profusion. An acre of violets. Heavy-headed lilacs. Shagbark hickory, butternut, pine, hemlock, oak, birch. An entire maple sugar bush.

We bought books. Wildflower identification tomes, bird watchers' manuals, mushroom handbooks, a field guide to small mammals and their tracks. A home handyman's encyclopedia. A text on masonry repair. Ten easy steps to making your own maple syrup. Landscaping with timbers. Raised-bed gardening. Twelve vegetables for the home garden. How to jell, can, and freeze a thousand and one products. Animal husbandry; the family cow; from sheep to shawl; your very own chicken house. And finally, *horses*.

Just across the valley from us a family-style horse farm was setting up a summer program. Our middle child, already skilled with manure fork and wheelbarrow from her protracted visits with horse-owning friends, joyfully signed on that first season.

Thus mildly began a contagion that was to consume us with converting the ground level of our barn to six box stalls with concrete foundations, the first floor to hay and equipment storage, and, slowly, hummock by hummock, swale by swale, fourteen of our craggy acres of gravelly glacial till to limed and tended and fenced grazing land.

From our friends across the valley we leased two riding horses each summer. Next, because they annually had a

crop of Welsh pony foals and Arab crosses, we took on two
newly weaned foals. Ultimately, we bought a horse. After
that, we saved a needy one. Once we were year-rounders,
still another cried out for a decent home. Before we knew
it, our how-to books embraced every aspect of equine man-
agement. We began to breed and raise our own young stock
for distance riding, a new sport.

Those first twelve years we managed to keep the level of
horse involvement down to something workable. We kept
our horses on the property summers and boarded them out
on free lease arrangements from Labor Day to June first. But
achieving a balance between city and country was a constant
acrobatic act.

Weekends that we stayed in Greater Boston felt like lost
weekends to me; I took to driving up midweek to counter my
frustration. In May I needed to stay longer in order to get
the garden planted. In September I had to put up jams and
jellies—and pickles. I had to make applesauce from our
own apples. I needed to shell out the horticultural beans
that had climbed and dried among the corn stalks. The farm
was a magnet; it held me fast.

Gradually the farm became the focus of our teenage
daughters' and son's social life. Their friends came by the
carload for the rustic delights of digging post holes, nailing
shingles, scraping old paint, and taking long walks in the
woods, ostensibly in search of wild mushrooms, old cellar
holes, or undiscovered logging roads that had gone back to
second-growth forest. Our area of New Hampshire had been
more densely populated in the 1830s and '40s, before the
good agricultural land of the Middle West was made accessible and a mass migration ensued. The almost forgotten
graveyards along overgrown trails had a special allure for
this new generation. They studied the stones and took rub-

bings, speculating on the events and epidemics of the late eighteenth century, discussing the poetry and pathos of the epitaphs. Without quite meaning to, we had become curators of an exotic and precious past.

In fact, most of what happened to us was serendipitous. My father was fond of quoting the old maxim, "Experience is a dear school, but a fool will learn in no other." If we were not foolish, we were at least ignorant. We learned about fencing by doing it. Our vegetable garden annually improved as we grew in wisdom (and horse manure). The wood we cut, split, and dried for our two woodstoves taught us patience with the process and skill with the tools. We learned to love the changing seasons with the abiding love of those who coexist in harmony with natural phenomena, and to admire the wisdom of the old settlers, who snugged our farmhouse halfway up the hill, out of the prevailing sweep of the north wind in winter.

But until 1976 we were mere dilettantes, choosing to go to the country when the weather suited us, choosing to burrow under the covers in a centrally heated suburban house when it did not. Once the last child had left home there were no compelling reasons to stay in suburbia. We screwed up our courage, rented our house, and moved to New Hampshire—on a trial basis, we told everyone. Victor continued to work as a consulting engineer, commuting to Boston twice a week to oversee his projects. As a writer, I had no allegiance to one place.

Rather, my allegiance was to the natural world, to "life near the bone," as Thoreau described it. Our trial year was hugely successful from my point of view. So much around me was new, full of small dramas to be observed, that I hardly ever looked back. And because I had always traveled to distant universities to give poetry readings and conduct workshops, I was able to schedule my days away from Pobiz Farm so that these did not conflict with my husband's trips to the city. Indeed, as we added animals, this kind of dovetailing became essential.

A year later we sold the suburban house and sealed the bargain.

The ensuing years have sped past. Increasingly, the poetry business pays the horse bills; horses continue to invade the poetry. We have stuffed the barn with critters, greatly enlarged the vegetable gardens, intensified the endless rounds of maintenance and improvement projects. We built a second barn to store the horse trailer, aggie truck, and additional hay. We built a lumber shed to house the leftovers, and a sheep and goat shelter for you know what. We added pasture, cleared bridle paths, logged 2000 miles in competitive distance rides, insulated walls, refinished floors and wainscotings, installed a dishwasher, freezer, clothes washer and dryer, created a greenhouse from the front porch and guest quarters from the old generator house, stacked twelve cords of wood per annum, and discovered the benevolent tyranny of what we had wrought.

I can't say that Victor has never looked back. He is given to periodic cravings for subways, skyscrapers, live theater, and political involvement beyond the local level. Although he has served faithfully on the executive boards of several voluntary agencies here in rural New Hampshire, he still misses the tumult of the city. He misses the ocean, and sailing, and from time to time he makes forays to gratify his longings. Does he miss the traffic, rescue wagons bleating to get through the snarl, helicopters scouting the expressways? Possibly.

As for me, it is a family joke that it is hard to get me past the mailbox unless on horseback. I am a transplant whose new roots go deep.

On the whole, despite some persisting ambivalence about our now total commitment to rural life, I would say that it has provided some unexpected bonuses. We came away from the city at a time of our lives when many of our contemporaries, their children flown, were undergoing great changes. This restlessness never afflicted our relationship; there wasn't time for it to overtake us. The exigencies of barn and garden, house and horses crowded in. We learned almost from the outset to work as a team, building and mending fences, mowing and mucking out, stacking wood, setting maple taps, and keeping a close eye on broodmares in the late stages of their pregnancies. I think our personal bond has tightened, for we are necessarily interdependent.

Living this way has made us both highly respectful of the land. We are custodians of 200 acres which shelter deer and bear, wild turkeys, coyotes and foxes, and hundreds of smaller creatures. Except for the porcupine population which annually bests our dogs, we wish to protect our co-inhabitants. With the increasing pressures on land that developers now exert, we feel more strongly than ever that we must join with others to save our open spaces.

On the downside, it's true that we almost never go to the theater, or dine out in gourmet restaurants. We don't attend the symphony, or tour museums and art galleries except on infrequent vacations. But we don't have to drive a hundred miles to view the fall foliage. We don't have to hunt for a farm stand when corn and tomatoes are ripe. We have enough maple syrup to pour recklessly over waffles and fritters.

This past summer we taught a visiting grandchild to dive off the rock into the pond, post on the correct diagonal, walk softly among the sheep, pick peas and pull carrots, and identify a dozen different birds on the feeders. We are infected with his enthusiasm for each new skill and we are comforted to think of the legacy we are handing on to him. My fondest hope is that our little dynasty here on the hill will go on.

A HORSE FOR FUN

The first summer that our restored barn was horse-habitable, we leased two placid schoolies from an equestrian facility across town. That early baptism provided a wonderful way to try the perils and pleasures of horse ownership. Coached by the stable managers, our once-a-week riding instructor, knowledgeable horse friends, and an armload of how-to books, we embarked on a new life in which horses gradually achieved year-round prominence.

Now we are horse ambassadors ourselves, helping new owners here and there, making suggestions, lending equipment, and from time to time biting our tongues not to criticize what we see as lapses in care. Over the years we have raised several foals, broken them first to harness, then to saddle, and seen some of these youngsters go on to careers in combined training, which involves dressage, cross-country, and stadium jumping. Others are now doing combined driving events. All of them pleasure-ride as well.

Early on in our horsekeeping, we learned that having a horse for fun means arranging to have a happy horse. The first step in this direction is to limit or eliminate confinement. A free-choice arrangement, where horses may roam a good-sized paddock or field and take refuge in a loafing shed or open barn at will, is the most desirable facility. All the luxuries of mahogany stalls, automatic waterers, knee-deep bedding, and piped-in music do not compensate, in our opinion, for lost freedom.

In his natural state the horse is a range animal. If he cannot roam a reasonable territory, he may express his frustration by developing some unpleasant or even health-threatening habits. Chewing on fences or stall boards may be followed by cribbing and wind-sucking, vices in which the horse bites down on a hard surface and swallows air at the same time, to the accompaniment of little grunts. (Some will argue that cribbing is a genetically acquired habit, but it is rarely seen in a horse at liberty.)

Further, a continually stabled horse may become a weaver, swaying from side to side in a restless, compulsive pattern. To me, this is as sad a scenario as watching a caged tiger pace back and forth behind bars. Cribbers and weavers, for obvious reasons, frequently develop digestive problems. The message is clear, then: as much turnout for as many hours as possible.

Good fences go along with this package of measured freedom. Our visible acres are fenced with rough-cut two-by-sixes nailed to pressure-treated wooden posts. The Herculean labor of digging post holes, carting lumber board by heavy board, and tweezing out splinters incurred in the process can never be forgotten, but the result is, modestly, splendid.

Our less visible, distant fields are fenced with single-strand wire, casually electrified when we plug in the charger a few days in the spring and again in mid-fall as a reminder. These fields back onto forest. The horses are not sorely tempted to commit bustication through thickets of blackberry bramble.

Besides, they are already in paradise—no reason to leave it. And because we live in isolation at the end of a dirt road, we don't have the agonizing worry of so many horse owners that if their horses break out they'll gallop down a busy street.

Where boundaries are less casual, temporary, portable, easily installed electric fencing utilizing fiberglass poles and electrified tape is now readily available. It's an easy way to move horses from one grazing area to another, or to separate groups of horses from each other, and it is, relatively speaking, inexpensive. A horse who will not respect a single strand of charged wire with bright ribbons dangling from it may surprise you by being very much in awe of the new, woven electrified tape, especially if it is presented in two strands. Somehow the added thickness and parallel lines must look to him like serious stuff.

Many other options, from rustic split rails to permanent vinyl, present themselves. One caveat: Barbed wire is terribly dangerous and to be avoided at all costs. Barbed wire punctures, rips, and shreds horseflesh impaled on it. We have spent years, it seems, removing rusty strands from unexpected places around the farm.

If you must confine your horse to a stall most of the time, as in a boarding establishment with limited turnout, you have an obligation to provide regular exercise. A stabled horse who does not get ridden or driven at least an hour a day or exercised on a longe line for twenty or thirty minutes will express his boredom, depression, or rage by attempting to demolish his surroundings. Without regular exercise, the stabled horse loses muscle and soon he no longer presents the elegant picture you started with.

The second step to a happy horse is to provide companionship. In the wild a horse is a herd creature. His mental health depends on having at least one other horse in his immediate vicinity. There are occasional exceptions to this dictum. The solitary horse can survive his isolation with some other companion—a goat, a donkey, even a pet rooster or cat—but many horse owners adopt an elderly pony as a companion. The supply of these is seemingly unlimited; the security Little Old Tanglefoot imparts is well worth the small additional cost to feed him.

Here and there in the equine population a loner will display indifference or even antipathy to others of his kind. The lone horse—especially one who has suffered at the bottom of the pecking order in a large group—may welcome solitude and develop a deep and abiding bond to his owner. While this is a plus, it also increases the owner's responsibility for his animal's well-being.

Step number three: Provide the right kinds of food and ample water. The horse is a grazing creature with a surprisingly small stomach for his size. Through it must pass a fairly constant stream of victuals. Hay, in amounts commensurate with his height, weight, and level of activity, is his major food source from autumn frost until the grass regrows in late spring.

Here in New Hampshire, we favor second-cut timothy and native grasses over alfalfa, which is higher in protein but can turn dusty by February. Alfalfa, in our experience, doesn't cure as well as timothy or orchard grass in our climate and it is too rich to feed in quantity, sometimes inviting colic. In drier areas of the country, alfalfa comprises the chief hay crop and is much prized for its high protein content.

Small amounts of grain fill out our horses' rations, a standard sweet feed mix available from the local feed and grain store. We buy it by the 100-pound bag and house it in a defunct chest freezer in a small, separate stall. Not only

does the freezer lock with a metal chain, but the stall door
has a double latch, and woe to anyone who fails to fasten it.
The quantity is adjusted according to work load. It is no
kindness to overfeed a horse. First, his ribs will disappear
under a layer of fatty tissue. Then he will develop a crest of
fat along his neck and more fatty swellings will make their
appearance over his croup. He will grow lethargic from obe-
sity.

On the other hand, if he is not getting enough groceries,
you will eventually see the stark outline of all his ribs. His
hip bones will jut out. In extreme malnutrition, almost the
entire skeletal framework of the poor starveling becomes
visible. You might think this underweight condition would
be obvious, even to the neophyte. But well-meaning people
with no prior experience do not always see the obvious. It
takes horse-sense, which comes with experience.

The advice and counsel of longtime horse owners and
professionals can be enormously helpful. Horse books and
horse magazines are also great educational tools. Little by
little, your eye becomes trained to weigh and measure your
horse from day to day. You begin to pick up more subtle
clues to his state of mind and body from the way he carries
himself, the way he rolls after you take his saddle off, the
corner he chooses to stand in when the sun is high, and so
on. Horses are creatures of habit; any observable break in
his pattern of behavior can alert you to a possible problem.
And every grooming session with curry and brush, hoofpick
and finishing cloth is an opportunity to learn to read your
horse's body language.

Bear in mind that roughage—grasses and weeds, twigs
and stems—is essential to the equine's digestive tract. If
you observe a horse at liberty in a pasture, you'll see that

he'll spend some time munching tender shoots, then move on to coarser material, including some scrappy-looking emerging saplings. His body knows what he needs.

If he doesn't have access to fiber *au naturel* he will acquire it by cribbing on fence boards, stall doors, and other woody items within reach. We've overcome this problem by providing our horses with stove-length chunks of poplar trees all winter long. They merrily de-bark these logs from first snowfall until the early green shoots of grass appear, whereupon their interest wanes. Old-timers routinely used to offer poplar in winter to their horses. It was thought to have de-worming (anthelmintic) properties.

Need we add that water is required to move roughage through the intestinal tract? Lots of water, up to fifteen gallons per horse per day, in fact. Easy enough in summer, far more of a chore in winter. Expecting Dobbin to compensate by eating snow is a big mistake. A horse cannot meet his liquid needs slurping up snow, and he may just risk hypothermia if he is driven by thirst to do so.

Frozen water buckets become a real test of faith for the horse lover. Dehydration colic, according to our vet, is the commonest winter complaint she sees. We've devised a way to keep a submersible heating unit (for sale in the aforementioned feed and grain exchange) in the trough just inside the open doors of the barn. The wire runs up through an aluminum downspout (away from inquisitive young noses) and is plugged into a grounded fixture over the doorway. Here, several horses can safely congregate out of the wind or sleet and enjoy 45-degree water at any time.

More often, though, they choose to stand out in the fiercest elements, looking woebegone and icicle-ridden, snow frosting their rumps. It takes some doing not to project our own shivering viewpoint upon them. But horses are really arctic-proof if they are permitted to grow out their winter coats untrammeled by clippers or blankets. It's a good idea to have a winter blanket on the premises in case of illness, but we've only seen one or two episodes of shivering in all the years we've been horsekeeping. And our expensive New Zealand rugs, purchased when we were still anxious beginners, remain folded away in the tack trunk.

A place to stand out of the wind is essential (in New Hampshire, a three-sided shelter is the law from November 1 to April 1). Some sort of bedding underfoot, shavings or sawdust, pine needles, shredded paper, straw or peanut hulls, is a reasonable amenity. Given these options, a horse will select his own comfort zone and come through the worst blizzard a happy camper.

Mucking out—the removal of manure and wet bedding from stalls, run-in sheds, and pastures—is best accomplished with a manure fork and a muck basket, which you drag behind you on a stout rope attached to one handle. Both items are available at the local feed store. A wheelbarrow is useful if your terrain is flat enough to make its use practicable and your manure pile is accessible. Hint: a small, deep heap will turn into compost faster if you keep it covered and cooking with added vegetarian leavings from kitchen, lawn, and garden. And the more assiduously you muck out stalls and paddocks, the smaller your resident fly population will be.

Access to a three-sided shelter, water at all times, minimal grain, adequate hay and roughage—ready, get set, go? Not quite. There is the farrier to consider. There is vet care. The first of these two items may be a minor expense if your family pleasure horse has strong, tough feet and is mostly ridden on grassy trails. Lots of Morgans, for instance, never wear shoes, nor do Icelandic ponies. Even without shoes, your horse will need regular trimming to ensure that his hooves are at the proper angle. Some horses may need shoes only in front (60 to 70 percent of the concussive force at the trot is absorbed by the front feet). But if you take up distance riding or three-phase eventing with its demanding cross-country and stadium jumps, your mount will need shoes throughout the season. On stony trails he may need pads as well. The farrier will pay regular visits, six to eight weeks apart.

A good farrier is worth cultivating. She can watch the way your horse travels and by judicious shoeing help to correct certain problems. Our best driving horse, for instance, has such a long stride that he sometimes overreaches, catching the heel of a front foot with the toe of a hind. With trailers on his hind shoes—little metal extensions that ever so slightly retard the moment the hind foot steps into the front print—he no longer injures himself. To a significant degree, your farrier establishes a bond with your horse, too. Because she sees him on a regular basis she may pick up some change in the way Dobbin is traveling before you become aware of it.

With luck, you may see your vet only once a year, in the spring, when it is time for the annual immunizations against encephalitis and rhinopneumonitis. (In some parts of the country, annual boosters against rabies and Potomac horse fever are also recommended.) Everybody gets a tetanus shot at this time, too. Horses who travel out of state or to rated shows and events will need Coggins tests to certify they are free of equine infectious anemia. These horses may also benefit from flu shots renewed in the fall as well.

Learning how to give injections is a practical necessity if you're going to have horses of your own. Somewhere down the road a course of penicillin may await one of your precious charges who has developed a deep abcess or a respiratory infection; you can't afford to have the vet travel to your barn every day for eight days to provide this service. Most vets are happy to teach the owner how to proceed. A good way to perfect your technique with the hypodermic is to practice injecting an orange. Its skin and the equine epidermis have fairly similar densities.

The vet will also lay out an appropriate worming schedule to follow. Not so many years ago, before the discovery of ivermectin, worming involved not only rotating several different classes of wormers but also the sometimes quite traumatic semi-annual process of tube-worming. Each horse had a plastic tube threaded through one nostril, down the esophagus. Medication was then pumped through the tubing into the stomach. A resistant horse was in for quite a struggle and frequently incurred a massive nosebleed in the process.

Nowadays, horse people worm their charges every eight to ten weeks with a paste that is easily squirted directly onto the animal's tongue. It's important to stay on schedule and not stint on regular wormings, probably more important than feeding on a regular schedule. A horse can survive a missed or delayed feeding, but there is nothing sadder than colic caused by parasite infestation. If the intestinal wall has been thinned by repeated and prolonged infestation, it may rupture, dooming the animal to a painful death.

Worming syringes have other uses. We always keep a used worming syringe clean and ready in case we have to medicate with aspirin or "bute" (phenylbutazone), a nonsteroidal anti-inflammatory drug that is commonly prescribed for swellings. The crushed pill or pills can be mixed with a little applesauce, spooned into the syringe, and delivered onto the ailing equine's tongue. In fact, we squirt unadulterated applesauce into our weanlings' mouths so they won't have a prejudice against the practice.

A run-in shed, a companion, hay and grain, fresh water, a farrier and a vet, appropriate wormings—ready, get set; time to find the right horse. If you're a first-time horse owner, our advice is to take your time.

Try not to fall in love with something unsuitable—a gorgeous, green-broke three-year-old, for instance. Look at lots of horses for sale and ask the seller to show you what the horse looks like under saddle before you climb on board. We think it takes about seven or eight years for a horse to settle down and take his line of work seriously, but maybe ours are slower to grow up than other people's horses. A young horse can be a wonderful investment for a knowledgeable rider, but it takes time, patience, and understanding to bring along a youngster.

Don't buy a Thoroughbred off the track even though he is only four or five years old and looks absolutely spectacular. The price may be right, but you will incur heavy expenses around the next bend when ligaments, tendons, stifle joints, and pasterns begin to show the wear and tear racing inflicts.

Rarely is a racing Thoroughbred a wise choice for a family horse, even if he's sound as a dollar. Inbreeding and breeding for speed have made him a restive, often edgy critter. His digestion may also be delicate from his almost constant confinement. Track horses rarely are given the opportunity to graze; some actually have to relearn a taste for grass. Never having had the experience of being turned out with other horses, a former racehorse may create a full-scale ruckus when you put him out with gentle Dobbin.

Appaloosas, Quarterhorses, and Morgans are breeds with a well-earned reputation for graciousness. Tennessee Walkers, with their four-beat "amble" in place of the standard trot, also have their enthusiasts. While there are always exceptions within the breed, in these categories you are more likely to find a calm, intelligent equine who will be fun to ride and fun to care for than in the Thoroughbred line.

These horses are usually in the 15-hand class, a solid, medium size for mounting and dismounting as well as going down the trail. (The hand is an ancient measure of four inches. A horse's height is determined at the withers, the high point of its back at the base of the neck.) Thoroughbreds and the increasingly popular warmbloods from Europe—Hanoverians, Trakehners, Holsteiners, and so on—may be considerably taller, ranging up to 17+ hands, which is farther to clamber onto and fall down from.

A "gift horse" may be worth exactly what you paid for him. Once your vet looks in his mouth, she can give you a good estimate of the animal's age from the condition of his teeth. (Of course, if he comes with registration papers, you will already know his age and breeding.) After she listens to his heart, lungs, and gut sounds, flexes his knees and hocks, runs practiced hands and eyes over every inch of his body, she can evaluate his general state of health. When she sees him trot away from and toward her, trot in a circle or figure eight, she can determine whether he paddles, is pigeon-toed, or has a perfectly sound way of going.

It is absolutely essential to have a prospective horse checked out by a veterinarian of your own choosing. Don't buy anything without a vet check. While it may not be necessary to x-ray the legs of an unraced, sound horse of ten or twelve, you may save yourself a lot of grief paying for x-rays if there is any suspicion of navicular disease or ringbone, common arthritis-like ailments that lead ultimately to lameness.

In the category of generic horse, sire and dam unknown, you may find your best buy. We once acquired a generic horse. The size of his feet and the "feathers" (long hairs) on his fetlocks pointed toward some ancestral carthorse blood. His head was big and Roman-nosed and it seemed that nobody wanted him. The vet pronounced him sound, healthy, and probably nine years old. This homely gelding became the king of our farm, a benevolent despotic babysitter who ruled over our young horses for many years.

Although Arabians constitute perhaps the best-known and most beautiful bloodline, they may not always be the best breed for first-time owners. Something with a little Arabian blood mixed in, however, may be a rewarding prospect, adding elegance but not too much bounce. The marks of Arabian blood are usually quite apparent in the high tail-set, swan's neck, and small, refined head.

Word of mouth in your own neighborhood is a reasonable way to find out about a prospective horse. Ads on the bulletin board of your local tack shop may turn up a good prospect, too. A nearby horse farm or livery stable with horses for hire may want to retire a school horse. For a first horse you can't beat an experienced schoolie. The change in his lifestyle will put a sparkle in his eye and take the plod out of his gait as well.

What you pay for your first horse will help to determine what kind of horse you acquire. The initial outlay can run from $700 or $800 for the generic horse of no special training on up to $10,000 or $20,000 for a registered animal trained to second-level dressage or confident over four-foot fences. Conditions of pasturage, hay prices, and farrier and vet bills vary so widely from place to place that we hesitate to put down even a round number for additional annual expenses. We've read lots of articles that claim you can keep a happy horse for $1000 a year, but here in the Northeast at least, we doubt it.

On the other hand, when you calculate all the other ways money leaks out of the family exchequer without garnering rich rewards, the healthy habit of horses in the family may almost balance the books. When we go out with windfall apples to catch our critters and they come bucketing in from the far pasture, glistening with good health and high spirits, we know we've caught the right magnificent obsession.

HAVE SADDLE, WILL TRAVEL

The poetry business is a curious occupation. You cannot make even a modest living writing poems, but you can keep body and soul together nicely by reading them out loud to people. Over the last thirty years I've flown from Boston or from Manchester, New Hampshire, to every contiguous state in the Union except Oklahoma and Wyoming to give readings and conduct workshops. Lately, po-biz has begun to seem onerous, requiring a higher level of mobilization of my resources than I feel up to. My notion is to lighten these trips away from the farm by "horsing around" whenever I get the chance.

At five this morning, in almost total darkness, I separated the mare and foal into two stalls for their hay and grain, then tossed extra hay to the others in the upper pasture for my husband to bring in after he had made the airport run with me. We have an hour's drive to Manchester. Once it was a little rural airstrip with propeller flights to Boston; now it is served by three major carriers and crammed at 6:45 A.M. with people as intent on going places as I am.

In Pittsburgh the airport corridors look like central Manhattan at the noon hour. The volume of traffic moving through this airport is overwhelming. Commuter flights are relegated to a lower-level holding pen. Testy announcements admonish everyone to pay attention. If you are not ready when your flight is called—if you're in the bathroom or on the telephone—you have missed your flight. No second chances. I practice deep breathing in the midst of this controlled bedlam and try to stay alert for the sound of Lynchburg on the PA system.

At least half the expendable energy of po-biz is taken up with this kind of rackety travel. I am clutching a sheaf of tickets, my toilet articles, and my books, having trepidatiously checked all else. I used to travel light enough so that I could tote all my possessions on board (and shoulder them through airports on the long hike from Gate 1 to 99). But once I added a saddle to my necessary equipment I decided to entrust my suitcase to baggage handlers.

My lightweight synthetic saddle, foam over fiberglass, adapts to the narrow and broad-of-beam equine without difficulty. It is seemingly indestructible. Ads show a truck driving over one side of it. And an old friend, a poet from Salt Lake City, gave me her saddle carrying case into which I can fit not only the saddle and girth but also my schooling helmet and boots. These last in turn are stuffed with two pairs of socks, rolled-up breeches, and a T-shirt.

It's October. Lynchburg, Virginia, is golden with autumn haze. The Sweet Briar official greeter waves to me. The saddle has also arrived safely.

"What kind of musical instrument is that?" a gentleman asks as I reach down to grasp the strap.

"Tuba," I tell him. He nods, then walks off looking thoughtful.

Although visitors to the stables at Sweet Briar are not generally welcome except as observers, the rules have been gently abrogated in my favor. At 2 P.M. I am signed over to a trusted student, one of the college's top equestrians.

For a while we stand in the outdoor ring and watch an intermediate class learning how to execute turns on the fore-hand. The students are impressive, riding with relaxed agility and near-perfect form. Most of these horses were tax-deductible gifts to the riding program. Some came off the racetrack, others were hunt-club mounts. A few students have brought their own horses to Sweet Briar, but it's a heavy added expense.

Immense, well-lighted, immaculate, the indoor facility creates for horse lovers an ambience that could be compared to that of the Four Seasons or Lutèce for gourmets. The barn makes me think of the old Bonwit Teller store, gracious and elegant purveyor of women's apparel, giving off a quiet aura of fame and propriety. The horses are stabled in large, airy stalls, bedded on crushed peanut shells, which the staff assures me are both absorbent and edible. Stall doors are customized mesh so as not to impede air flow. Saddle pads are laundered on a daily basis. Tack is cleaned almost immediately by its user in a washroom appointed with doz-ens of glycerine soap bars and sponges, towels and polish and neat's-foot oil. Outside, two wash areas for the horses have hot and cold water, hoses, buckets, sweat scrapers. In short, except for a lack of open space for horses to be at leisure in, paradise.

My guide and I set out for a lazy cross-country hack, over rolling terrain where Holstein cows from the college dairy graze. The fields are divided by counterweighted gates you can tug from horseback so as not to have to dismount to open and close them. The succession of pastures is also accessible via chicken-coop jumps, but students are not allowed to leap over these except under supervision. I am somewhat relieved. My jumping skills are rusty and those of the rotund Appaloosa under me unknown. His trot is longer-strided than I expected from my ground-level view of him, and this is pleasing. His canter is rollicking and rideable. His attitude—school horses all too seldom get out of the ring—is that of an enthralled tourist. Except for his breadth (he weighs 1400 pounds) I am enjoying the trip.

By nightfall my hip joints ache. It is the familiar ache of encroaching arthritis, clamorous enough to merit two rounds of ibuprofen. Usually I try to avoid such sprung-ribbed horses, but when you are a guest you take what you get. It is humbling to be mounted on something so broad and massive and to strive, for the sake of my reputation, to maintain a balanced seat thereupon. But it is good for poets to undertake prose from time to time, and it is good for the rider to adapt to a different way of going.

Transient humans at Sweet Briar are housed in capacious, attractive motel rooms on campus. The sliding glass door of mine leads onto a patio. Beyond are mixed oak and tupelo woods, sunlight streaming through the now-depleted branches and lending a glimpse, this late afternoon, of two deer. They are smaller than the New England deer in my home woods, but they provide the accidental-tourist touch that enhances my sense of comfort.

In this calm twilight before the dinner before the reading, I am able to stretch out and catch forty winks. In the background, persistent cicadas strum. They are certain to go down tonight in the predicted hard frost.

The ability to nap before a reading has only come to me

in the last five years or so. My anxiety quotient seems to have receded gradually. I still welcome a serious drink or two, or at least a carafe of wine at dinner—for it is the rare reading that is not preceded by dinner with several faculty members, and / or students—but the Old Devil Panic has been superseded by nothing more than nervous tension.

Sometimes I wonder if that old terror of podium and microphone hasn't been subsumed by the total jitters I feel at the start of every competitive trail ride. Trying to stay in possession of myself and an overeager horse while waiting for my number to be called is harrowing. The first five miles of the ride are just like the first poem.

Every poetry audience is different. Some are formal and ominously silent. Others laugh easily, carry your books, and follow your poems as you read them. There is no way to predict how it will be. You take a deep breath and begin . . . in a matter of minutes, you know. In the first five miles your horse comes to terms with the fact that he is surrounded by other horses; he settles down. Or doesn't.

This evening's reading goes well. Everyone connected with the program seems pleased by the size of the audience and the enthusiasm of students who linger for the reception. Many of them have studied some of my poems in class, which always defuses the tension associated with having to sit still for the distant poet, isolated on stage. There are books for sale and lots of people want theirs signed.

Next morning, after breakfast, the quick run to the airport. I hate to leave this landscape of rolling hills and pale autumn foliage. I fly, wrong way, it seems, south to Charlotte, then north to Newark, once again entrusting my luggage to the airlines.

•

A young woman from the College of St. Elizabeth meets me, recognizing me easily, she claims, from the publicity photo. It is always a relief to be plucked out of anonymity by the unknown person delegated to meet your plane. We proceed to the baggage-claim area, where my saddle, still snug in its vinyl case, rides up the conveyor belt almost immediately.

A long and anxious wait for my other bag ensues. The conveyor belt finishes its task and is shut down. Just as I am about to seek someone official, an attendant rushes up to me.

"This yours?"

The look on my face is his answer.

"It didn't get off-loaded with the rest. Got stuck behind the cargo door; I just found it."

I thank him profusely. I've lost bags in Gainesville, Austin, and Miami that I can remember. Selective amnesia is shielding me from other occasions; I'm grateful this is not to be a rerun.

There are no horses associated with this small women's college in New Jersey. For exercise, though, I get an hour's walk on a gravel strip designated as a bike path along the New Jersey rail line. A mockingbird greets and follows me for a bit. Several trains clatter past, both express and locals. I feel dizzy; I am nowhere. In *A Bend in the River*, V. S. Naipaul says, "The airplane is a wonderful thing. You are still in one place when you arrive at the other. The airplane is faster than the heart."

A glass of wine and a sandwich before the reading, which takes place at 7 P.M. to accommodate commuting students and the many continuing-ed students, older women, who

attend college on a variety of schedules, nights and weekends.

The room is jammed with enthusiasts, filled to overflowing. The nuns seem a little startled by the turnout. My companion, who made the arrangements, was responsible for the
publicity and she is of course delighted too. Alas, she has
failed to arrange for books to be sold, always a downer for
the traveling poet. But the evening ends early and I have a
quiet night, broken every hour or so by the invasion of trains
crossing the foot of my bed. Next morning my friend is
punctual and drives me back to Newark Airport in good time
for my early flight west.

A long day's travel to El Paso, with a change in Dallas. I
have again checked saddle and suitcase through to my des-
tination. The connection is smooth and my El Paso host
meets me at the gate. We drive to her charming little house
on the larger ranch of a cardiologist / gentleman farmer. I
am to spend tonight here in the desert to facilitate an early-
morning ride tomorrow. This afternoon there is time for a
brief nap before supper and the reading. I don't sleep but
am soothed by the sound of the wind in the cottonwoods
imitating rain, and by the presence of a big house cat, Gam-
ine, who seeks me out at once and lies purring beside me.

In spite of overlapping the World Series (postponed by
the earthquake to this date), the reading draws a good audience. Books are for sale there, and at a private party at a
student's house after the reading, the dining table groans
with homemade delicacies. But by 10 P.M. jet lag has overtaken me. And three readings three nights in a row, no matter how you vary the poems, take their toll. Moreover, tonight
there was no microphone. The acoustics in the auditorium

were splendid, but I feel extra fatigue from having had to project my voice beyond its usual range.

Driving back from town into the desert I am not too tired to note a beautiful, healthy-looking coyote with a great bush to his tail. He stands transfixed in the headlights as we turn up the driveway; rarely, says my chauffeur, do they look so well fed and bold.

Finally, to bed! Sleep carries me off almost instantly. I come awake a few hours later to the several voices of coyotes, at first barking in concert like dogs, then building up the scale to a series of yelps that precede the full-fledged howl. This cacophony entertains me; I am not unhappy to be wide awake in the desert. When the orchestra finally fades, I am able to sleep again.

My host and her neighbor have planned for the three of us to ride up the mesa, make a broad circle, and descend the other face. I am to ride a borrowed polo pony, a 15½-hand Appendix Quarterhorse–Arab cross. This eight-year-old gelding is rigged like a battleship, with breastplate and draw reins attached to a Pelham. This is slightly off-putting to me, as our endurance horses go in snaffles with a figure-eight noseband to keep their mouths closed on the bit. Sometimes in early spring when they are rambunctious, we switch to a Kimberwicke and curb chain. But I often question whether the additional control outweighs the added fussiness. I haven't ridden with double reins since I was a child in suburban Philadelphia, and was taught to ride saddle seat, hands high and legs parked straight out in front of me.

It is a splendid morning, warming, but with a good breeze. We all walk for about a mile, loosening up. My mount starts out a little behind the formidable bit but soon rounds over, gratefully dropping his nose to my light contact. He is a comfortable fit and instantly responsive to my legs. Going up through dense scrub growth of mesquite and creosote, we sight at least a dozen jackrabbits. They leapfrog in front of us, close enough so that I can see the veins coursing inside their fluted ears, which stand straight up at a considerable height. New England rabbits are smaller and furrier; they carry their ears at an angle and slick them back as they run.

Soon we pick up a steady trot. Everyone breaks a sweat; we all feel good. My horse has a high, competent stride. I concentrate on changing diagonals round every swerve and keep my hands light to encourage him to take more of the bit. We canter a long stretch. This is clearly his most secure gait and it is very comfortable. I really love this guy!

In about an hour we come out on top of the mesa, from which we have a 360-degree view. The Franklin Mountains are on one side, the Organ Mountains on the other. We can see El Paso spread out beyond us in the valley. Except for the city, miniaturized from here, the area feels timeless. The mesa and its arroyos have been here since the Ice Age, unchanged and unchanging.

A drivable dirt road winds its way up here. I am startled to see a pickup truck emerge out of a dust cloud and bear down on us. A little farther on we come to a dump—the polite term is landfill. My host says she found a dead calf up here one day. She circled it, repelled, thinking it would decay and stink. But each day as she rode back to inspect the corpse she found it further diminished, odorless, soon reduced to its essential bones. Dry air, hot sun, possibly turkey vultures?

Her allegiance to the desert is touching. Like so many other transplants I meet out here, she has bonded to the landscape. She loves the subtle changes from daybreak to dusk, season to season. My eye is not practiced enough to see gradations of brown and gray. The desert saddens me, at least on this limited acquaintance. The view looks static, like clay contoured by a careless hand. It feels depleted, if not dead. There are no birds, little wildlife. We see no road-runners, no wild pigs, no rattlers. It is too late in the year for snakes. People wander out here casually to shoot their guns. Someone is always conducting target practice. The *thunk!* of rifles accompanies us as we cross the mesa and start down the other side.

Back on the valley floor, we ride around a big Quarter-horse ranch, with some very well-made horses following us curiously along the pipe rails. Yearlings cavort in one corral. Weanlings are in separate pens, wearing halters with long ropes attached. My companions explain that this is the western way of breaking them to the lead rope. They are invited to step on it and come to an abrupt halt. Back East we would decry this as dangerous. Horses seem more expendable here, to my biased easterner's perception.

As we travel single file along this sand track, I realize how much my eye depends on the sight of companionable horses, grazing, moving from hummock to knoll, to pine grove and back. These great dry paddocks with wire fencing depress me.

Much as I love to roam the woodlands of New England on horseback, pastures are even dearer. I see the landscape with the instincts of a farmer. Now that we're back down in the valley, cantering on the berms of great irrigation ditches, I feel lighter-hearted, more at home. There is iceberg lettuce in the field still. Most of the cotton has been harvested, but here and there a section waits to be picked by huge mechanical pickers.

Out here, alfalfa is a major irrigated crop, grown as a perennial. Cut and laid in windrows, it is baled soon there-after. The climate is so dry that spoilage is seldom a problem. Alfalfa will cure in the bale, they assure me. I see it stacked two stories high under a covered pavilion on farm after farm.

On the way home we detour slightly so that I can see someone's pet llamas in their enclosure. Four or five of them stand looking bored in their sandy pen. In the far corner one llama seems to have his head down under the door to the storage bin.

"Is that guy stuck?" one of my buddies asks, immediately concluding that he is. She does a flying dismount, throws me her mare's reins, and shinnies up the chain-link fence, under the electric wire—I never find out if it's turned on—and drops into their pen. Because she is horsewise, instead of tackling him frontally she circles around the critter, slips into the storage area through an adjoining stall, and opens the door from the other side. The poor prisoner recovers his neck with the head still attached, blinks, and stands perfectly still, giving us the once-over. No sign that he had ever been pinioned in that awful cramped position.

"Lucky we made the detour. The owners don't visit every day," my host says.

I ride back silently cursing absentee animal ownership, these casual possessors of creatures they have so little feeling for. If only you needed a license to own a horse or llama, like a driver's license. . . . If only the world were kinder and people more educable. Horses die out here from sand colic, which is another name for dying of boredom and neglect. With nothing to forage for in their bare paddocks, unable to crib on wooden fences or tree trunks—vices we do not condone but understand—some horses ingest sand particles as they nose about their enclosures. Impaction colic can result.

That evening we cross the border into Mexico to meet some students for dinner in Juárez. We spend an hour or so cruising through the local museum and then the state-sponsored crafts shops. Faced with handsome examples of Mexican art, my sales resistance wavers, then holds fast. Enough baggage!

My colleague escorts me to a downtown hotel from which, she assures me, there will be limo service early the next morning for my 6:30 flight out. I leave a wake-up call for 5 A.M. and secure everything for a dawn departure. I am still a bit anxious about the supposed limo. I've experienced their late or non-arrivals elsewhere and spent a day fuming, trying to find other connections out.

The next morning I discover I had nothing to worry about. The pilot of my flight to Dallas, as well as several other pilots and flight attendants, slept here, too. We all get a cup of coffee in the lobby, then board the same limousine. They are very chatty, want to know what brings me to El Paso, what is my line of work.

What a strange life! Horses appear in it wherever I go. It turns out that the pilot has a Morgan mare. He's thinking of breeding her to an Arabian stallion and asks my opinion. His daughter rides English and wants to learn how to jump. As tactfully as I can, I counsel him to look for a different stallion, a Thoroughbred if possible, to provide the kind of bone a jumper will require.

I almost never have to admit I am a poet in public. When asked "What do you do?", "I raise horses" meets with interest, even approval. "What do you do?" "I'm a poet" invariably invites, "That so? Ever published anything?" If you say you are a doctor or a lawyer your credentials go unchallenged, but to be a poet is immediately to be set apart as somehow incomprehensible.

When I deplane in Dallas to reconnect to Newark and finally to Manchester, the pilot / horse owner is waiting for me at the door of the plane. To my astonishment he is holding a copy of my book, *Nurture*, with my photograph on the back. "I knew I'd seen you somewhere. My daughter went to your reading night before last." He creases the book open to a particular poem, "Sleeping with Animals." And then I remember the adolescent girl who asked me to sign her copy on that page.

I've been found out.

"Have a good trip back," he says. "It's clear weather, all the way."

GONE TO THE DOGS

Today the mason appears to repair one of the two elderly chimneys this house is blessed with. The chimney has been leaking creosote inside on the second floor for the better part of two centuries.

This is a skilled and expensive mason who was expected a month ago. He arrives complete with dog, an aging black part-Labrador bitch who rides in the back of his pickup. She is just enough dog to tantalize our two Dalmatian puppies, who are trouble enough without an accomplice.

Our houseguests from Middlebury arrive *in medias res* with their dog too, a mutt from the local pound and smarter than the three aforementioned animals. His name is Byron, which does not necessarily have anything to do with the poet Byron. The husband wanted to call the dog Clank. The wife protested that you can't go around calling a dog, "Here, Clank!" It doesn't work, one harsh syllable like that.

She wanted to call the dog Guido. The husband said that you can't go around calling a dog Guido, for Pete's sake, it sounds like a restaurant. So they compromised on Byron, with equal accents on both syllables, which makes a spondee, and is a very callable name.

While we are conducting this amiable discourse, large, tricolored (part Great Dane?) Byron sits grinning. Evidently he has heard this explanation before.

The mason is on the roof by now, ripping out bricks and casting them down at a great rate. He is also ripping out the original authentic ancient chimney tiles and dropping them. He finds the offending leaky tile and begins his repair.

The situation gets a little heady on the roof, what with his shifting the ladder, lifting bricks in great clusters, hauling up cement by the bucketload. Before any of us can think to mention what may happen, the mason puts ladder and self through an upstairs storm window. The sound glass makes as it shatters is quite musical.

In the midst of all this, or perhaps as a result, the two Dal puppies disappear with Byron. The visiting wife and I are selected to go find them. We hike up the hill toward the strawberry farm, our nearest neighbor in a westerly direction. Grueling through clouds of mosquitoes and almost visible humidity, we call Byron and the puppies, whose names, if they paid any attention to them, are Gus and Claude. Byron at length appears. The puppies have gone disobediently elsewhere.

We return. There is a long confab as a result of the fallen glass, which is everywhere. The puppies materialize out of the woods, stickered with burdock burs. We close the dogs on the porch, turn our backs on the work scene, I get lunch on the table, and we enjoy a relaxed meal. It is pleasant to entertain old friends. We push back from the table in a mood of mutual self-congratulation.

The houseguests now pack to depart, as the husband has a lesson (he sings) in Middlebury and they will just get back in time for it if they hurry. Consternation seizes us: Byron is missing, and along with him, the black Lab belonging to the mason.

Leaving the mason on the roof to contend with the remnants of bricks, tiles, glass, and the like, the visiting husband and my husband set out to find the missing Byron and Ophelia (the less pedigreed the dog the more elegant its name). They decide to search the strawberry fields of the neighboring farmer, one alp above our own, but will do so by driving down to town, cruising under the highway, and up the other side of the hill to the berry farm.

The visiting wife and I, after a conference in which we agree we can do nothing, decide to lie in the sun and have a beer. Just as the men vanish downhill Byron reappears, dripping wet from the pond. We leap into the visitors' car and take off to intercept the men in hopes that the husband can leave early enough to have his music lesson after all.

Halfway down the hill the car feels sluggish, unwilling, lumpy—flat-tired. Byron, panting in the back seat, threatens heat prostration. We feed him ice cubes out of a cooler and lean back, waiting for the men to return from their fruitless search for the dog now in our possession.

Four or five hours later, our houseguests depart. The mason leaves with his rediscovered Ophelia. He does not clean up behind himself; he is too highly skilled for that. Less highly skilled, I sweep up half a ton of cement dust, pick up several shards of glass that have escaped his casual scrutiny, and find a safe place in the barn to store the broken storm window frame.

The chimney is clean and does not leak. Inside the house at the chimney cleanout—a little trap door that would be eye level for a mouse—there is an additional pile of creosote and dust. Thank you, expensive mason. This chimney is now certified for winter. The cost of certification would possibly have paid for installing an oil burner and filling it for a season.

A day later, the next houseguest arrives two hours after the time agreed on for a carefully planned Saturday picnic lunch. He comes carrying a huge floral arrangement from the last place he visited. It's too late. My husband and I were so hungry we have already eaten, but we go through the motions.

This guest is not allergic to poison ivy. His annual house present is to pull up great swatches of it all around our pond, where it is creeping luxuriantly. We celebrate its removal with the first swim of the season. The puppies stand on the diving rock and bark frantically as their master and mistress disappear into the enormous drinking-water dish. They will not be coaxed into this element. If God had intended them to swim, they say, they would have webbed feet, right?

Suddenly Ophelia appears, crashing through the underbrush, and does a racing dive off the rock. It is clearly a rescue situation. She is intent on saving any one of the three of us she can reach. As the houseguest is the closest to shore, she goes for him. Only our vigorous intervention keeps him from drowning in the grip of her enthusiasm.

The expensive mason has refigured his bill and wishes now to adjust the amount he was paid downward by $12.75, which he judges to be the replacement cost of the fractured pane. He was in the neighborhood anyway, so he thought he would just drop by. Finding no one at home, he adduced that we might be using the pond. His words exactly. As for Ophelia, it is in the breed to fetch things from the water. The long scratch down our houseguest's forearm attests to her zeal. The mason promises he will clip her toenails tonight.

After only a brief palaver, we all repair to the house for

iodine. Husband and houseguest seem to think the situation calls for beer, and the mason is right behind them as they peer into the refrigerator. Before either of them can straighten up, Ophelia is gone again, and with her the puppies.

ENOUGH JAM
FOR A LIFETIME

January 25. Three days of this hard freeze; 10 below at dawn and a sullen 2 above by midday. After the morning barn chores, I start hauling quart containers of wild blackberries up from the basement freezer. I am a little reluctant to begin.

Last August, when the berries were at their most succulent, I did manage to cook up a sizable batch into jam. But everything peaks at once in a New England garden, and I turned to the importunate broccolis and cauliflowers and the second crop of bush beans, all of which wanted blanching and freezing straightaway. Also, late summer rains had roused the cucumber vines to new efforts. There was a sudden spurt of yellow squash as well.

Victor went on picking blackberries. Most mornings he scouted the slash pile along upturned boulders, residue from when we cleared the last four acres of forage pasture. We've never had to fence this final field, for the brush forms an impenetrable thicket on two sides and deep woods encircle the rest.

We've always had blackberries growing wild here and there on the property, good-sized ones, too. But never such largess, such abundance. I wondered what this bumper crop signified, after a drought-filled summer. Were the Tribulation and the Rapture at hand?

Long ago I wrote in a poem, "God does not want / His perfect fruit to rot," but that was before I had an addicted picker on my hands—whose enthusiasm became my labor. It is the habit of the deeply married to exchange vantage points.

Even the horses took up blackberries as a snack. Like toddlers loose in a popcorn shop, they sidled down the brambly row, cautiously curling their lips back so as to pluck a drooping cluster free without being stabbed in the muzzle by truly savage thorns. It was a wonderful sight.

Making jam—even though I complain how long it takes, how messy it is with its inevitable spatters and spills, how the lids and the jars somehow never match up at the end of the procedure—is rich with gratifications. I get a lot of thinking done. I puff up with feelings of providence. Pretty soon I am flooded with memories.

My mother used to visit every summer during our pickling, canning, freezing, and jamming frenzy. She had a deep reservoir of patience, developed in another era, for repetitive tasks; she would mash the blender-buzzed, cooked berries through a strainer until her arms were as weary as a weightlifter's at the end of a grueling workout. She prided herself on extracting every bit of pulp from the purple mass.

I find myself talking to her as I work. I am not nearly as diligent, I tell her, thumping the upended strainer into the kitchen scraps pile, destined for compost. I miss her serious attention to detail.

Scullery work used to make my mother loquacious. I liked hearing about her childhood in the southwestern hilly corner of Virginia at the turn of the century, how the cooking from

May to October was done in the summer kitchen, a structure loosely attached to the back of the house, much as many New England sheds and barns connect to the farmhouses they supplement. I liked hearing about my grandfather's matched pair of driving horses—Saddlebreds, I gather, from the one surviving snapshot that shows my mother's three youngest brothers lined up on one compliant horse's back. My mother talked about the family pony that had a white harness for Sundays. I wonder aloud what a white harness was made of in the 1890s. Perhaps she had imagined this item, but fabricated it lovingly so long ago that it had become real.

One spectacular late summer day we took my mother down North Road along Stevens Brook in search of elderberries. We hiked up and down the sandy edge of the water in several locations before coming upon an enormous stand of the berries, ripe to bursting, branches bent double with the weight of them. After filling the five-gallon pail we had brought with us, greedily we started stuffing whole racemes of berries into a spare grain bag.

I had not thought much about dealing with the booty until we had lugged it triumphantly home. Mother sat at the kitchen table well past midnight, stripping the berries from their slender finger filaments into my biggest cooking pot. Even so, the great elderberry caper took two more days to complete. We prevailed, eventually boiling the berries with some green apples from our own trees so that the released pectin would permit the mass to jell. I don't believe in additives and scorn commercial pectin, but I will lean on home-grown apples or rhubarb in order to thicken the berry soup.

It was amazing what those elderberries had reawakened in my mother; she was transported. There was the cold cellar, there stood the jars of pickled beets, the Damson plum conserve larded with hazelnuts; there, too, the waist-high barrel of dill pickles weighted down with three flatirons atop a washtub lid. Potatoes and sweet potatoes, carrots, onions, and apples were stored in areas appropriate to their needs— apples in the dark far corner which was the driest (and spookiest), and so on. There was the springhouse, where milk from the family cow cooled unpasteurized in a metal can set down in a cavity of rocks, and a butter churn which took hours of push-pulling the paddle to turn the cream into a finished product.

It was never an idyll Mother described. She remembered sharply and wryly the labor, the peonage of childhood, when the most menial and least absorbing tasks were invariably assigned to the smallest children, especially the girls. She could not escape the chores of housekeeping for the imagined dramas of field and barn. But interestingly, chickens seemed always to have been relegated to the care of females.

Mother loathed the chickens that pecked her feet when she went into the coop to scatter their scratch. She detested egg gathering, having to shoo brood hens off their nests and then be quick about plucking the eggs into the basket; eggs from which fluff, feathers, and bits of crusty manure had to be removed. I never saw my mother eat an egg, boiled soft or hard, poached, or sunny-side up. They were a bit too close to nature for her taste.

Another kitchen thing I hear my mother say as I work, this cold January noon: "Warm the plates!" she croons to me from the Great Beyond. She abhorred the common practice of serving hot food on cold china. *Common* is the epithet she would have applied to it, a word that carried powerful connotations of contempt.

This wintry day, then, I reduce five gallons of blackberries to serviceable pulp, measure out three cups of sugar to every four of berry mash, and set it boiling. We will have successive batches on the stove the rest of this day. I have already rummaged for suitable jars from the cellar shelves and these I will boil for fifteen minutes on a back burner. Toward the end I will grow more inventive about jars, for there are never enough of the good, straight-sided variety.

But for now, the jam puts up lacy bubbles, rolling around the top third of my giant cooking pot at a full boil. Despite candy thermometers, the only way I trust to gauge when the jam is ready is dip and drip. From a decent height, off a slotted spoon, I perform this test until the royal stuff begins to form a tiny waterfall. This is known as sheeting; all the cookbooks describe it, but it's a delicate decision to arrive at. Stop too soon and you have a lovely blackberry sauce to serve over ice cream, sponge cake, or applesauce. Continue too long and you have a fatally overcooked mess of berry leather.

There is no quality control in my method. Every batch is a kind of revisionism. It makes its own laws. But the result is pure, deeply colored, uncomplicated, and unadulterated blackberry jam, veritably seedless, suitable for every occasion. After it has cooled, I pour melted paraffin on top of it, tilting the glass to get an airproof seal. Modern science frowns on so casual an approach to shutting out microbes, but I don't apologize. If the wax shows a spot of mold growing on top after a few months on the shelf, I can always remove it, wipe the sides clean, and pour a new layer of wax over all.

My mother would go home from her summer visits with a package of pickles and jams for her later delectation. When she died, there were several unopened jars in her cupboard.

I took them back with me after the funeral. We ate them in her stead, as she would have wanted us to. Enough jam for a lifetime, she would say with evident satisfaction after a day of scullery duty. It was; it is.

MUTTS

When I come out of the grocery store, of course they've both jumped into the front. The pseudo-white German shepherd, betrayed by his upwardly curling tail and misaligned biscuit-colored ears, is in the driver's seat. The mostly German shepherd with an all-black muzzle and a collie's white vest sits at attention in the passenger seat. Staring straight ahead, both co-conspirators ignore me.

"You're not driving," I say to them, I always say to them. "Get in the back!" After the second repetition, they do.

"What interesting-looking dogs!" people say if they pass by during this discussion. "What breed are they?"

"Generic farm dogs," I tell them. If my husband's answering, he says it more emphatically: "They're just a couple of mutts."

Both of them are foundlings. Josh, the white one, came to us first, while our last Dalmatian was still alive. He arrived as a four-month-old puppy, rescued by our new neighbors from a bad situation in which he was always confined, either penned or chained, and handled little. Our neighbors couldn't house him because they were already sharing close quarters with two teenagers, four cats, two dogs, and three birds, but it was summer and he had the run of their barn.

When he first came up the hill half a mile to live with us that fall, he made daily forays back to his Other Home. After he saw the girls off to school in the morning, he returned with something in his mouth: a halter, a leg wrap, a curry, or a brush. Often, a barn boot from the back stoop. We diligently returned each of these items at the end of the day. Gradually, the girls developed stricter barn-keeping habits and reduced the number of articles available for Josh to deliver.

Deprived of equine objets d'art, he learned how to navigate the steep staircase up to a storage area in the barn loft and began to pilfer far more ambitious items. A bag of curlers, a baby doll, some winter socks. His most inspired retrieval was a pair of ice skates, tied together by their laces, which he laboriously fetched up the hill ten feet or so at a time, pausing in between to sit down and catch his breath.

Eventually, a door was installed at the top of the stairs and Josh slowly unlearned his foraging habits. For several months, though, he seemed to feel it his duty to trot downhill to see the scholars off to classes. Sometimes Gus, our aging Dalmatian, went with him, but for the most part he found it a long haul down and up and preferred to stay at the top, overseeing Josh's excursion.

Gus tolerated the newcomer with surprising good grace, given his tendency toward lassitude and the puppy's toward perpetual motion. Josh wanted to wrestle constantly. Neither his play growls and mock attacks nor his nonstop nipping and chewing seemed to bother Gus very much; he was a deeply jowled and wrinkly fellow with an ample supply of loose flesh. Sometimes we would see the two of them racing downhill, the younger one's teeth fastened into Gus's cheek or neck, his puppy feet hardly touching the ground as they sped off. But when Gus's arthritis made it impossible for him to climb the stairs to sleep on the rug at the foot of our bed, Josh, who had happily shared that spot, retraced his steps to sleep beside him on the sheepskin rug in front of the woodstove.

We were down to one dog for several months after Gus died. Neither of us quite wanted to begin again with a new puppy. Maybe one dog was enough, we told each other. Josh was so easy to live with. He stayed faithfully on the property even if we drove off to do errands. He got along well with the horses and he coexisted with the sheep. He had been around through a couple of foalings so we knew he could be trusted around equine newborns as well.

At the end of April I went to New York City to a literary awards ceremony. An editor I knew only slightly was, according to the seating plan, scheduled to join our table. Since he was nowhere to be found, eventually the proceedings got under way without him. An hour later, he and his wife burst wild-eyed on the scene.

They had a harrowing tale to relate. Driving down the West Side Highway from Riverdale, they had caught sight of an emaciated young dog dodging traffic, narrowly escaping sudden death several times under their horrified gaze as drivers swerved, their brakes screeching. Horns honked on all sides out of frustration. Stanley pulled the car over, leapt out, ripping his belt out of its belt loops as he ran, and took off in pursuit of the dog. At that point, the terrified creature hurdled the median divider and ran into the jaws of oncoming traffic. Somehow, Stanley managed to overtake him, downed him with a flying tackle, and collared him with the belt.

He and his wife, Jane, wrestled this apparition into the back seat of their station wagon. En route to the Poetry Society dinner at Gramercy Park, they stopped to buy some bottled water and a can of dog food and, using the widemouthed lid of a thermos, offered these alternately to their captive. Although quivering with apprehension, he was both hungry and thirsty. After that, he was willing to be patted and soothed and only whimpered briefly when they left him in the car.

When the speeches were over, several of us trooped down the block to where Stanley had providentially acquired a parking space. He was a skeletal pup, all right, but he didn't shrink from the several pairs of hands that reached in to feel his head and neck. Stanley wasn't sure what he would do with him. He was afraid they wouldn't be able to socialize him with their aging male dog, but he hoped his vet could find a proper home.

I allowed as how we might try him in New Hampshire.

Stanley beamed.

The little audience assembled around the station wagon breathed its approval. I could feel myself being elevated to sainthood.

Hastily, I amended: "Of course, it depends on whether Victor agrees or not."

Everyone nodded solemnly. Those who knew my husband personally knew he was a soft touch. Hadn't he already taken in a couple of waif dogs and a series of abused horses? On the other hand, how many times can you go to the well before it runs dry?

When he hears *this* story, I said to myself, he won't be able to resist.

A week later, a newly inoculated, deloused, dewormed, bathed, and somewhat less disreputable-looking dog arrived with Stanley and Jane at our farm, along with a list of his immunizations, some feeding instructions, and thirty pounds of a very high protein kibble. The New York vet had pronounced him dehydrated, malnourished, and suffering from exposure. He thought the dog was possibly a year old. Since he had virtually no toenails, the vet concluded that he had probably been out on the streets most of his life.

"Born behind a garbage can," Victor said, after introductions had taken place. "And nourished by one, from the looks of it."

It was true that the entire framework of dog was still visible. You could see where each rib depended from the shelf of backbone. The head seemed strangely knobby, too, the face drawn almost into a grimace. And the dog's chest was tiny, in proportion to his body and leg length, most likely the result of his chronic malnutrition.

Positively portly by contrast, Josh was instantly agreeably disposed toward the newcomer. They rolled around amiably together, pretending war over the possession of a stick, then strutted around sharing it.

"Well, what do you think?" Stanley asked.

"It'll take quite a while to fatten him up," Victor said.

"Meanwhile, how about lunch?" I suggested neutrally. It looked as though the dog would stay.

A little controversy arose between husband and wife over the conferring of a name. Victor wanted to call the dog Bernstein, in honor of the author of *West Side Story*. I wanted to name him Rilke, after the visionary German poet, who had also been sustained by angels.

I pointed out that Victor had named the barn cats Abra and Cadabra, after I had wanted to call them Emily and Lavinia.

"That was ten years ago."

"Well, he *is* mostly German shepherd," Jane said. "And we *did* bring him along to a Poetry Society dinner."

No further protest was lodged, but I must confess that Rilke tried us sorely over the ensuing several months. An enthusiastic digger, he totally demolished my perennial bed, which used to butt up against a stone wall. Small things that lived in that wall were harried from their homes by Rilke.

House etiquette was unknown to him, as was the concept of house. On the rare occasions that we left him behind, he had to be sequestered in the back hall because he demolished everything in sight in his outrage and terror. Happily, he is now housebroken, and he does not howl or act out when we leave him.

He must have learned his bird-stalking skills in quest of pigeons in Manhattan. Here in New Hampshire he crouches like a panther and advances stealthily on unsuspecting ground doves, a species that has grown fat and abundant hereabouts, crowding chickadees and nuthatches from the feeders to dine on black oil sunflower seeds. He is so adept at catching mice and an occasional red squirrel that one wonders if he honed this skill on urban *Rattus rattus*.

Chipmunks, however, are just a hair too quick for him. So are the cats, with whom he seems to have an agreement. Some days they agree to be chased and some days they stand their ground, hissing. In the latter case, Rilke turns aside, pretending not to be interested. But snakes drive him wild. He stands above them barking hysterically, then makes little feints and jabs as they coil and hiss in bewilderment.

We have an abundance of garden and black snakes, several of which have always traveled freely into and out of the crawl space that extends under the back part of our house. In his zeal to get at one, Rilke excavated so frenetically under the foundation that he managed to rip away the phone line as well. "Can't imagine how this happened," said the repairman, installing a new one. We couldn't either, we said.

Given his fierce demeanor, I was worried how Rilke would behave with a new foal. Or with the sheep, for that matter; a little band of ewes comes to us every May when it is time to wean their lambs. To my surprise, he proved to be a model of decorum on both counts. He is equally trustworthy with small children, putting up with a lot of investigatory poking and grabbing.

On the downside, he cannot resist rolling in fresh manure or dead animals; apparently they smell the same to him. He leaps into any body of water, be it river, pond, or puddle, quenching his thirst as he fords the hazard. Muddy wallows are his favorites but he quivers with terror when you tie him to the barn in order to give him a bath. An indefatigable explorer, he bounds over stone walls, races through scrub growth, flies across pastures, and returns matted with clumps of burrs, which have to be picked out while he squirms and carries on. He still, alas, chases pickup trucks unless you are on the site rattling the chain you are ready to throw at him. And an unchaperoned horse, allowed to walk down alone from the upper pasture to the paddock and thence into the barn, produces the same reaction.

Victor and Rilke have gone to dog school for nine sessions. The instructor—the chain was her idea—says there is nothing more she can teach him and that it will be another six months before he is dependable. Dependability means minding a command even when distracted, or in the presence of other dogs, or especially when you don't want to. You have to practice a lot to become dependable, so we have thirty-minute sit-stays and several down-ups. Josh, a graduate of this same course, went along on a few of Rilke's sessions, just for a refresher.

Rilke outweighs Josh now, and he often plays too rough. Whenever I see him wrestle Josh to the ground, grabbing him by his neck hair, I think of Josh as a puppy tormenting Gus. By non-poets, this is called poetic justice. This poet calls it divine intervention by the Great Overdog, the one who placed him in Stanley's path and ultimately delivered him to us.

CHILDREN OF DARKNESS

The first wild mushroom I ever ate was a little pear-shaped puffball, its inner texture and whiteness that of angelfood cake. I sliced and sautéed it in butter somewhat trepidatiously. Even though it is the simplest of all fungi to identify, I approached it with caution, my head full of dark tales of poisonings and emetics, emergency rooms and funeral parlors.

Since, as a writer, my business is words, I tend to put my faith in the printed page. Much of what I have learned about the natural world came to me from handbooks. Where animal husbandry, maple-sugaring, and the construction of dry stone walls are concerned, I feel I have been well served. But the mysteries of mycology run murkier than those of wool production.

It seemed that every mushroom book I consulted contained a generous interlarding of horror stories. While one or two took the novice on a tour of the simple non-gilled and therefore easily identifiable fungi—puffballs fall into this category—hardly any of them said comforting things such as: If you can distinguish between a head of cauliflower and a head of broccoli, you can learn to tell the difference between a puffball and a deadly amanita.

European cultures are at home with these "children of darkness." In France, when chanterelles are in season, the woods are alive with foragers who jealously guard their secret places from one another. Russians, Poles, Italians all treasure the specialties of their regions. Open-air markets in autumn display a wondrous variety of species for sale. In Switzerland on the weekends many cantons have a mycologist on call at the fire station to identify questionable finds. If you eat out, it is not unusual to encounter two or three choices of wild mushrooms on a restaurant menu.

One memorable lunchtime, in a French restaurant near Orange, I was treated to an immodest feast that featured not only morels en casserole, but a distinctly purple *Tricholoma* known as a blewit. Neither my host, the poet Thérèse Plantier, nor I was fluent in the other's mother tongue, but to share poetry and mycophagy was enough to create a magical afternoon.

On another occasion, backstage at the Library of Congress, I first met Nobel laureate Czeslaw Milosz a scant ten minutes before I was to introduce him to his audience. In the awkward isolation of the dressing room we hit upon wild mushrooms as a shared enthusiasm. As a boy in Lithuania he had foraged with his mother; he had perfect recall for the species they gathered and for their Latin nomenclatures. In the language of the ancients we were able to compare items of what the Romans called "food of the gods," which comfortably disposed of the enforced wait before we went on stage.

But Americans in general are wary of any mushroom that doesn't bear the sanitized imprimatur of the supermarket.

Southerners, I have found, are the least trusting. I base this on an admittedly small sample. At the Bread Loaf Writers' Conference in Vermont held annually in August, the foraging was often superb after a few days of wet weather. The director, John Ciardi, who had dubbed me the Witch of Fungi, frequently designated me to lead a group of enthusiasts on an afternoon expedition. During cocktail hour in the staff house it was our custom to offer to the assemblage sautéed specimens of the day's bounty—chanterelles, chicken of the woods, meadow and oyster mushrooms, and the good, meaty international boletuses called *cêpes* in French, *steinpilz* in German, *porcini* in Italian. Invariably, the southern writers avoided these hors d'oeuvres and focused steadfastly on the cheese.

A fair amount of my mushroom knowledge came from field trips with experienced foragers. One golden fall I took a field course conducted by the president of the Boston Mycological Society. Each expedition was followed by a viewing of colored slides of the species we had seen.

Another time, in the Cascade Mountains of Washington, I was treated to *in situ* discoveries by a mycological expert from the University. Afterward, he took me back to the lab for a lesson in how mushroom spores are stained and mounted for microscopic identification.

Morels, uncommon in New Hampshire, pop up as readily as dandelions in the hills outside Lexington, Virginia; one early April a local writer friend and I gleaned hundreds of them in an afternoon. And once, in the sandhills of the Cape Cod federal preserve, my husband and I encountered a group of Russians who were enthusiastically gathering a tough-stemmed boletus they assured us was delicious; we gathered a dozen to try, but found them rather fibrous and undistinguished.

Puffballs, boletuses, and other non-gilled fungi were a good introduction to the sport. But as I cross-checked my finds in the various textbooks I was beginning to accumulate, each new encounter began to seem fraught with ambiguity, if not downright peril.

On the printed page, the first caveat I encountered was in the preface to the *Field Guide of Common Mushrooms,* one of Putnam's quite admirable Nature Field Books series. The author, William Sturgis Thomas, M.D.—the medical degree is cited, I infer, to convey an additional gravity to this already weighty matter—quotes from two experts at Johns Hopkins University: "Unfortunately, there are mushroom 'handbooks' in this country which are unfailing sources of misinformation and they have evidently been written by people of no training and poor judgment."

Nor was I suitably encouraged to read in Linus Zeitlmayr's *Wild Mushrooms* that while many animals such as guinea pigs and rabbits can eat poisonous species of fungi without ill effects, human beings seem to be excepted. "Dr. Limousin of Clermont-Ferrand has based a special treatment of Amanita poisoning on this fact. It consists of feeding to the patient a brew made from finely-chopped, raw, rabbits stomachs and brains. Unfortunately, this is said to be quite ineffective."

Nevertheless, on the fateful fall day in 1968 that I ate the puffball nothing dire ensued. A few months earlier, I had undergone back surgery. Because walking was recommended as the therapy of choice to improve my mobility, I was inspired to forage farther afield. We were not quite newcomers to the country, but we had barely explored the perimeter of our considerable and craggy acres of second-growth woodland, ledges, and boulders. That spring I began to investigate the interior.

Mushrooms are not a fast food. When time is more precious than taste buds, the Golden Arches prevail. But finding mushrooms is its own slow feast. Collecting becomes a sport, pursued without ski pole or tennis racket. It's a kind of slow hiking which develops acuity of vision. A neophyte hunter can spot a chanterelle—easy, since they're yellow—at twenty yards, but only an experienced forager is going to spy those even tastier clusters of horn of plenty, ashy-gray little trumpets camouflaged by leaves under the beech trees.

I carried a flat-bottomed basket, the kind that graces illustrations for Red Riding Hood, a roll of waxed paper, some brown-paper lunch bags to contain the specimens individually wrapped in wax paper, and a knife for digging the mushroom up whole. Other members of the family and various drop-in visitors often took part in these expeditions as well. Weekends became a huge around-the-kitchen-table (indeed, the only table) identification scramble as we sorted out specimens and pored over a gradually enlarging collection of mushroom books.

We used a hand lens to examine gill or pore structure. We learned how to take spore prints under an ordinary water glass; we began rather glibly to use scientific terminology, reveling in a language of specific distinctions. Gills were decurrent, adnexed, adnate. Caps were dry, hairy, viscid, had warts. The stem had a ring (annulus), a veil; the bottom of the stem was contained, or not, in a cup (volva). For just as poetry builds on a detailed jargon of dactyl and spondee, enjambment, quatrain, and pentameter, so does mycology flourish under a rain of specific terms, almost all of them drawn directly from the Latin.

O, that I might dial the grave and tell Miss Juanita Mae Downes, my high school Latin teacher, this new application of the language I so painstakingly labored over for four years in my adolescence! *Volva, annulus, pileus*, Miss Downes, I would say. *Coprinus, lactarius, atramentarius*. And I would lead her by the hand into the pasture, there to make the acquaintance of *Agaricus campestris*, the common meadow mushroom, which is the wild and tastier ancestor of its supermarket relative. For the Romans were enthusiastic mycophagists. *Ubi uber, ibi tuber*, wrote Apuleius: Wherever it is fertile, there is the truffle. For in the Latin lexicon, tuber referred not to potato but to that rarest of fungal delicacies, the truffle.

Or, to quote from the famous Roman satirist Martial: *Argentum atque aurum facile est, laenam togamque mittere; / Boletus mittere difficile est*. It is easy to dismiss silver and gold and fancy clothes; to leave good mushrooms untouched is difficult.

H. Kleijn, the same author to whom I am indebted for the line from Martial, is former president of the Royal Society of Natural History in Amsterdam and a lively stylist. After cautioning the would-be forager to study the natural surroundings in which various fungi grow, he says, "After all, one does not look for water lilies on a moor!" I wonder about this translation from the land of dikes and polders, obviously rendered by an Englishman.

Here in New Hampshire, where I sit remembering these mycological beginnings and paging through my still-growing collection of mushroom texts, a hard frost has ushered in November. The season of foraging and finding, of gleaning along woodland trails and pastures where I did not plant seed, has passed.

Ever since May, I have peered through the underbrush, scanned the trunks of decaying trees, and crawled into bosky dells in search of various edible treats of this netherworld. Late spring was disappointing. Summer was dry and nonproductive. But the fall was lovely, abundant, even—nature's way—super-abundant. Pig food, squirrel's bread to some, these gleanings are delicacies to my palate. I made appropriate soups and stews and sautéed and froze quantities of good specimens for winter use.

On the cutting edge of winter, there is time to return to underground literature, the world of illustrated handbooks, trail guides, hefty encyclopedias, slenderer nomenclatural classifications, and cookbooks. A lilting folk language has given us shaggy mane, lawyer's wig, inky cap, oyster mushroom, hen of the woods, brickies, honeys, Devil's snuffbox, dog stinkhorn, dryad's saddle, horn of plenty (also, but unjustly, known as trumpet of death), Scotch bonnets, and the parasol mushroom. These and other colorful epithets vary from one culture to another. The first three in the list above all refer to the same genus, *Coprinus*. What looks like a shaggy mane to Americans evokes a lawyer's wig in Great Britain. Because the genus deliquesces with age—indeed, the Pilgrim fathers collected this juice and used it for ink— it acquired its third nickname, inky cap.

Other names combine the Latin term with descriptive English modifiers. Once I thought of writing a murder mystery based on characters called Perplexing Hypholoma and Slippery Leotia. For the butler, Fat Pholiota. Suspects could be Fetid Russula or Waxy Laccaria. The murderer of course would be the Destroying Angel, the Deadly Amanita.

In addition to popular or folk names, the literature of mushroom books is full of changing—because still evolving—nomenclatures. Mystery, science, fallacy, suspicion, and intuition enter as well. The texts piggyback on one another in much the same way that honey mushrooms—*Armillariella mellea*—crowd the base of a dying tree. Popular illustrated guides to the edible species, with darkly specific information about the deadly poisonous ones, abound. A year never passes without the publication of a new, purportedly easier-to-use, tuck-in-your-backpack handbook. By now I have accumulated a goodly assortment of these, ranging from coffee-table-size art books to briskly practical Michelin-guide types, labeled, for instance, *Wild Mushrooms of Field and Forest: How to Recognize, Collect & Cook*. I never tire of dipping into them.

Some difference of opinion seems inevitable where matters of taste are involved. But, along with good advice, a note of asperity and sometimes of snobbishness does creep into these assessments. Here are a few of my favorites:

Nina Marshall, writing in 1904 *(The Mushroom Book: A Popular Guide to the Identification and Study of Our Commoner Fungi, with Special Emphasis on the Edible Varieties)*, offers that "frequent cases of poisoning occur in all classes of society. The mistakes resulting in death have been frequent enough to inspire the timid with an overpowering dread of all fungi, while the damp and grewsome [sic] places in which many fungi flourish have caused them to be despised by others." Published as Volume 10 of a very ambitious Nature Library, this text is rich in hand-colored or -tinted photographic illustrations of various fungi and represents what must have been an enormous undertaking at that time.

In a vivid instance of class condescension, a Dr. Badham describes his book, *A Treatise on the Esculent Funguses of England*, published in London in 1847, as "a work whose chief object is to furnish the laboring classes with wholesome nourishment and profitable occupation." Apparently foraging for fungi was seen as an appropriate leisure-time activity for those already bent double by the Industrial Revolution.

Alexander Smith and Nancy Smith Weber in their updated

University of Michigan Press handbook write with macabre jocular intent: "It has been said that there are old mycophagists, bold mycophagists, but no old bold mycophagists." On the other hand, chewing on the gristle of this statement, I remember my father tartly saying: "There's no fool like an old fool." If bold is synonymous with foolhardy, then perhaps some members of the latter category have survived.

Another admonishment I treasure comes from Phyllis Glick's *The Mushroom Trail Guide:* "A police whistle is handy to keep in touch with your wandering companions. It's easy to lose your sense of direction when walking head down in the woods." I confess I have misplaced my way in our own woods several times, but comfort myself with Thoreau's dictum, "For a man [or a woman?] needs only to be turned around once with his eyes shut in this world to be lost. . . . Not til we are lost . . . do we begin to find ourselves."

One Thousand American Fungi, a hefty compendium by Charles McIlvaine, president of the Philadelphia Mycological Center, and Robert K. MacAdam, who is never further identified, was first published in 1900, then reprinted in 1902. Luckily, it was reissued by Something Else Press of Glover, Vermont, in 1973, because it is a large and valuable text.

No sooner had I put my faith in it, however, than I encountered Louis Kreiger making this off-putting remark about it in *his* mushroom handbook: "The colored illustrations are not so good, and the advice as to the edibility of certain kinds might be questioned." He then goes on to praise "Miss Marshall's less pretentious book," referred to above. A little mycological back-biting, not unlike contemporary politics or the tenure struggles of academe.

When it comes to myco-myopia, McIlvaine does not mince

words. "Let us clear away the rubbish and superstition that have so long obscured the straight path to a knowledge of edible toadstools. Let us bear in mind that a mushroom is a toadstool and a toadstool is a mushroom—the terms are interchangeable. If toads ever occupied the one-legged seat assigned them from time immemorial, they have learned in this enlightened age that the ground is much more reliable, and so squat upon it, except when exercising their constitutional right to hop."

But my favorite passage from McIlvaine—I assume it is McIlvaine and not MacAdam speaking—occurs in his discussion of the merits of *Marasmius oreades*, the fairy-ring mushroom, also known as Scotch bonnet or mountain nymph, a common and easily identifiable comestible. He tells us: "The most delicate stomachs can digest it. The writer saved the life of a lovely woman by feeding her upon it when nothing else could be retained. . . ." I visualize the mycologist keeping a lovely lady alive in the woods during some dark incident of rivalry and skullduggery among the mushroom experts. A passionate love affair while deceived into losing their way in a vast forest, perhaps? Alas, we are never to know.

A not dissimilar account is provided by the redoubtable Zeitlmayr, who cites a German general hemmed in with his troops in German East Africa in 1918. He "managed to save them from starvation and to hold out for some months against superior forces by encouraging them to supplement their meagre rations with whatever fungi they could find." I do wish Zeitlmayr or his general had been more specific. What mushrooms did the troops dine on, gleaned from forest or savannah, in German East Africa, now Tanzania?

Then, in Judge Samuel R. Rosen's little book titled *A Judge Judges Mushrooms*, I read that in Scandinavian countries and Iceland from the ninth to the twelfth centuries, bands of "Berserkjers," so named for a legendary hero who sallied forth into battle wrapped only in a bearskin, terrorized the countryside. They did so under the influence of a toxin contained in the *Amanita muscaria*, the toadstool of Alice in Wonderland, a squat but showy creation of bright yellow/orange with white warts atop, which adorns our woodland trails in midsummer. It is also called the fly agaric, for its ability to attract flies and other insects. Throughout human history it has been treasured for its hallucinogenic properties. Some ancient tribes fed the mushroom to their cows and then ingested a milder form of it through their milk.

Rosen further offers the useful information that in the Yucatan mushrooms were held sacred by the ancient Mayans, who claimed they were the result of sexual intercourse between a bolt of lightning and the earth.

To the Egyptian pharaohs mushrooms were thought to convey a special prowess because of their observed ability to spring up overnight; they decreed that mushrooms could only be served at the royal table. Truffles, unknown on this continent, where air freight shipments of them command lavish prices, have always been greatly prized. (For a while it was rumored that truffles had been discovered in, of course, California, but I have not been able to validate this claim.)

In Europe in the Middle Ages, the elusive truffle was thought to spring up from deer semen, which accounted for its seasonal and eclectic appearances. And there are dozens of folk tales about fairy-ring mushrooms. Kreiger retells one. In it, "gnomes and hobgoblins buried their treasure within the confines of such rings. Dragons, resting momentarily from the labor of scaring simple folk out of their wits, breathed living fire, thus scorching the greensward about them." The scientific explanation for these formations rests on the gradual outward spread of the mushroom mycelia; some rings have continued to form over a period of several hundred years.

It's good winter reading, this shelf of books. I don't mean to slight the texts devoted to mushroom cookery, either. Jane Grigson's *The Mushroom Feast* is a storehouse of fine recipes. I treasure even more highly her personal account of mushroom hunting in the countryside of the Bas-Vendomois. "Sunday is the occasion. Woods which have been silent most of the week, come alive. . . . One is isolated, all sense of time goes in the velvet warmth of the young trees. . . . Tolstoy could have written a scene from that Sunday afternoon, adding love disappointed, the coincidence of discovery. Or he might have been content, as we were, with family peace and mushrooms."

Robert Graves, the British poet, novelist, and essayist, deserves to be heard. "People of British stock are quite content to dismiss mycophobia as a social phenomenon hardly worth discussing. 'After all,' they say, 'most mushrooms are poisonous, so why not play safe? There are plenty of other things to eat. Why grub around under rotten tree stumps for nasty-looking fungi? Leave that to the Slavs.' You might as well refuse raspberries because the deadly nightshade is poisonous; or apples because of the terrible manchineel."

Like the dreaded amanita, this West Indian tree has acquired a lore of its own. Its fruit is poisonous and the milky sap it exudes can raise blisters on the skin. Not content with these facts, early naturalists reported it to be so toxic that people died from taking a nap in its shade. It is rumored that the Borgias judiciously stirred pulverized bits of poisonous amanitas into libations at banquets to dispatch their enemies.

Some things we will never know. But even as we avoid sleeping under manchineels and nibbling amanitas, let us not stint on apples and *Armillariella*.

JICAMA WITHOUT
EXPECTATIONS

Long ago, in a handkerchief-size suburban backyard dom-
inated by a huge maple tree that admitted very little sunlight, I raised half a dozen spindly tomato plants and first
made the acquaintance of the fearsome zucchini. Burpee's
was my catalog of choice back then; indeed, I doubt that I
knew any others existed. The prolixity and seductive lure of
today's catalogs almost exceed my desire to leaf through them.
It is not roses I seek; I am in search of the perfect vegetable.
Open-pollinated, disease-free, all-season producer, easy to
harvest, fun to cook, and heaven to eat. What cultivar is
this, as yet unborn?

I have lived long enough to see the sugar snap pea survive
its trials and move into the glossy pages of Harris, Stokes,
Shepherds et al. I have seen the great viney winter squashes
shrink into manageable bush types. A white eggplant has
swum into my ken, as have seed potatoes, and giant onions
that spring up from seed in a single season. The red brussels
sprout has arrived. There is an ongoing revolution in the
pepper world: Orange, red, yellow, chocolate, and now white
peppers are all said to be possible.

Lettuces of every hue and configuration have all but obliterated the boring iceberg head, and Japanese vegetables are so numerous that they now command their own category in the catalog. Central and South American varieties are not far behind, although I have only this winter tried to jump-start jicama, a delightfully crunchy root I first met on an hors d'oeuvres platter in Texas ten years ago. To my surprise, it has a vining habit and will want something comforting to twine itself on.

Climbers of the leguminous persuasion, from heirloom shelling-out beans to a strain of leafless peas, all do well in our soil. Frankly, I am deficient in the pepper department. *Capsicum*'s podlike fruit mostly just sit and sulk in my garden, although the long green Buddhas, which I haven't deliberately planted in a decade, continue to volunteer in all the wrong places. As do Oriental poppies, broadcast by unseen birds. These refuse to be transplanted into some other location but dot themselves among the carrots and beets at will.

For just shy of twenty years now I have been gardening in the same spot abutting the forest out of which emerge such outlaws as raccoons and woodchucks, skunk, deer, and black bear. I long to have my garden closer to the house where it would be less subject to depredations. The dogs could keep an eye on it there. But our hilly farm yields only this distant tabletop a hundred yards above the house and barn, and it must serve as garden space. The earth dries out slowly there, backed by our pond. But it stands open to full sun and yields 800 pounds of produce in a decent season.

Substantial credit for this prodigious yield goes to the *New York Times*, which arrives Monday through Saturday in the mailbox at the foot of the hill, courtesy of the RFD mailperson and her jeep. On Mondays or Tuesdays the *Times Book Review* comes via the same route. I don't subscribe to the

Sunday edition, partly because it is too heavy to carry half
a mile north, and partly because it would usurp every Monday to work my way through it.

It makes no difference that the news is a day late when I
carry it up the hill, usually on a horse, sometimes on foot.
For breadth and depth of coverage, the *Times* has no peer.
Certainly no other newspaper can match, inch for inch, its
thick accretion of words, stacked and ready at all seasons
in the mud room.

In March, when I start seedlings in flats on top of the
refrigerator and dryer, little cutouts of wet newspaper line
the trays and help hold in the moisture. New York City's ten
best Szechuan restaurants underlie Johnny's new hybrid
pepper seeds, which seem to take forever to wake up and
grow. My almost-antique celery seeds which have not failed
in four years lie atop Charles Schwab's ad for how to open
an IRA account. Germination rates may exceed interest again
this year.

By early April, seedlings strain up to the fluorescent lights
in three locations in my kitchen and crowd every south-
facing windowsill. Once they attain a certain size, the hardy
ones move out to the porch to make room for such tender
beginners as basil and eggplant. Another week or two and
onion and lettuce flats can proceed from porch to terrace to
harden off, followed by broccolis and cauliflowers.

Later, when the winter's weight of horse manure has been
turned into the garden and the early May sun has dried the
soil to a workable stage, these cold-weather crops go into
the ground. Broccoli, cabbage, cauliflower, and celery
seedlings, wearing their *Book Review* cutworm collars closed
with paper clips, appreciate being mulched early with whole
sections of Home and Living, covered over with sweepings
of old hay from the barn floor.

Peas prefer to stand alone, unweeded between and crowding in on each other for support before they start to climb the wire fencing. Respectfully, I paper only between their rows to keep out interlopers.

A little later in the growing season such directly sown vegetables as beets and green beans are also mulched with "All the News That's Fit to Print." Once the individual plants are well organized with their second set of true leaves showing, I enclose them, tearing slits in three or four thicknesses of paper to fit around the whole plant.

This is tedious and time-consuming, but pays off mightily in shutting out weeds and preserving the soil temperature that suits each variety. Green beans, for example, like warm soil, but want to be mulched before summer's full heat strikes. While kneeling to put paper around them, I can catch up on an enormous range of topics that eluded me when they were current events. If it's windy, though, I have to hurry and weight down the papers with mulch.

Since our own leavings don't yield enough, I collect spoiled hay from other sources, some of it saved from the preceding season and piled outside the garden in late November when I dismantle the rows and topdress with manure. Each year, though, I scrounge moldy bales from neighbors with a leaky barn loft or a leftover supply from two years back. (It goes against the New England ethic to have to pay for spoiled hay.) I think it is not possible in this life to have too much mulch. When we re-dress the rows in the fall, old sawdust bedding from the run-in sheds mingles with and lightens this pile.

Cucumbers and various squashes begin indoors in my house in cut-down cardboard milk cartons. These seedlings are very susceptible to root damage and need to have their underpinnings protected in the transplanting process. Once the soil is hospitably warm for them (usually the first week in June), I tear the bottoms off the containers and tuck the seedlings into the garden, then paper them about with more pages of the *Times*. Since squash must sprawl and run before it fruits, it's useful to have prodigious amounts of newspaper available to cover the ground it plans to overtake. Otherwise, poke and burdock and other deeply rooted nuisances will crowd the edibles and cut down on the yield.

The *Times* is entirely permeable. Rain, when it graciously falls, and droplets borne from the pond, when it doesn't, penetrate hay and newsprint and soak into the furrows.

A vegetable garden just below a pond, just inside a field bordered by hundreds of acres of forests, clearly needs to be fenced and refenced. To keep down weeds that take tenacious hold in, around, and through the original buried chicken wire fence and the later additions of hardware cloth, screening, and other exotica thrown into the breach when emergencies arise, fat sections of the *Times* can be stuffed into the gaps and pleats, then mulched for appearance's sake.

All around the outer perimeter, whole sections of the newspaper lie flat, weighted and stained with handy rocks. Before I climb over a stile of poplar chunks and into my garden, I sometimes stop to marvel at the Roche Bobois furniture ads, the gorgeous lofts in Chelsea, the halogen lights and sunken marble baths of the back pages. Here where tomatoes overgrow their cages and Kentucky Wonders climb chaotic tepees of sumac branches, I admire engineered closets and beds that fold up into walls.

My corn is not sown here, but in an inviolate space facing south in the uppermost and hottest pasture. A year's worth of *Book Review*s, exactly the correct width when opened out, serves as carpet between the rows. And an opened-out page folded into thirds slips between individual plants, once they're six inches high. It's an Augean labor, but only needs to be performed once. Hay and / or sawdust mulch covers the paper, and nothing further is required except to eat the ears when they're of a size. No, I misspoke. Just before the corn really sets ears, I need to energize the two strands of electric fence that keep raccoons at bay.

Next April, when a general thaw makes it possible to turn the garden once again, nothing much is left of the *New York Times*. A few tatters with mysterious pieces of words on them are in evidence, but, thanks to thousands of literate earthworms, not enough remains to construct even a minimalist story.

Cultivating a garden satisfies at least some of my deep yearnings for order. Everything else has a ragged sort of shape to it. In an old farmhouse, cobwebs cling to exposed beams. Pawprints muddy the floor. Doors have to be propped open with stones, the stair risers constructed 200 years ago are amateurishly uneven. Wisps of hay ride indoors on our sweaters. It's a comfortably down-at-the-heels atmosphere. Sometimes, guiltily, I think of my mother, who would never have tolerated this welter. But the garden is composed of orderly rows and blocks of raised beds. Weeds do not penetrate the deep mulch. Serenely, plants grow, blossom, set fruit. All is as workable as Latin grammar: *amo, amas, amat* among the brassicas; *hic, haec, hoc* in a raised bed lively with parsnip foliage.

You cannot justify a garden to non-believers. You cannot explain to the unconverted the desire, the ravishing need, to get your hands into the soil again, to plant, thin, train up on stakes, trellis onto pea fence, hill up to blanch, just plain admonish to grow. From Pliny to Voltaire, from Thomas Jefferson to Saint-Exupéry, gardening has been an emblem of integrity in an increasingly incomprehensible world. Even

Thoreau, who wanted to break with the past and start over as a sort of new Adam, an innocent in Paradise on the shores of Walden Pond, was susceptible to the blandishments of growing things. He narrowly escaped enslavement by hoe when he "made the earth say beans instead of grass." In *A Week on the Concord and Merrimack Rivers,* he pronounced gardening "civil and social, but it wants [lacks] the vigor and freedom of the forest and the outlaw."

There is an intimacy to the act of planting as tantalizing as possessing a secret. Every seed you sow has passed through your fingers on its way from dormancy to hoped-for fruition. "Trailing clouds of glory do we come," Wordsworth wrote. Thus come the little cobbles of beet seeds that separate when rolled between your fingers, the flat, feathery parsnip ones that want to drift on air en route to the furrow, the round black dots that will be Kelsae onions, fat and sweet by September, the exasperatingly tiny lettuce flecks that descend in a cluster, and the even harder-to-channel carrot seeds.

Some of my seed packets are ten years old but they've lost little vigor. Stored out of season in an unheated closet, they have amazing keeping qualities. But consider the lotus seeds found under an ancient lake bed in Manchuria. Carbon-dated at 800 years old, they grew into lotus plants of a sort that had never been seen in that particular area. Such extravagant longevity makes me hopeful that we humans too will ever so gradually advance into new forms, a higher level of lotus, as it were.

A few years ago, early in May, while upending a wheelbarrow load of horse manure onto the pile, I noticed some splayed green leaves emerging along the midriff of this sizable mountain. They were not poke or burdock. They had a cultivated look. By tacit agreement my husband and I began to deposit our barrow loads on the north face of the pile.

By mid-June the south slope was covered with a dense network of what were now, clearly, squash leaves. Male blossoms, visible on their skinny-necked stems, were popping up and a few bees were already working the territory. *Let this not be zucchini*, I prayed to Mother Nature.

Around the Fourth of July, green swellings could be seen at the bases of the female blossoms. The solo plant had overrun the manure pile and was now racing along our dirt road, uphill and down. Every few days I policed the road's edge and nipped back each of the brash tendrils that thought, like turtles, to cross the right-of-way. Thwarted in this direction, the heroic squash began to loop upward, mounting a huge stand of jewelweed in its eagerness to get at a telephone pole.

Well before Labor Day we knew what we had: Sweet Mamas of an especially vigorous persuasion. About ten of these pumpkin-shaped winter squashes were visible from the mountaintop. Several looked table-ready.

We watched and waited, despite several frost warnings, secure in the knowledge that the warmth of the pile would protect this crop from an early demise. A two-day downpour flattened some of the luxuriant foliage; we could see that the plant was still setting fruit, heedless of the calendar. After several sunny days when things had dried out a bit, I poked around a few of the giants at the top of the mountain. They had orange streaks and some of the stems were cracking.

Harvest time was at hand. I began yanking the vines hand over hand, as if coiling the ropes of a seagoing vessel. In all we garnered thirty-five beauteous volunteers. Not a single squash bug anywhere. No chipmunk toothmarks, no tiny gnawings of mice or voles. It seems that even the lowliest creature disdains a manure pile.

We compost all our garden and table scraps, from elderly

broccoli plants to orange peels to onion skins. The simplest method is just to dig a hole anywhere in the brown mountain, deposit the leavings, and backfill with a few shovelfuls of the usual. Leftovers disintegrate in a few days; sometimes I catch a glimpse of grapefruit rind or eggshell not fully digested. I re-inter them without a backward glance.

Late November is manure pile demolition time on the farm. As much of the mountain as can be moved manually or by machine is returned to the gardens, pastures, and riding ring. In the course of upending and hauling, some ancient Sweet Mama cotyledon must have been stirred to germinate. I like to think of the seed lying there through several seasons before the right combination of sun and warmth, moon and rain awakened it.

Early in October, in Geese Go South Moon, leaves rain down with a muffled sideslipping sound. Dust motes spin in sunlight like flour sifting in puffs onto the beginnings of batter. For the horses this season is heavenly. We haven't had a killing frost yet. All of our fields are open to them, and they wander like sleepwalkers from one area to another grazing intermittently, sometimes standing for long thoughtful moments silhouetted against the backdrop of forest or granite outcropping.

This is the season when tails at last become superfluous. The biting insects have fled, migrated, died off, or entered hibernation. Except for the usual small ectoplasms of gnats that still hover in quiet air, all is benign and salving in the ether. Gone the vicious little trapezoidal deerflies that draw blood from animal and human. Vanished too the horn and face flies, bot- and horseflies. The ubiquitous black flies, that penance of the north country, never quite disappear but they are greatly diminished. And this summer's long tenure of mosquitoes appears to be over.

We are in the briefest and most beautiful moment of stasis. Along the perimeter of the pastures, fall-flowering asters, tiny blue florets with yellow centers, flourish. A few late blackberries go on ripening, daintily pursued by the greedy broodmare, who rolls back her lips in order to nip them off, one or two at a time, without getting pricked by thorns. The Jerusalem artichokes, harbingers of frost, are in bud and threaten to open in today's sunlight. Toads in the vegetable garden, deprived of their prey now, have begun retreating to the woods after a long and profitable summer. Mushrooms appear everywhere—two brain puffballs in the dressage ring, little pear-shaped lycoperdons dotting the pine duff like misplaced miniature golf balls, smoky hygrophorus clustering in the dark corners of the pine grove, and in the rocky acre allotted the ewes, brickies—*Hypholoma sublateritium*—spring up, breaking their gray cobwebby films. The chanterelles we prized and ate all summer are gone, but clusters of honey mushrooms at the base of decaying oaks are now ready. Sometimes, traversing the woods on horseback, we spot a full bloom of oyster mushrooms swelling on the trunk of a dying tree. Foraging for mushrooms has its own visceral pleasures: We reap where we did not sow, paper, mulch, or water.

The war against the thistles continues. Day three of eradication, extirpation, elimination, waged by me with a large serrated breadknife and by my helper with a presharpened post-hole shovel. I bobble along on my knees, repositioning the kneeling pad that was a birthday present, scraping my knuckles against the inside of these thistleproof deerhide gloves. I infer from what I see that the thistle is a biennial plant. The great green overlapping swords I am digging up— though seldom does the entire taproot come with the plant— will be the stalk and flower of next summer. The dried vicious pickets we can pull out, thereby scattering 10,000 new seeds for the future, are no threat for the immediate season. While we're about it, we yank any surviving nettle plants, which ovines will eat if desperate.

Nothing on this farm ever reaches the desperation stage. The several ewes who summer here, leaving their home pasture to the newly weaned lambs, make little single-file trails, over to the pond, behind the pond to the woodlot, thence along the fenceline back to the rockpile, and in the heat of the day, into the run-in shed where they lie on green pine sawdust in a flaccid heap like dirty laundry. We are their sabbatical. They arrive sheared and anxious in May and go home in October woolly, plump, and totally at ease, to be bred once again.

In the garden broccoli continues to bud, the Kentucky Wonders still put up beans, and the cauliflower plants left unpulled have, to my wonderment, made multiple tiny new heads. We've pulled and dried and braided our onions. Carrots, too, cannot stay in the ground, as voles and mice begin to nibble them. Two years ago I left parsnips in their bed to winter over and found not a trace of them by spring; last winter I pulled and scrubbed them, dried them off, and froze them, on the theory that they sweeten in the frozen earth if undisturbed. My theory proved itself, for we ate them with relish all last winter in soups and stews.

Kale, brussels sprouts, leeks, celery root, and three purple cabbages remain. Two five-gallon pails of tomatoes, last of the line, are ripening on the porch. A small group of gargantuan zucchini, somehow overlooked, has already been converted into zucchini bread and / or grated, salted, squeezed dry, and frozen to be sneaked into next winter's recipes a little at a time. Zucchini blend unnoticed in winter soups and are barely discernible when spread on pizza dough before the sauce and toppings are added. The freezer is packed with the summer's haul of strawberries, raspberries, peas, corn, green beans, and aye the rest. Part of me—the weary part—longs for frost. The other, frugal self is happy to receive each day's reduced yield.

November 15. Now I am removed by a thousand miles from my farm and garden. A wet snow is falling in central Illinois, locus day and night of mournful diesel whistles at grade crossings. Here, the campus grounds are littered with crab apples and I find myself mourning that no one cared enough to gather the harvest and make jelly. I think of my own shelves full of blueberry, strawberry, elderberry, and grape jams, and the five gallons of blackberries waiting in the freezer for a January nor'easter so they can be cooked into "that tar-thick boil love cannot stir down."

There are still brussels sprouts to be picked and half a dozen daikons—Japanese radishes—to be pulled, but otherwise the garden is done for. And with it the unremitting labor. Dilled green beans and bread-and-butter pickles crowd the storage shelves, abutting bottles of decorative purple-pink chive blossom vinegar. Mint, tarragon, and dill plants are drying in paper bags hung from the porch rafters.

Visitors fall into two categories: the urban admirers, nostalgists who long—but only in their imaginations—for gardens to tend, and The Others, who see this as madness. It's not cost effective, they remind you. Look at the money you spend for seed, blood meal, Dipel, whatever. Look at the fencing (which is now deplorable and needs to be redone). On the other hand, nothing we eat has been drenched with pesticides or fertilized with chemicals. There's also the deeply Calvinist satisfaction of knowing you have earned by the sweat of your brow this delicious feast of fresh asparagus, new spinach, sweet corn, either harvested *in situ* or now, at this season, brought up from the capacious freezer in the cellar.

"The poet," Thoreau wrote in *A Week on the Concord and Merrimack Rivers,* "is he that hath fat enough, like bears and marmots, to suck his claws all winter. He hibernates in this world, and feeds on his own marrow."

December. Home again, to bountiful snow. Such good cover we can open the fields again, as soon as hunting season passes, to the horses to wander at will. This is the Moon That Parts Her Hair Right Square in the Middle, so styled because of the shortest day of the year and the welcome beginning of longer days. December and the arctic months that follow belong to the writer in a leisurely way, to read, think, scribble, declaim aloud, and develop a dozen fantasies of fulfillment. In January's Help Eat Moon—stay inside; too cold to do anything else, so eat more—and during February's Moon of the Eagle and Hatching Time of the Owl I will suck my claws.

Ruminating in February, I read through a stack of old *Smithsonian* and *Natural History* magazines, my favorite provender. When I lift my eyes to the hills that surround us, all visible activity is suspended. This could be a glacial prehistoric era but for the two woodstoves radiating a hospitable warmth indoors and the two domesticated wolves several times removed dozing on the hearth. As I muse on the tenacity of the life force—the mice and voles unseen, running along their narrow tunnels under the snow, deer bedded in a hemlock grove far from any road—I come upon an article about suspended animation. The technical term is cryptobiosis. Brine shrimp, which flourish in brackish water that other plankton cannot tolerate, manage to survive even after the ponds dry up. They stop consuming oxygen and simply encyst their embryos until conditions improve.

Researchers have carbon-dated some cysts retrieved from sediment found to be 10,000 years old. Amazingly, several of these hatched when placed back in water. I am comforted, and it is not a cold comfort; it cheers me to learn that certain kinds of brine shrimp reproduce by parthenogenesis and have persisted without male assistance for millions of years. This is less a feminist statement than an affirmation of reproductive forces.

Now we have arrived at Groundhog Day, an increasingly trivialized ceremony in this epoch of electric lights and central heating. Once it was an event that pledged the faith of human beings in the approach of the vernal equinox. Early Slavic peoples celebrated a holiday that translates as "butter week," when, as an act of sun worship, they devoured mountains of the pancakes we know as blini or blintzes, slathered with melted butter. Preparing, chewing, and swallowing were meant to ensure halcyon days to come with abundant crops, golden marriages, and sturdy offspring to till the fields. I like this story much better than Pennsylvania's Punxsutawney Phil, dragged out of hibernation and paraded before the television cameras to make the feature page of every newspaper in the East.

We have forgotten that we celebrate the coming of the growing season. Most of us are so far removed from the acts of cultivation that we would be unable to recognize a tepee of horticultural beans at twenty paces. But we are evolved from East African hominids that once subsisted on a totally vegetarian diet. This line of herbivorous pre-humans possessed incredibly powerful chewing teeth about five million years ago, but the species did not last. Our molars and premolars have shrunk, our craniums have enlarged, and we are less robust omnivores, and what has it profited us?

It's fascinating to realize that the formal notion of agriculture, of actually sowing, weeding, and reaping plants from the soil for human uses, is only about 10,000 years old, a mere blip on the screen of human / pre-human history. We seem to have evolved in response to varying temperatures, "successive cooling plunges," anthropologist Elisabeth Vrba calls them. Wet forests gradually shrank into dry grasslands and then climatic upheavals probably reversed this action several times. Rainfall amounts and geographical boundaries tend to isolate animal populations, limiting the exchange of gene pools. These smaller groups may then diverge to permit the development of new species or they may simply die out—more's the pity—as did our very early vegetarian ancestors. I read that the biosphere is "a living layer, stretched thinly over the globe, responding rhythmically to the beat of the earth," and I think of the holes we are poking in this thin curtain that sustains us. What new species will evolve once we have destroyed the atmosphere we require in order to breathe? What new brine shrimp will we become?

This past winter I've had a sleigh at my disposal, a little two-seater built by the Excelsior Sleigh Company of Watertown, New York, around the turn of the century. At some time in the past hundred years an importunate horse's hoof kicked a crescent-shaped hole in one side of it but this in no way limits its serviceability. With new shafts and a few mended braces, it's sturdy enough to drive across the fields and, before the plow arrives, down the road as well. Twice we sojourned with it to Vermont to attend festive sleigh rallies that looked like events recorded by Currier and Ives.

When conditions are optimal—about six inches of snow over hard-pack—going sleighing is as exhilarating as the daredevil bellyflopping runs of my childhood. Down the steep of our backyard that connected with the Kellys' driveway, around Devil's Elbow and out onto Pelham Road we flew, perilously side by side, in Germantown, Pennsylvania, long ago.

My half-Arab, half-Standardbred gelding loves to pull. Once he overcomes inertia and the sleigh begins to glide, he finds it all but effortless to keep it skimming. I have to hang on tight; I drive him with the reins on the lowest (most severe) slot of his Liverpool bit. In summer with the two-wheel phaeton, I can trust him with just a snaffle. The term "mercurial" accurately reflects changes in equine temperament according to the vagaries of weather. When the mercury plunges, their exuberance rises proportionately, and vice-versa. In winter our horses are very shaggy, volatile, and round-bellied from free-choice good hay. By midsummer, freed of those heavy coats and in regular work, they are sleek, supple, and almost obedient.

There's a place we love to go, on horseback or by phaeton and now by sleigh; it's a protected stretch of wetlands under federal jurisdiction, crisscrossed by a network of driveable trails. Weekdays we are usually the only travelers. The dogs go with us, sprinting into the woods to follow some elusive scent, bounding back to catch up with us around the next bend. In winter we cross-country ski here, too, along paths that weave through managed stands of red and white pine, hemlock and some few larches. Only an occasional patch of sunlight makes its way here. The prevailing northerly wind is deflected by the abundant growth. The stillness is so palpable I would risk calling it holy.

Rhythmic hoofbeats and arrhythmic sneeze-snorts echo like gunshot in these vasty rooms. Although I have never seen the taiga, I think it must look like this, with a three-abreast hitch of caribou flying over the tundra, outstripping their wolves. We seldom raise any wild creatures here as there is very little understory for browsing, but once, around a bend in the trail, we came upon a magnificent coyote, well nourished, tall at the shoulder. There was barely enough time to admire him before he was gone. Oddly, our dogs never picked up his scent but continued their dilettantish feints around the bases of trees up which a few squirrels had scampered.

These are the best of days. At noon when the temperature peaks in the twenties, the fresh powder of last night's little snow squalls squeaks under our skis or runners. My horse is shod with borium caulks on all four feet. In front he wears snowball poppers, pads designed to keep the snow from balling up in the concavity of his hoof known as the frog. He is surefooted and a little too eager! We fly along in an extended trot until he wears down the edge of his enthusiasm and will come back into my hand.

Is it dangerous? Of course. A spill in cart or sleigh is far more fraught with peril than an unceremonious dumping from the saddle. The horse's life, too, is at risk when he's in the traces and upsets. But I mind the trail, squint in a sudden stretch of sunlight, settle into a long easy trot on the flat, and ask him to walk the last mile back so he can cool out without chilling.

In March the lambs—singles, twins, and triplets—begin to be born to various small-farm and hobby-farm breeders. The professionals who raise lamb in quantity for the market breed early, risking losing some newborns in order to have table-lamb, as they call it, in time for the Easter trade. It's baby chick and rabbit time, too, most of them destined for oblivion in eight to ten weeks. Goat farmers are happy to have infant bucks on hand for the Greek Orthodox Easter market in Boston, where roast kid is considered a delicacy.

I can't blink these facts but I'm grateful I don't have to participate in them. By and large, the small breeders raise their animals for slaughter in a far more humane fashion than the animal factories of agribusiness. Around here, veal calves are not confined in slatted cages in the dark, chickens scratch in capacious barnyards and are not debeaked, sows farrow in full-size pens or in the open. Does it matter how they live, since they are all going to die to feed us? I think it matters mightily, not only because these uncrowded creatures need not be shot full of antibiotics to survive to marketable size, but because how we treat the animals in our keeping defines us as human beings.

April is punctuated by the geese going over, baying like beagles in the dawn sky. Our hundred maple taps run grudgingly around midday, then seal up tight until the next day's warmth releases them again for a few hours. Traditionally, George Washington's birthday is the first acceptable date to go out with brace and bit and bore holes in preselected trees. This year, blizzards and relentless cold delayed the start a good three or four weeks. Sugaring-off time depends on the freeze-thaw cycle of March and early April. This hasn't been a good run compared to last year, but the deep snow cover is prolonging it clear to the end of the month, which is unusual. Things have a way of balancing out, a fact it has taken us thirty years here to accept. Drought one season, monsoon the next.

For the first time in our long tenure here, the spring peepers have been all but inaudible. True, we've had a slow, cold spring, but except for a few tentative pipings, no evidence of *Hyla crucifer*, whose high, shrill whistle ordinarily raises a deafening chorus every night during mating season. Some nights I've even closed the bedroom window on the lower-pond side to reduce the noise pollution. Now I find myself straining to hear that high-pitched stridulation.

Reflecting back on last summer, the population of bullfrogs in our upper pond, normally abundant enough to keep our dogs busy startling them off their sunbathing perches, seemed to have diminished. There were sporadic late-afternoon jug-a-rums announcing the locations of various kings, but the usual clumps of tadpoles in the shallows sprouting forelegs and gradually absorbing their tails were greatly reduced.

The salamander density seemed undisturbed, especially in the red stage on dry land when they are known as efts, a useful Scrabble word. The salamander is voiceless, so far as I know, but consider this lyrical outburst from my sobersides bible, the *Complete Field Guide to American Wildlife, East, Central and North*, by Henry Hill Collins, Jr.: "The cries of the ancient frogs may well have been the first voices in the springtime of the Age of Land Vertebrates. For millions of years before the coming of the songbirds, the calls of various frogs and toads must have been the most musical sounds on earth."

Another mystery is the absence of great blue herons from the rookery in our secret beaver pond a few miles away. For years we've gone on horseback every few days beginning at the end of April to keep tabs on this enormous nursery, where a dozen or more nests decorate the tops of dead pine trees still rising from their flooded bases. So far this year, no activity is evident. No crying and flapping, no *ack-ack-ack* of hungry fledglings, not even any tardy parent brooding over her eggs. Are we simply in a new cycle of birth and decay, have the herons relocated to a better, even more remote pond, or is the culprit manmade: acid rain?

Still, the geese go over barking in formation, the rusty-hinge sound of the red-winged blackbirds announces that insects are once again abroad. Tongues of snow retreat in the woods, the ubiquitous mud ebbs, pastures begin to green around the margins, fiddlehead ferns poke their spokes up through the woodland wet, and the first harbingers of spring, wake-robin trilliums, which will send up their distinctive burgundy blooms, announce the tidings with their earliest leaves.

Everything resurrects in May. Nettles first, followed by wild mustard, then dandelions and clover and tender grasses. The hardwoods flush faintly red with new buds, prelude to leaves. The willows sprout catkins, then laces of yellow strings. Wake-robin is followed by bloodlilies, violets, lady's slipper, and the whole procession of miniature blossoms that dot the grudgingly greening pastures.

In the bird department, phoebes are the first to return after the blackbirds; I worry what they will find to eat before the air fills with insects. Robins next, then all are smothered in a brief snowstorm. (I put out raisins and hope for the best.) Finches, both purple and gold, hung around all winter, as did the evening grosbeaks, but here come the song sparrows with their *old-john-peabody, peabody, pea* refrain, and finally the rose-breasted grosbeaks, spectacularly jousting at the feeders.

How joyous the first light is now, with all this territorial music! How lucky I feel to come awake to the overlapping trills and calls, a symphony of screes, caws, and warbles, many of them distinctive and recognizable, some tantalizingly elusive, even unknown. It is deliciously noisy at 5 A.M. Everyone is staking a claim. But what falls so happily on human ears actually reflects a tense struggle to survive and procreate. Life is not harmonious for the insectivores, it seems to me, who must sieve the air from dawn to full dark for enough protein to sustain a clutch of nestlings. Prodigal nature dictates their stern routine: two, even three batches of babies in a season to guarantee the future of the race. In much the same way, nature sends down a deluge of volunteer dill into my vegetable garden, along with torrents of sprouting jewelweed, chickweed, lamb's quarters, and half a dozen extra-prolific others to bedevil the deliberately planted cultivars.

It's a penance of sorts to rise extra early and get the horses out on grass for a few hours before the wings of midges and black flies have dried. By 9 A.M. you cannot inhale outside without ingesting black flies. Even with face masks in place, the horses are driven wild by them and prefer to be in their stalls. We will endure black flies until the mosquitoes overtake them, but even this plague is self-limiting. In a few weeks, once the richest flush of growth has passed and with it the danger of founder from too much grazing, the horses will be out on grass all night. The cruelest pests—deerflies, horseflies, bots—are diurnal. Admittedly, mosquitoes raise welts on equines as well as humans, but they are more easily deterred with repellents and oily lotions.

One dawn's reward: a pair of loons crying their thrillingly demented cry overhead. That same week, wood ducks overnighting on the lower pond. The next morning a great showy splashing on the big upper pond. Two pairs of mallards, and later, one hooded merganser. What can you do with these treats? Like the winter's wild turkeys parading across the back lawn, the daily visitations by pileated woodpeckers, the late-summer fawn still speckled with camouflage who bounded out of the tall grass like an enormous rabbit, these are honoraria to share with like-minded friends. We commingle our passions with a small band of other beast-bird-and-flower fanatics, like a secret cell of Communists. Some of them have snapshots of moose, blurry because the photographer's hand was shaking with excitement, some have up-close black bear sightings, one has even come into the presence of a bobcat. Such events make us celebrities of a sort.

A Montana visitor in May, however, complained that the world of New England was far too verdant for her eyes. She could not differentiate the variations; all was a huge humid sea of green vegetation in her parched sight. Her retina longed to record the yellow and brown vistas of her native heath, the open plains and craggy mountains, canyons and draws that comforted her.

Especially you know what not to rhapsodize about. Nothing rhapsodic about the enormous male raccoon who seems to have taken up permanent lodgings in the grain room of the barn. He sprawls over the cats' feeding shelf while they wait respectfully on the back sill, and it takes a snap of the longe whip to drive him off. I am a bit leery, given the recent rash of reports of rabies in New Hampshire. All our animals have been vaccinated, but we humans are certainly vulnerable. Now I remove the cat dishes every evening, hoping to deprive our adoptee of the easy pickings he seems to have come to expect. Bad enough to feed a flock of forty aggressive evening grosbeaks year-round. Am I destined to deliver cat kibble to the multitudes of masked bandits?

One afternoon our raccoon arrived just as I was feeding the cats. Abra growled, a sound I have never heard her utter before, and instantly decamped. I looked up into the coon's handsome feral face; he paid no attention to my shouts. I snapped the longe whip at him but he stood his ground. The next crack caught him across the shoulders but hardly dislodged him. He retreated twenty paces into the broodmare's stall where she totally ignored his presence and went on eating. A raccoon that bold by daylight? We called the town's animal officer, who offered us the loan of a Havahart trap.

"Take him at least ten miles from here, or you'll have him

back next morning," he said. "Course, last time I did this, I got a skunk in the trap. If you catch a skunk instead, throw an old blanket over the cage before you pick it up so he won't spray." (Do I believe this will work? Not for one moment.) "Try peanut butter and if that don't get him, tuna fish."

Peanut butter didn't work but the trap was sprung. We continue to reset it with various baits, but this fellow is apparently a graduate of Havaharts. He gets the goods and goes free. The cats and he seem to have agreed on a non-aggression pact. The dogs, too, have grown quite used to him; the horses treat him with total indifference. His hide-out lies between the double walls that separate the brood-mare's stall from the sawdust bin. He materializes and fades away as soundlessly as the Cheshire Cat. Often now I find him resting comfortably on the top ledge of that divider, eyeing the general proceedings. He is extremely handsome with his narrow feline face and foxy ears. I count five rings on his great tail.

Now I look over my shoulder before I open the grain bin, expecting the marauder to leap in unannounced. And as if raccoons weren't enough, Rilke, our mostly German shepherd, came home from a trail ride today with ten porcupine quills in his face. Luckily, we were able to yank them out with needle-nose pliers while distracting him with dog biscuits. Dozens of other times with our other dogs, particularly with the handsome but ineducable Dalmatians we used to raise, we had to make emergency runs to the expensive open-all-night city vet to have forty or fifty quills removed under total anesthesia. "The reason we don't learn from history," my poet friend Howard Nemerov once said, " is because we are not the same people who learned last time." Dogs, it seems, are never the same dogs who learned last time. Every porcupine, every skunk is newly imprinted on the brain pan, which then reverts to tabula rasa.

After a week of imprisoning one barn cat after the other in the Havahart—each seemed perfectly content there, having polished off a plate of tuna fish—our raccoon took the original bait of peanut butter. He slept most of the way to Mt. Sunapee State Park, lulled into slumber by the gentle motion of the automobile, leading me to suspect that he has made this journey before, but came awake at once when the trap door was opened. He snarled, leapt out, and shot up a tree. We hope we are permanently delivered of raccoon.

In mid-June we take our first delivery of next winter's hay, a hundred bales of first-cut timothy, insurance in case the second cutting, which we prefer for its better keeping properties, comes late or, heaven forfend, not at all. (There is always Canadian hay in an emergency, but the bales are wire-tied and the contents are coarser.) The farmer who supplies us is an old friend by now. He takes a proprietary interest in the well-being of our horses, especially my driving horse, who took him for a few fast passes in the cart one day, and he is a source of rich anecdotes about the past in this corner of New England. His family has been here since, as he puts it, the back of the beyond. Steer are his specialty but he also raises up a fine crop of local boys who hire on with him for summer jobs as soon as they are tall enough and strong enough. His work ethic is stringent but kind. Graduates of his school go on with better biceps and enlarged self-respect.

And so we grope our way into high summer again, into the time of strawberry picking, followed by the first peas. If rain is bountiful there will be hundreds of *Coprinus* mushrooms, our first available fungus, to make into soup. The green beans will ripen all at once, there will be too much broccoli, and when the yellow squash and zucchini begin to set fruit, there will be no sane way to cope with their over-abundance. We will wait on the cusp of August for our first vine-ripened tomato. Turn around twice and they will be too many.

Just as we ate asparagus every night for three weeks when the crop gushed magically forth in May, so will we devour corn on the cob every night for those few weeks—if we're lucky!—at the end of August and into early September. A little melancholy will creep in when the corn is done. I know I will grieve as I stand there feeding the succulent shucks to the horses, as one does when a wonderful novel draws to its close. "What do I want of my life?" Stanley Kunitz asked in a poem. "More! More."

Another year, please. Another year of the same. Hay in the barn, heavy snows, ten cords of dry firewood, split and stacked. Send in the black flies, let a new crop of nettles emerge, may the broodmare bring forth a healthy foal. Next year I promise to plant a smaller and thriftier garden. If I get another summer like this one, I vow to spend an hour every afternoon sitting by the pond or swimming in it. I will cultivate leisure as tenderly as jicama, which, by the way, made splendid vines and never cared to develop edible roots. I will grow jicama again, without expectations, simply to cherish it, along with the dogs and horses, the cats, even the raccoon, if he returns to raise a family, a not unlikely prospect.

LABORS OF LOVE

In 1976, our first foal, a fawn-colored, spindle-legged filly with a white star and snip, was born. Her mother was a maiden mare, an abuse case Victor and I had intercepted two years earlier on her way to the slaughterhouse. We bought her for 30 cents a pound. Taboo was liver chestnut with a star and looked to be part Standardbred with very wide-set eyes, east / west-pointing ears, and a long but not unrefined face. In the course of her physical rehabilitation, we discovered that she had been harshly "cowboyed." A half-inch-thick scar ran like an elastic band all the way around her tongue. She had two muscle scars in her neck, indentations the size of a dime and deep enough to absorb your thumb up to the first joint. It seemed likely that in the course of being broke, someone had looped a wire around her tongue, snubbed her up tight to a post, and left her to fight it out.

Despite huge rations of tender loving care, Taboo never overcame a certain standoffishness, a lack of trust in human beings. Sturdy and smooth-gaited, she was wonderfully brave on the trail, unfazed by flapping laundry, working cherry-pickers, or kids on bicycles doing wheelies, as long as she was out alone. But she could never be safely ridden in company, for the sound of hoofbeats drove her wild and she invariably bolted whenever she heard another horse approaching.

I read articles on how to deal with this problem. I consulted trainers and owners, and everyone had a different theory. Some advised letting her run off and then making her gallop further after she was exhausted. Others suggested starting over with lots of groundwork on the longe line. Still others put their faith in a variety of headgear and bits. I tried them all.

Eventually, I gave up on martingales, Kimberwickes, hackamores and Pelhams, bosals, war bonnets and draw reins, and I rode her alone in a snaffle. We were happy together but I had to revise my hopes of using her as a competitive trail horse.

Because breeding was said by the local pundits to exert a calming influence on the fractious, we bred Taboo to a nearby Arabian stallion who had sired several amiable get. She was easy to handle, easy to breed, and she seemed to enjoy our solitary hacks during the long months of her pregnancy. Toward the end of it, I rode her bareback in fly bonnet and Easyboots painted orange in case one flew off at a trot. People pointed to us and snickered.

Taboo's filly was born at nine on a June evening. We arrived on the scene before it managed to get to its feet. The next several hours were a horror show, for the mare would not allow this interloper, this ghost that had somehow appeared in her stall, to nurse. At midnight I called the vet, who brusquely advised us to twitch the mare, back her into a corner, and get the baby on a teat "or you'll have a dead foal by morning." Thereupon he hung up.

Victor and I struggled through the next twenty-four hours, taking turns staying in the stall, positioning the mare where her hind feet could do the least damage and maneuvering to get the foal attached long enough to acquire the mare's antibodies through her colostrum. We then removed the foal to its own stall and began feeding her mare's milk replacer (Borden's Foal-Lac) every four hours by bottle.

Within a week she had learned how to suck up the liquid gold from a bowl. Soon thereafter, she began to nibble the milk replacer in pellet form. Nutritionally she throve, grew sleek and shiny and beautiful.

Although her sire was a bright red chestnut, this filly gradually turned dun color with a dorsal stripe, dapples, black points, and grulla markings over the withers. She socialized comfortably with the other horses, including her uncomprehending mother, but grew up to be an incorrigible tail chewer. She bobbed all the other compliant horses' tails, robbing them of efficient fly swatters the following season (tails, alas, grow rather slowly). This depraved appetite persisted until she was four years old, doubtless a response to that major early deprivation.

Over the years Boos Boomer, as we had named her, distinguished herself as a tough-minded, surefooted, competitive trail horse. She trailered fearlessly from New Hampshire to Maryland, Maine to Pennsylvania, acquiring a roomful of ribbons and winning several best-of-breed awards—half Arab—along the way. Whatever confronted her on these rides—a flock of turkeys in the road, tricky railroad ties to negotiate, rivers and streams to ford or even swim through—Boomer prevailed.

At home she has become the alpha mare of a constantly shifting population of young horses whose hay piles she scrutinizes and assigns, whose allotted spaces in run-in shed and barn are at her whim. She greets the farrier, who has handled her feet since her infancy, with teeth bared and ears plastered flat back, then stands perfectly still on cross-ties while he trims and hot-shoes her. "Hi, Smiley," he says to her; they understand each other perfectly.

Toward strangers she is unfriendly but not aggressive. Allow an unknown on her back and she will tolerate, even obey, this novel person, but the position of her ears and the continual wringing of her tail let the world know what she thinks of this situation.

When Boomer was twelve and had completed 2000 miles in endurance competition, we decided to breed her to a newly arrived Arabian of impeccable bloodlines. It was our thought that her grit and his royal lineage would make a useful combination. Several experts had assured us that foal rejection, which occurs in one out of 10,000 cases, was not an inherited characteristic.

We trailered Boomer across town in every heat cycle to the stallion of our choice only to have her violently reject his advances. Although she would flag to any equine visitor when she was in heat at home, upon arrival at the stallion's enclave, she would clamp her tail tight and insist there had been some dreadful mistake. We tried having her spend the night in an adjoining stall in hopes that the hormonal message would creep up on her, but to no avail. The entire breeding season passed in this fruitless charade.

By the following summer we had acquired a new vet— one of a triumvirate who rotates weekends so that someone is always on call—and a new outlook. He was certain he could get Boomer to settle and he, too, was reassuring about the rejection syndrome. In nine out of ten cases, he said, the early difficulty can be overcome by patience, the judicious use of tranquilizers, or even stronger painkillers if required. In the years since Boomer's birth, we had raised several foals by our other broodmares and felt vastly more competent than we had been in that innocent first encounter.

Although many mares are very casual about being palpated—one of ours would simply stand unhaltered and half asleep in the field while the vet examined her—Boomer, of course, had to be tranquilized. We subjected her to this indignity on the observable fourth day of her May cycle, but we had apparently misread the cue. There was no follicle on the ovary.

As if forewarned of our intent, in June Boomer displayed no signs of heat to a variety of invited geldings whose appearance at the fence rail would normally have elicited flaggings and squealings. Somewhat daunted but still determined, we counted days, watched, waited.

Early in July she appeared to be cycling. Another tranquilizer shot, another palpation. Possibly a follicle, but too early to tell. We waited forty-eight hours, then tested again. The time had indeed come.

A nearby draft broodmare, fortuitously, was in season. She was used as a jump mare, the semen was collected in an artificial vagina, and our vet roared uphill to our barn with the precious fluid. "Don't drop it," he admonished, thrusting the vial at me. I held it securely in two hands.

By now, Boomer had made the connection between this man in the green coveralls and that lovely floating feeling he provided. She practically stuck out her jugular for another shot of the good stuff. In her euphoric state it was no problem at all to instill the semen.

The next eighteen days passed excruciatingly slowly. Was

she settled or wasn't she? Was her putative hormone defi-
ciency, which had kept her from responding to the stallion's
amorous advances, going to keep her from conceiving?

The answer was no. The ultrasound (another tranquiliza-
tion required) revealed an embryo. Praise be! Our mare was
pregnant.

Boomer's pregnancy was much like Taboo's before her.
She was relaxed and contented, almost gracious in demeanor
toward every caller, a born-again mother-to-be. We continued to ride her throughout her term, slacking off in the final
month once her shoes were pulled.

On May 22, I moved out of the house into the barn. A
straight stall abuts our foaling stall; in it we store the sawdust we use for bedding. We had taken the precaution of
filling it to the brim about a month before Boomer's due
date. I smoothed it as level as possible, spread out the same
old foam pad I had used in each of my other foal watchings,
topped it with my sleeping bag and pillow, and hung up a
trouble light to read by.

I had also assembled: two bales of straw for the actual
event as straw is thought to be a safer and cleaner medium
for the newborn foal; two baby bottles with nipples, in case;
a can of Foal-Lac, returnable if unopened; extra-strength
iodine to saturate the umbilical cord; and a Fleet enema in
case the foal had any difficulty passing meconium. Victor
hooked up the intercom system we always used to relay
information from mare-side to bedside.

Boomer quickly got used to this new arrangement. She
did not resent being confined to her stall at night with a good
ration of hay. The other horses had free access to the barn
floor. I discovered that they had established a certain routine, visiting companionably with Boomer for a longish while
after full dark, then absenting themselves to forage on the

back fields, ambling back to the lobby about 4 A.M. for a
good nap and gradually coming awake, blowing their noses,
urinating, and so on, at about 5:30 or 6. It was a question
of available light. Dark mornings they tended to sleep in.
As the season advanced and the sun rose earlier, so did
they.

Once everyone was up and about, I too arose, put each
horse in its correct stall, fed out rations, and retreated to my
indoor bed for a quick fix of slumber before the day properly
began. For some reason I was confident that Boomer would
foal only in the dark. I could afford this early-morning nap;
Victor was theoretically awake and ready to stand duty.

Boomer's due date came and went. In spite of the fact that I
felt I was being educated in ways not immediately apparent
to indoor sleepers—I could by now distinguish each horse
not only by its breathing and snoring pattern but also by its
preparatory lying-down sounds and wiggles—the nightly ritual in the barn was beginning to pall. Mosquitoes now made
reading in bed infeasible. I slathered my face and neck with
repellent and toughed it out.

The night of Boomer's thirteenth birthday, she was strangely
restive. Toward morning she began to circle the stall, kick-
ing out from time to time to drum on the walls, an unlovely
habit she had developed as a yearling to register her dissat-
isfaction with the way we humans were running things. But
this time the kicks were accompanied by grunts of pain. It
looked like a classic case of colic.

I turned on the trouble light and entered her stall. I spent
about half an hour doing T.E.A.M. (Tellington-Jones Equine
Awareness Method) circles and ear pullings, belly lifts and
so on to try to relieve her discomfort. Then I gave her some

hay on the theory that her gut was probably empty and con-
tributing to her uneasiness. She munched and settled down
and even fell asleep for an hour.

Firm believers in the usefulness of T.E.A.M., my horse
helper and I had been using the relaxation techniques on
Boomer for several months. Mostly because we so feared
that she too would refuse to nurse her foal, we had worked
her udder daily, massaging the teats with vitamin E oil and
trying to simulate the bumps and bludgeonings a foal would
soon visit on her.

The morning of June 3 dawned. There was no apparent
change in Boomer's condition. The pseudo-colic of the night
before had vanished and she tucked into her two quarts of
sweet feed with her usual relish. I fed the others and sorted
them out; we were keeping Boomer by herself in the field
that adjoined the barn area. After breakfast I walked down
to the barn to clean stalls and redo water buckets, and Victor strolled into the field to check on the mare.

He walked back in before I had actually finished the first
stall—not Boomer's but one next to hers.

"There's a foot sticking out," he said.

"Front foot or hind foot?"

"Can't tell. Maybe you'd better go see."

I hurried out. The moment she caught sight of me, Boomer
asked to come back in. Even though it wasn't bedded in
straw I put her in the one clean stall and she promptly lay
down.

"Call the vet!" I whispered. I went on being businesslike
at half speed, trying to keep to a calm rhythm. After all,
this wasn't our first baby by any stretch. But it was our first
second-generation baby and I was terribly emotionally
involved.

Boomer kept getting up and lying down. Now both feet

had emerged and to my relief they were clearly the front ones, properly positioned. Victor returned to say that the vet was on her way—one of the triumvirate on call, as this was a Saturday morning.

As we watched, the head appeared, tightly encauled. Boomer appeared to be resting, gathering her forces, but that tightly wrapped head was worrying me. Theoretically, the foal was still on its mother's life support and did not yet need to breathe, but if the cord was being pinched, if anything else was not quite right. . . . I slid the latch, entered the stall, and knelt down by the head. I tore the caul and hiked it back over the ears. The foal opened its eyes and as I watched took a breath of outside air. Boomer pushed. It was now half born, out to the hips.

The mare was sweating and grunting. In another minute she had expelled all but the lower third of the hind legs. The baby not yet fully born took this occasion to whinny. It was a high-pitched, eerie, but unmistakably equine whinny.

The expression on Boomer's face was one of total bewilderment. At that moment she did not appear to have any notion of what had just happened.

Dr. Peck arrived at that juncture and we stood companionably together as the foal struggled to get to its feet. I had already saturated the navel stump with iodine while it was still lying down, the easiest route to avoid splashing iodine on everything else as well, but I had not at that point made the gender determination.

Dr. Peck did. "It's a filly," she whispered.

Praise be! A filly.

But the hardest part was still to come. A perplexed and hurting mare, Boomer did not want anyone or anything near her udder or indeed behind her. She had not yet passed the placenta and a good portion of the afterbirth was trailing out of her vagina. Every time the foal began to zero in on the milk supply, Boomer would squeal and strike out.

I was deeply pessimistic. I foresaw that we were in for another round of Foal-Lac by bottle, another orphan, another depraved tail eater for years. Dr. Peck was far more sanguine.

We kept trying, one of us holding the mare, the other guiding the foal toward the milk supply. I finally managed to squeeze one teat, spraying a little milk on the foal's muzzle, but Boomer foiled her attempt to get more than half a swallow.

"We just have to be patient," Dr. Peck said. "We'll give it an hour and if that doesn't work, we can always tranquilize the mare to get the baby started."

Although she didn't want her to nurse, Boomer was beginning to display some motherly affection, nudging and licking the foal. She didn't really speak to it but allowed herself a very small nicker, a hopeful sign.

An hour and a half later, the foal got her first solid drink. Dr. Peck departed. Victor and our part-time horse helper and I took turns staying with the mare in two-hour shifts through the rest of the day and the ensuing night. Each time the baby arose and staggered to the fountain, whoever was on duty also arose and held the mare's rope shank. We feared that left to her own devices, she might not let the baby nurse.

Boomer was still in pain. She had not yet manured or urinated and did not do so until the crucial twenty-four hours were almost up. The placenta passed just before the maximum allowable time of eight hours had been reached. Beyond that time, the risk of infection would mean antibiotics and some intervention.

Only minutes before Boomer was due to receive a gallon of mineral oil by stomach tube, she manured. Shortly thereafter she urinated. Our relief was almost as great as hers. From that time on, she was very accepting of the foal and we felt safe in leaving them unsupervised.

The little filly was in great shape. She had passed meconium within minutes of getting to her feet, thereby obviating the need for the Fleet enema. She was a vigorous nurser, pumping away at Boomer's distended udder, pulling back only briefly if Boomer squealed a protest.

To our chagrin we discovered that Boomer would only allow the foal to nurse from the left or near side, although we observed that she was able to suck from both teats in this position. We realized then that all our T.E.A.M. massagings had been conducted from the near side. It was three or four days before Boomer relented and accepted the baby on the right side as well.

This new foal began as a pale buckskin, almost palomino, with one hind sock and a white striped front hoof. Her mane and tail were tricolored gray, black, and white. She has her mother's star and snip but no sign, at least yet, of the rich darker dapples Boomer possesses. Everyone admires her refined throat latch, nicely slanted shoulder, and powerful hind end, legacies from her sire. She follows people around like a pet dog; we are hard-pressed not to spoil her.

And now the tenth baby in our amateur career of raising horses is "in the oven." Although when Praise Be was born, we dubbed her "Final Filly," we don't seem able to stop. I, at least, am unwilling to give up this grand annual gratification. Although Victor says *he* is ready to call it quits, I note that unasked he's in the barn remounting the intercom. He's tuning in, readying himself for the impending arrival.

In a way unmatched by any other daydream, the prospect of another innocent on stilt-like legs racing across the pasture in midsummer takes the bite out of a New England winter. When I close my eyes on the night of a February blizzard I need to see healthy horses on broad pastures in my mind's eye, and among them an expectant mare or two. My partner in this ongoing folly is more detached. He will recount the nights of lost or fitful sleep, the suspense, the breeding fees, the angst of autumn weanings. A Johnny-come-lately where horses are concerned, he only took up riding, showing, and breeding fifteen years ago.

I, on the other hand, was born with my obsession. From kindergarten on I lobbied mightily for a pony. Before Christmas, before every birthday, I prayed ostentatiously on my knees under the bewildered gaze of my parents that a pony be granted me. Failing a pony of my own, I took on the world's sad horses. I passed out my brothers' camp blankets to the occasional carthorse who still plodded by in our suburban neighborhood, hauling a load of potatoes or clothes props. On a regular basis I filched sugar lumps from the kitchen pantry to have at the ready for any policeman's horse I chanced to encounter.

The most that was allotted me was an hour a week on the local livery stable's rental horses, faithful schoolies of no hope and little spirit who carried wistful children like me on their bony backs. I arrived early, stayed late, and appeared on non-riding days to make myself useful. Here I learned how to clean stalls, soap saddles and bridles, pick pebbles and manure out of elderly hooves. It was a useful beginning.

I never outgrew that childhood obsession, or the impulse

to rescue neglected quadrupeds from bad situations. Along the way, I fell in love with Arabians as a breed. Well suited to distance riding, they are slim and fleet, tireless at the trot, quick to size up the terrain and handle themselves accordingly. They form an abiding bond with their rider and they love to go forward. Aficionados of the breed often refer to them as "the dogs of the horse world" for their native intelligence.

Boos Boomer, fifteen this year, is once again ponderously in foal. While she no longer competes in distance events, she is a family pleasure horse and gets ridden almost daily. As she approaches due date, she wears her old leather foaling halter.

We never leave halters on our horses unattended; an unbreakable nylon one is an accident waiting to happen. This worn leather headpiece is guaranteed to come apart if she catches it on some unlikely protuberance. But if she lies down in labor too close to the wall . . . if she needs to be caught outside and led in . . . if for some unforeseen reason she needs to be restrained, the halter is in place.

Boomer's udder is full and hard, the muscles around her tail have softened. The bulge in her undercarriage that for months has looked like a fireplace log wedged sideways now appears to be moving backward. I begin to feel nervous about not being at her side all night long. Misgivings about what I hear over the intercom, rustlings and chuffings that I can't easily interpret, begin to overtake me. I move into the barn.

This ordeal, to which I am more or less inured after the last waiting period of twelve nights, is slightly ameliorated by a thermos of hot cocoa fortified with a dash of coffee liqueur. In my damp sleeping bag I try not to review all the breeding information, complete with horror stories, that I

have amassed from attending clinics conducted by veteri-
narians, or from the considerable literature on the subject.
Filtering out everything but happy outcomes is necessary to
my well-being. All possible equipment is at hand. The vet's
phone number is engraved on my brain pan. When the time
comes, I will beep the intercom that connects to our bedroom.

Victor is wonderful to have on hand because he is calm
and sensible. I am invariably in a state of exalted terror,
telling myself to go slowly, move at half speed, stay alert
and relaxed so as not to transfer any of my own tension to
the mare. I am focused on all the things that can go wrong,
and on the fact that even at full siren, it will take our vet
thirty minutes to get to us in an emergency. If, heaven forfend, there is a malpresentation—breech, for example—we
will have to get the mare on her feet and walk her to delay
contractions until the vet arrives. And failing that, the plastic gloves.

Most foals are born at night; nature seems to have selected
darkness as a safer time for the mare to lie down and deliver
her offspring. Because we had one stillbirth along the way
when a foal was born with no one in attendance, I am determined to be present just in case any intervention is needed.
It was heartbreaking ten years ago to wait out an eleven-
month-long gestation only to lose a big, beautiful filly who
never drew breath.

That was the firstborn of a very gentle Quarterhorse mare
we had bred to a handsome Thoroughbred stallion. Presum-
ably, the caul over the foal's nostrils never ruptured and the
bewildered mother didn't intervene. I thought afterward that
I had heard a kick in the barn just before dawn but didn't
rouse myself to investigate. Some things we never forgive

ourselves, even though that mare went on to deliver two other half-Thoroughbred fillies and is still an exemplary mother.

Despite my vigils, I have missed two other births—one by mere seconds when I went back to the house to get a cup of coffee, the second by half an hour when the Quarterhorse mare casually decided to foal out in the pasture in midmorning (so much for my cover-of-darkness theory).

On that occasion, I had gone back to bed in the house at dawn with a terrible stomachache. Victor had fed and turned the horses out at 7 A.M., but hadn't segregated the expectant mare. He dutifully went out to check on her every hour throughout the morning, as he thought she looked imminent—there is no other word to express that slack-muscled stance when the foal has begun to move backward toward the birth canal but the mother-to-be is still cropping grass and acting insouciant.

Just before noon he burst into the house to tell me the news. I staggered out with him to our farthest pasture to find a sturdy little filly up and nursing while my gelding was attempting to lick her dry.

A fine rain had just begun to fall. We had to make multiple trips to remove the terribly curious non-parents from the vicinity, then haltered the mare to begin the quarter-mile trek across the pasture and down a craggy hillside to the barn. The baby bopped along merrily, unfazed by the rain, terrain, or distance. (She is now a big, bold jumper of four-foot fences.)

Obviously, we are amateur breeders. Amateur in the true sense of that word, *lover*; financially, it is a losing proposition. My other life, as a poet and writer, supports the horse passion. Here on Pobiz Farm the two of us supply most of the labor involved, but we must buy hay and grain, pay the farrier who trims and shoes our horses on a regular basis, and keep abreast of our vet bills. Routine health matters such as wormings and inoculations are within our expertise, but in any given year we are sure to encounter at least one ailment we are uncertain about treating on our own—an abcessed hoof, persistent cough, swollen knee, or exotic rash.

As amateur breeders and trainers, we raise youngsters to live out of doors as much as possible. They are invited into their stalls twice a day at feeding time and they are handled daily, groomed, fussed over, taught from an early age the etiquette of behavior with humans. Unlike many show horses who are rarely out of the artificial environment of the barn or indoor arena, ours go out on the trail to encounter brooks and boulders, on the road to come to terms with trucks and bicycles and children. By the time they leave us they are roadwise and confident, though shaggier than their show-ring counterparts. Clearly, we do not operate at a profit.

Is it feasible to make money breeding in our corner of the world? A few stalwarts manage to hang on, usually through a combination of skills—boarding horses, training young-sters, showing horses for wealthy owners, teaching riding at levels ranging from rank beginner through fourth-level dres-sage, as well as working with horses and riders in cross-country and stadium jumping. Breeding is better adapted to a warmer climate, where horses can be out on pasture most, if not quite all, of the year; where hay crops can run up to four or five cuttings in a season instead of the stingy two we can expect here in Zone Four. New Hampshire forage pas-tures, no matter how well kept, cannot compete with Ken-tucky bluegrass. The limestone underlay makes a rich growth. Granite underpinning, alas, does little to improve our tim-othy and clover.

A few outstanding stallions can be money-makers for their

owners in any geography. Winning racehorses retired to stud command huge breeding fees. Imported warmbloods, big Trakehners, Hanoverians, Oldenburgs, and the like, are very much in vogue right now. Televised show events have created a new interest in jumping competitions as well as in dressage, where horse and rider execute predetermined figures, comparable in some measure to those demanded in ice skating competitions.

The big warmblooded horses, developed from skillful crossbreeding of Thoroughbreds and old-timey workhorses (some Arabian and Morgan loyalists have been known to refer to them as the warm dumbbloods), have for the most part wonderfully serene dispositions. While they may be bold movers with giant strides between fences, they are remarkably tolerant of the tight discipline required in the dressage ring. A professional breeding establishment with one or two well-known stallions imported from Holland or Germany can indeed turn a profit from stud fees.

But Arabians never go out of style. Always in demand for his versatility, the Arabian can perform well in a variety of disciplines. In addition to marathoning and racing on the flat, this breed makes a refined carriage horse, a fancy saddle-seat show horse, an amiable Western pleasure mount, a talented dressage horse, a rewarding family pet. By and large, Arabians are not gifted jumpers because of their naturally elevated head set, but there have been some notable exceptions.

Because of our interest in distance riding, we have gravitated toward crossbreeding with Standardbreds, the trotters of harness-racing fame. A bigger-boned, less refined, and generally more phlegmatic breed developed from Morgan and Thoroughbred stock, the Standardbred can bring size and a slightly calmer attitude to the offspring. In my experience, the pure Arabian is not notably tolerant of human foibles. Adding in the cooler blood of another breed, be it Appaloosa or Quarterhorse, Morgan or Standardbred, can ease the situation.

The rewards of breeding successive generations are largely aesthetic and personal. I can see my old runaway mare Taboo shining through her two-year-old granddaughter Praise Be, this three-quarters Arabian filly who stands at the gate nickering for attention. She recognizes the car that has just driven up the hill; it may disgorge a person who will come down and speak to her or proffer a carrot. If, on the other hand, it's the monthly meter reader, she will ignore its passage.

I can also see, objectively, that this youngster is quite an improvement on her ancestor. Because we crossed a long-backed mare with an Arabian stallion, we developed a more closely coupled animal (the Arabian traditionally has one fewer vertebra than other breeds). She has her grandparent's broad chest and substantial heart girth, plenty of room for lungs to expand. While her graceful head with its dished profile and her tiny ears are typically Arabian, her legs are not quite so fine as a pure Arabian's. She has good "bone" and solid joints. Her pasterns, the joints which connect the prominent bone of the lower leg to the foot itself, slope slightly more than is common in the Arabian. This gift came from her Standardbred ancestry, as did her powerful hindquarters and solid, round hooves. Here she carries a stronger musculature than the traditional Arabian, for if the Arabian has any consistent conformational defect, it can be seen in the sickle shape of the hind legs, the lighter bone, the deerlike oval hooves. This time we were lucky. The next cross may emphasize other, less sought-after traits: big Standardbred jughead and east / west-pointing ears, a short neck set low in the chest, a long back, a deep body on delicate legs.

Since we've only had two colts in nine rounds, chances are Boomer's unborn foal is a colt. Chances are it's a buckskin, or almost. The old hybrid mare Taboo was a liver chestnut; her descendants have dorsal stripes and bicolored manes and tails. Praise Be is a buckskin, Boomer is a mouse dun. Another buckskin of the same size and conformation would be lovely—a potential driving pair.

On the other hand, at least we know it isn't twins. Our vet checked Boomer with his ultrasound scanner when she was a mere three weeks along. The embryo then was little more than a dot on the screen. Ultrasound has become a major diagnostic tool in breeding. If multiple fetuses are detected, a skillful vet can pinch off all but one. For despite her size and strength, the mare cannot normally house two embryos. Almost always the mare will abort well before term. If she carries twins to term, rarely will both be born alive.

Final colt? Final filly? We are only into the second night of my vigil when I come abruptly awake at the unmistakable sounds of beginning labor. It is a moment of high drama, as the panting mare begins to circle restlessly and finally flops down with a harsh grunt.

The first time Boomer goes down she is too close to the wall, but before I can intervene to move her, she rises, circles again, and this time positions herself right in the center of the capacious stall. Labor is swift and seemingly effortless. Hallelujah! It *is* another filly. The little one whinnies even before her hips are in this world and Boomer, wise now in the ways of parturition, nickers a welcome.

Although bonding this time takes place without full-scale intervention, Boomer once again has some difficulty with her let-down response. We rotate shifts to oversee the first few hours of nursing. Boomer's bountiful udder is full to overflowing; it takes courage—or merely powerful instinct—

for the little one to persist in suckling when the edgy mare squeals and threatens to kick out. But once nursing relieves this pressure, Boomer becomes a gracious and attentive mother.

Booms Hallelujah, known as Lulu, is an exact color-copy of her mother, from star and snip to part-white hind hoof. As she matures, it gets harder to tell mother and daughter apart at a glance. We joke, saying she was cloned rather than sired, but the truth is, she descends from impeccable Arabian bloodlines. On closer inspection, Lulu is more finely made and shorter backed, a showier version of her tough-minded dam.

Praise Be and Hallelujah. I'd like to try for Amen, but I fear I will be overruled.

PART II

STORIES

Fiction is like a spider's web, attached
ever so lightly perhaps, but still attached
to life at all four corners.

VIRGINIA WOOLF,
A Room of One's Own

SOLSTICE

It was shocking to see that the reindeer had had their antlers sawed off, leaving what looked to Moira like stubby candle holders. Her first day on the job at the Arctic Biology Station she was told that this was done to keep them from stabbing each other. They were such herd creatures; the way that they pressed together in their fenced-in compound there made her think of fish schooling up.

Here in Alaska, people called antlers "the top story," as if these animals were merely trees for pruning. Well, it was true, in a way. The exotic headgear would regrow next season. But shorn like this, she thought they looked pathetic, like a pack of enlarged mice.

The musk oxen stank, as she had been told they would, in the middle of July. When the cold weather came she thought she wouldn't notice it as much. Their calves were endearing, already so shaggy and unkempt and, well, *planted*. The adults were stodgy, but even the youngsters didn't move around much. It was easy to see them cast back in prehistory, mammals that had survived the Ice Age intact.

The Arctic Biology Station tried not to serve as a pound for all the orphaned animals of Alaska, but a couple of times a year someone would arrive with a starveling moose calf whose mother had been shot, or hit by a truck on the main road out of Fairbanks, and then what could you do? Moira hadn't been on the job a week when this little bull calf, half dead from hunger and fright, was hauled in in the back of a pickup, and the director more or less turned it over to her. She named him Golly, short for Golliwog, and got him started on a calf nipple.

Her job was mostly mucking out the animal pens and holding a twitch on various caribou from which blood samples were being drawn weekly to isolate the virus that attacked them in the wild. Every afternoon she drove the tractor out onto the tundra to drop hay for the assorted tame herds.

As jobs go, it was pretty low-key. Even so, she'd gotten it through pull. Her father, Rich Maginnis, an electronics engineer in Massachusetts, had called a colleague who called a colleague at the University of Alaska. The idea was for Moira to get out of town for a while before she fell apart.

Moira's mother had died six months before, still bald from the chemotherapy treatments that were supposed to have saved her life. That had been early spring. Earlier, once they had found out that the cancer had spread, Moira had dropped out of Smith to be at home with her mother. She was an only child—there was nothing else she could do.

During that period, when people commented on how well she was bearing up, she couldn't think of anything appropriate to say back to them. That language hasn't been invented yet. For the first time in her life, Moira felt really close to her mother. It was as if Death had opened a forbidden door and Moira had been allowed to peek in on a new place full of raw feeling. Dealing with all this fervor was almost as scary as facing the fact that her mother's life was ebbing.

Her mother was bright and cheerful about the chemother-

apy treatments and made up little jokes when her hair started
to fall out. She wore turbans whenever anyone came to visit,
and she and Moira kidded around a lot pinning costume
jewelry in the middle of the fold. "The Maharini Maginnis!"
Moira would announce, helping her mother down the stairs
to be embraced by an old friend.

It was her father who couldn't handle it. He kept going to
work and coming back in the middle of the morning; then
he'd change his mind and drive forty miles back down 128
to Burlington. When her mother started having trouble
keeping solids down, Rich Maginnis began throwing up in
secret in the lavatory off his study. When she was dying, he
began to black out in the weirdest places—on the stairs, in
the laundry room, once in the bedroom closet. Moira covered him with a blanket and canceled his meetings. She
kept the house picked up, too, at least until close to the end
when there were nurses and Hospice people everywhere,
and, afterward, she answered letters and phone calls from
well-wishers.

It was funny, the things she remembered. She remembered how thrilled her mother had been when Moira was
twelve and got her first period. Her mother told her father,
which mortified Moira. Her mother practically wanted to make
a public celebration out of it. That night they had a rare
roast beef and a sparkling white wine that was almost like
champagne, but sweet. Rich gave his daughter a tooled leather
five-year diary. Even then, her mother couldn't let it alone,
but followed her into the bedroom. Perched daintily on the
bedspread, redoing her shell-pink nails, she asked, "How
do you feel about it, Moira-bird? Are you happy? Are you
sad?" To which Moira replied, "Well, really, Mother, there
isn't anything I can do about it, is there?"

They looked at each other for a long moment. Moira's

mother, normally a kittenish, sociable little person, finally rose with a sigh. Moira knew she had disappointed her, but in those days she didn't care. She didn't feel very close to her mother. Privately, she regarded her as an airhead.

Now, looking back, she wished she had given her mother a different answer. She wished she had been enthusiastically her mother's daughter, had let her take pleasure in Moira's first blood and their complicity as women.

In the beginning of the bad time—she was ashamed to remember—she had recoiled from her mother's body. But she cleaned up her vomit and washed and powdered her bony frame. She began to love her with a terrible, stabbing love. Moira marveled at the pain of it. They were women together, bonded like sisters. All her life she had wondered what it would be like to have a sister, someone to share the root hairs of childhood. Someone to wrestle and giggle with, to stay awake with half the night while in the other room the parents entered into their mysterious compact.

At the same time, she couldn't bear it. In a way, all this love was liberating but it pinned you down, too. Moira had a fear of being trapped. After the memorial service—they hadn't had a formal funeral, it would have seemed awkward and stiff after so slow a dying—Moira wanted to escape.

Rich Maginnis agreed that she needed a change. "Where do you want to go?"

"Somewhere far away and cold." When she said it she hadn't realized that she would be starting over at a very basic level.

"But nobody ought to have to watch her mother die," she said months later in Alaska to Greg, who had recently become her live-in boyfriend. Actually, it was the other way around

since the cabin was his. It was a log cabin five miles out of
town on a gravel road that narrowed beyond them and finally
petered out in the bush.

He agreed. By then it was late fall. "And nobody should
have to live alone in this climate." They were feeding two
cast-iron woodstoves but still woke one morning to find a
ball of steel wool frozen to the windowsill. The rime of ice
coating the window glass thickened day by day. Moira envi-
sioned them living inside an ice mountain. One day, she
thought, the door simply won't open and we'll look out and
see that the world has stopped.

At night, often, holding her, Greg quoted, "It is not easy
to make love in a cold climate. There is never the time or
the place." It was probably the only line out of Orwell he
knew, left over from his English lit course six years ago in
California, when he dropped out of San Francisco State.

Their relationship was a convenience, like a royal marriage, Moira thought. Love didn't enter into it. Moira didn't
think she had ever really been in love. She had slept with
four different men before Greg and sometimes she wondered
what all the fuss was about. In fact, after the first time, in a
nice enough motel in Williamstown with a boy she had dated
all through high school, she had dressed and crept out alone.
It was just past midnight. She walked around town hugging
her body to keep it from shivering. She wasn't a virgin anymore; there wasn't anything she could do about that. The
boy swore he loved her, he wanted them to get married.
Married at eighteen? Ridiculous! And then she saw that she
had wounded him, belittled what they had done. But he
slept like a baby, and she prowled the New England town
of white clapboards that looked in the moonlight as if they
had been freshly waxed.

Greg had all the survival skills that Moira envied. When

he first came to Alaska he worked on the Pipeline. Now, summers, he was part of the University road crew. Fall and spring he mended fences, installed gas tanks, insulated plumbing. As long as he was busy with his hands he was content.

Hundreds of young people lived like them in cabins in the bush, without amenities. It was too cold up here for privies. Instead you used a honeypot. A well, if you had one, froze solid before Thanksgiving. You bought your water by the tankful and hauled it in the back of a pickup. "Everything has to be kept indoors to guard against freezing," she explained in a letter to her father. "Every parking lot you go to has a stand like drive-in movies, only instead of earphones there's a plug for the electric heater you put under the car hood."

Her father's letters, written every other Sunday on his home computer, all began "Dear Moira-bird" and contained assurances that he was managing pretty well on his own. He was playing squash after a ten-year lapse; he stopped off evenings for a few beers with some of his bachelor colleagues because going home to an empty house was the hardest part. Speaking of which, he was terribly glad she had found such a congenial young man. He referred to Greg as Moira's Significant Other, a term she detested.

But Greg was going on about arctic conditions. "Talk about cold," he told Moira. "There's this rich collector in Fairbanks and he had all these old hand-carved ivory pieces, tusks and stuff. Some guys broke in and took it all. They stashed it in an outdoor shed over by that abandoned mine I took you to."

She nodded.

"Well, all of it blew up over the winter. Exploded like little bombs."

"What do you mean?"

"Well, you know ivory was once living tissue, okay? The residual moisture in it froze, little by little, and then it just shattered. Blew apart."

The long Alaskan night didn't affect Greg the way it did Moira. She got so she could hardly bear the midday rising of that pale sun. The way it smudged out of sight two hours later filled her with resentment. "Eternal night," she called it. "That's what this is, rehearsal for the nuclear winter."

"Wait till summer solstice. You'll love it. Wait till you see little kids running around playing stooptag at two in the morning. Nobody bothers to put their kids to bed in June. When they get tired enough they just lay down somewhere and take a nap."

"Lie," she said automatically. "Lie down." But she couldn't picture it.

In March, her father wrote to say that he and Peggy Dowling, a technician who also worked at Sanders, were getting married. "She's not much older than you are, Moira-bird, but she's had a hard life." He enclosed a snapshot of a slim, self-assured-looking woman leaning back against a tree trunk. The collar of her jacket was turned up. Her lips were slightly parted. You could see from the space between her two front teeth that she needed orthodontia. The wind had driven a lock of hair against her cheek; she looked as if she were about to brush it back but had stopped for the camera.

"Oh, shit," Moira kept saying. "Shit, shit, shit. I can't believe it!"

"What does your daddy do?" Greg asked, looking over her shoulder.

"Weapons. He designs weapons systems, whatever that

involves. I guess he designs them and she fits them together, it looks like."

"What kind of weapons? Guns? Rockets? Missiles?"

"I don't know. Missiles, I think."

"You *think!* Conventional or nuclear?"

"Oh, what's the difference! How could he *marry*, just like that?"

"Everybody needs somebody." He drawled it, playing air-guitar.

"Greg, he is old enough to be her father!" Moira pronounced both syllables.

"Live and let live, Moira-bird."

"Don't you dare call me that!"

But a few days later she wrote back and congratulated them. First she outlined the letter. Then she made a first draft and let it cool down overnight. Finally it was possible to copy out "Dear Daddy, I'm very happy for you and I know Mummy would be too, as no one should have to live alone. It is wonderful that you have found someone who shares your professional interests. She looks like a lovely person and I hope you will have many years together."

She worried about that last part; did it suggest that she thought he was robbing the cradle with Peggy Dowling? Then there was a paragraph about the work going on at the Station and Golly's general good health. A third paragraph about the weather described a recent whiteout. She did not ask him whether the weapons he and Peggy Dowling were collaborating on were conventional or nuclear or whether he thought there would be a first strike in her lifetime.

She tried to figure out why she was so angry about her father's remarriage. She ought to feel happy for him, and relieved. She ought to be grateful to Peggy Dowling for taking on the responsibility.

"Instead, I feel like an orphan," she told Greg.

"Listen, you're entitled."

"You mean, like now I really am?"

"Like first you were running away from the whole mother-father scene. And now you've been up here long enough, you're not numb anymore."

"I'm thawing," Moira said. "You're right, it's twenty below out and I'm beginning to melt."

In April, Rich Maginnis wrote to say that he and his bride were planning a cruise to Alaska. They had booked on a ship that came up the Inland Waterway to the Skagway Peninsula. "We'd love to have you meet us in Juneau and do the Glacier Bay trip with us."

Moira made a face.

"Why not? If your old man wants to pay for it, I'm up to doing the blue ice and bald eagles bit. I mean, we're going to Juneau anyway for the rally, right? So let's try to cooperate."

"Dear Daddy, Your trip sounds like a wonderful idea. I assume you were inviting both of us? We are planning to come down to Juneau for the solstice and annual Freeze rally, and we'd love to meet your ship when it docks."

She decided not to go into detail about the nuclear-freeze rally. It was hard to strike the right tone on paper. Probably he would dismiss the march as a lot of misguided nonsense.

Mornings came earlier now, and the afternoon sun hung in the sky minutes longer, but the dry cold continued. It was hard to believe in spring. Golly moose was enormous. He lived with the musk oxen now, but still recognized Moira and would trot up to her to have his neck scratched. In midsummer they would reinsert him into his natural habitat. The Arctic Biology Station had reinserted eight other orphans and six of them, as far as they knew, had made it. Moira didn't want to be there when, in the middle of June, they hauled Golly off into the muskeg and left him there.

In May, corn and tomato seedlings were already up in the University greenhouse. Pretty soon they were transplanted outside into circles of old tires. As they grew taller, layers of tires would be added as supports.

"What a neat idea!" Moira approved of recycling.

"Yeah, one thing Alaska has plenty of is old tires."

Alaska had plenty of backpackers, too. By the first of June it looked as if the entire population of the state had moved outdoors. Everyone wore bandannas to catch the trickles of sweat that they hoped they would work up in the good sun. It seemed to Moira that people walked around with their heads tilted back to keep the rays on their faces.

Moira's father sent them a check for the airfare to Juneau. Then, at the last minute, Greg, who seemed to have friends all over the state, got them a ride with a bush pilot who flew errands for half a dozen businesses in Fairbanks.

First they stopped at a little airport that served a cluster of towns along the Alaska Highway, to drop off some medical supplies for cattle. As they came in for the landing, a herd of bison moved a bit raggedly off to the west, like football linemen.

Next, there was a long southeast run along the Alcan, skirting the Wrangell Mountains, slicing across Canada where they put down briefly in Haines Junction for fuel. A brief flight took them into Skagway at the head of the Lynn Canal. The last leg, a short hop, took them low over the Mendenhall Glacier into Juneau.

The two men sat up front and talked. Moira was content

just to sit behind them and study the passing scene below. She saw herself homesteading here and there on a spit of land poking out into the bay. The wilderness was so densely forested that no road or path was visible beneath them. The plane cast its shadow on the treetops. And then, across the next inlet where spruce and fir crowded down to the shoreline, she spied an acre of untroubled greenery, a flat, probably boggy, plain unvexed with trees, across which some sort of grass had crept. Here, she thought, the house; there, the garden. Craning her neck as the patch vanished behind them she placed the barn, and then a toolshed. . . . It was 1880, she had come north by packet boat, all her worldly goods in two satchels. She would begin again where no one had ever lived, scratched soil, burned fire.

But this was the latter part of the twentieth century. Technology flushed every remote corner of the North with two-way radio communication, with satellites beaming television sitcoms into Eskimo villages even above Nome. Southeast Alaska was awash with discarded beer bottles, cast-off oil drums, derelict cars. In the spring bears stumbled into town to search out garbage. Every week another bear was rounded up downtown—shot, usually, that being easier than tranquilizing and relocating. The outcry from the conservationists died down just in time to deal with the next miscreant.

In Juneau they spent the night with friends of Greg's, above the city proper, where all the roads dead-ended against craggy mountain slopes. The house was built into the slope so that you could walk from a deck off the living room directly onto a mountain trail. Guests wandered in and out with drinks in their hands. It was eerie, Moira thought, the way twilight began, then melted into dawn. The sun merely skirted the horizon, then recommenced climbing into the sky, as if it had come to a decision.

In the morning they toured the city. Bald eagles swooped overhead, as common as seagulls, circling the Juneau dump. There was a carnival atmosphere on the main streets. Signs all over town advised where to assemble for the march.

By eleven, the dockside park was crammed with flowers and banners. Musical groups held forth, surrounded by their devotees. Babies were strapped to the fronts and backs of parents, and toddlers coasted along in strollers. Business in helium balloons was brisk; already several had escaped their owners and were drifting festively overhead. There seemed to be a contest in T-shirt statements. Vendors hawked Sister Corita posters, hot dogs, and homemade strawberry ice cream. The Sierra Club booth solicited new members. Greenpeace and Friends of the Earth were also on hand.

"You can see it's a perfect metaphor," the lawyer-owner of the house was saying to an official-looking visitor. "Solstice and the rally. 'The sun will not set on our efforts for world peace,' that sort of thing."

At noon the mayor of Juneau made a brief welcoming speech. He was followed by one senator, who read a message from the governor. The band played the national anthem and everyone sang.

When the Cunard *Princess* steamed into sight, it was agreed to delay the start of the march until the ship had docked.

"The same thing happened last year," Greg said. "It's a setup, for publicity."

But the ringing in Moira's ears made it hard for her to hear what he was telling her. She recognized the sensation. It was anxiety. It had been brought on by the speed-typing tests in the eleventh grade, the starters' litany at relay races, rising to deliver the winning rebuttal in a college debate. God! She hoped she wasn't going to wreck everything by crying when she saw her father.

The passengers came down the gangway in twos and threes, a confection of lime-green pantsuits and Hawaiian floral shirts. Rich Maginnis was dressed in a seersucker suit that enhanced his tan. His new wife wore a white flannel skirt with a navy wool blazer and good pearls. Moira noticed that the blazer buttons had little sailboats on them.

"What is this, some kind of Alaskan luau?" Rich asked, hugging her. "Does the whole town turn out like this for every cruise ship?"

"Daddy, no. The idea is to keep the world going. This is Greg."

"Pleased to meet you. This is our annual nuclear-freeze rally. It's summer solstice, that means the sun will not set," Greg said.

"Well, whatever it is, let's get out of this crowd. Here. Let me do the honors. Meet Peggy."

"Goodness. I feel like we've already met, I've heard so much about you. You're even prettier than your pictures, Moira. And this is Greg? Hello, Greg."

Moira saw that Peggy Dowling would make an excellent social director. It didn't seem to matter if she and Greg said anything. Peggy would fill all the spaces.

The Cunard customers were to be taken in launches across the harbor to a salmon bake.

"Best salmon in the world," Greg said. "We can meet you here after."

"Will you come with us?" Moira's father asked her.

"Daddy, I told you. I can't. We're marching to Douglas Island."

Several people from the cruise ship fell into the line of marchers. Moira thought they looked splendid in their pastels and spectator pumps mixed in among the wilderness set. It gave the whole leisurely line of marchers a certain tone. As they moved through the streets of the capital, kites and balloons jousting overhead, bearded marshals with armbands stepped off the curb and trotted back and forth to consult with one another. Peggy came over and stood with Moira. Rich wavered, then turned back and leapt into a launch that put-putted off across the water. Greg didn't notice. He had dropped back to talk with some old buddies from his days on the Pipeline.

"I wonder about those shoes," Moira said, after they had gone two blocks. Peggy wasn't quite limping, but it wouldn't be long before a blister or two popped up.

"I'm not exactly dressed for this."

"What did Daddy mean in his letter, you'd had a hard life?"

"I guess he was referring to my parents. They passed away when I was only ten."

"Who raised you, then?"

"I was a ward of the state until I was eighteen."

Moira had a vision of cruel foster homes and hand-me-down clothes. "Are you happy? I mean, you *look* happy."

"I love your father. He's a good man."

"So how come you joined the peace walk? You know he thinks we're all a bunch of Reds."

"People can love each other without having to think like clones."

Somewhere behind them a band struck up and people were singing "Give peace a chance."

Afterward, the four of them had dinner together on board the *Princess*.

There was no way you couldn't like Peggy Dowling; she

won you over by being so totally nice. When they got back
to the ship, she had gone down to the stateroom and changed
into sneakers and designer jeans and taken off her pearls.
Moira tried to remember her father on the floor in the closet.
She wanted to feel close to him. His new marriage was sticking up between them like the Berlin Wall. Or maybe it wasn't
even the marriage. Her father was in the weapons business
and they were on opposite sides.

"Do you think the world is going to blow itself up?" she
asked him between courses.

"Not in my lifetime."

"But do you?"

"Maybe. Maybe when you're very old. Or after, when your
children are."

"But doesn't that . . . change anything?"

"You can't live your life that way. You can't live as if this
were a dress rehearsal for disaster."

Greg and her father ordered cream puffs with ice cream and
chocolate sauce for dessert. Moira remembered the kitchen
stuffed with food that people had brought to the house after
the memorial service. Her mother, the doctor had said, had
simply starved to death. People made that decision, he said.
Not wanting to go on, they just stopped eating.

Moira said she guessed they would have to save Glacier
Bay for another time. She said the Arctic Station really
couldn't spare her, they were shorthanded right now because
of everyone goofing off for the solstice. Greg just looked
down at his plate and traced circles in the melted chocolate
with the tines of his fork. This was her family, he was letting
her handle it.

•

On the way back, she and Greg splurged with the money they hadn't spent on airfare and went to Denali to roam around the parkland for a couple of days. While Greg was climbing Mt. Healy, she joined a nature class that had come up from Anchorage with its own leader. The professor was trim and trig in his chamois shirt. He was wearing a telephoto lens, extra-power binoculars, and a magnifying lens for examining petals and sepals. Everything about him expressed confidence in the worth of the project in a way that made her think of her father.

People in the group kept looking up, sighting a jaeger or wheatear to add to their life list of birds, then squatting down to examine whatever he pointed to. Alpine azalea, crowfoot, anemone, alp lily, members of the heath family— the dicots, their leader affectionately called them. "Now this shy little fellow," he said, fingering a blossom, "has hung on here since the Eocene Age." People sketched the petal formation in their notebooks.

Moira felt a sudden twinge of jealousy. She wanted to care that much about something. She wanted to be as involved as that.

When she was only seven or eight, her father began to take her on leaf walks. He showed her how to press the perfect leaves between sheets of waxed paper with a warm iron. Afterward, she attached them to a sheet of notebook paper, and underneath, she printed Norway maple, red oak, honey locust. Her mother helped her tape the specimens flat and get the spelling right. On rainy days, Moira pored over the pages, dreaming of labeling every tree and shrub in North America. She remembered how happy she had felt then, encircled by known leaves and her quietly breathing parents. Whatever happened to that old scrapbook bulging with ginkgo fans and the crumbs of red sumac plumes?

When the fall semester began, Moira enrolled as a full-time student—the University accepted her as a junior—majoring in biology. She kept her old job at the Station five afternoons a week as a part of student aid, and she was on emergency call the rest of the time.

Rich Maginnis was delighted with her decision and said she should have the tuition bills sent to him. The letters from her father now contained long postscripts by Peggy Dowling, who had also taken to sending Moira various cold-weather items. Down booties, mittens with lambswool lining, and silk long johns arrived serially. Peggy was clearly thinking ahead to the arctic winter.

Greg was thinking ahead, too, thinking about moving on, maybe homesteading in British Columbia. He guessed he might go back home for a few months over the winter, then back to B.C. as soon as the ice went out. Moira could stay on in the cabin. He would leave her the pickup. He hoped she would fly down to meet him over Christmas. He'd like her to meet his family. Moira was amazed at how long-range his plans were.

She was amazed, too, at how much she didn't want him to go. At first she wasn't going to say so, but once she began, it got easier to let him know.

"So you see, we're not splitting up," Greg said afterward. "We're still connected. You come down for Christmas and I'll come up for Easter."

Two weeks into the new semester the road crew brought in another moose calf. They had pulled it out of a culvert under the highway. The mother lay nearby, apparently shot by poachers, who carved out the best steaks, then left the carcass for the crows. The calf was three months old, extremely dehydrated, too weak to stand. The vet ran an I. V. line to drip in electrolytes. There was some discussion of rigging a sling. Left too long on its side, the calf would accumulate fluid in its lungs and that would finish it.

Every two hours Moira and a helper lifted the suckling calf to its feet and held it there for ten minutes, propped against the stall. The rest of the time Moira worked over it, dipping her fingers in warm milk, pushing them into its mouth to get it sucking. She sat cross-legged on the straw and cradled its floppy head in her lap.

Unbidden, the Sunday suppers of her childhood flew into her mind. Invariably, there was cream of tomato soup with little oyster crackers to sprinkle on top. She could see herself catching the crackers one at a time in her spoon. There were the everyday clicking sounds of a spoon against bowl or plate. There was her mother, dusting Parmesan cheese across the surface of her own portion. Sometimes her mother, who had finished first, poured Moira's soup back and forth from one bowl to the other to cool it for her. Then she leaned across Moira to replace the full bowl and Moira smelled the rich perfume of her housecoat. Her mother had to hold back the fullness of her sleeves as she reached across, and the fine blond hairs of her forearms caught the light. From the way her mother was smiling at her, Moira guessed she was very little—four or five years old. Her father was not in this picture.

The doctor had said that starving to death was not a bad way to go, but Moira knew he was only being kind. Starvation was terrible, she had seen it for herself, life stretched taut on a thin wire.

Moira crooned to this creature, crooned and stroked its neck. Late in the day the calf responded, languidly at first, but she could feel the fine sandpaper of its tongue working against her fingers.

Then the calf began to suck more vigorously. She rose, filled a nippled bottle with milk. As it sucked, drawing the milk down with a rich froth of bubbles, Moira let her tears wash across its wrinkled muzzle.

BEGINNING
WITH GUSSIE

In a way, Tweedie's out-of-wedlock pregnancy—did people still call it that?—was mostly her grandmother's fault. Augusta James, born in the opening year of the twentieth century, an internationally respected botanist in the forties, was always exhorting her, "Follow your star, Tweedie. 'Extra vagance! It depends how you are yarded.' "

There was something in Gussie's past, hinted at, darkly alluded to. Tweedie could never tell if it was real or imagined. There were so many sides to Grammy James. She was earthy, iconoclastic, politically naive, with an underpinning of good family, old money, and the lingering traces of a private-school accent.

Forcibly retired from the faculty of Smith College at the age of seventy, Gussie had not yet given up field trips to alpine meadows. The year she became *emerita ejecta*, as she called it, she had made a modest find. A species of Arctic rhododendron had been named after her.

Gussie and Tweedie had bonded early. Sometimes Rebecca felt that her mother had pounced on the baby like some fierce, infertile tabby determined to acquire a kitten of her own. She had carried the child off with her every summer to her unrestored farmhouse in the Berkshires, in spite of Rebecca's protests.

"It's good for a baby to grow up in nature. And besides, it's important for children to have a sense of the generations. Would you deny me my rights as a grandparent?"

"What about my rights as a mother?"

"Sweetydarl, you have her ten months of the year."

"But all summer . . ."

"You will have her the rest of your life," Gussie pronounced.

Grandmother and grandchild shared the dusty, cluttered space in Becket with an array of creatures. One year it was a bummer lamb, the last-born of triplets, being raised on a bottle, and an orphaned raccoon in his own playpen. A nest of baby rabbits saved from the sickle bar, kittens from an adjoining farm slated to be drowned, were commonplace. Succeeding summers produced comparable rescues.

Tweedie at four, the only child of an only child, explained to her parents' dinner guests, "It isn't fair to a mother cat to let her have so many kittens. Grammy James says she should be spaded."

"The word is 'spayed,' darling," Rebecca said. "Do you know what it means?"

"Spaded means to have her kitten room taken out. And the daddy cats should be neutraled, they just snip off their pepsicles."

Gussie had been a bluestocking graduate of Barnard in 1922 and took a Ph.D. from Columbia six years later. She taught for several years before marrying an astronomer, who died of pneumonia not long after. Although she never married again, her daughter Rebecca, who could only dimly remember her father's beard and his pervasive aroma of peppermint, noted the ease with which Gussie attracted younger men.

Rebecca James Gruber, a Ph.D. in history, heading into college administration, was fond of calling her mother "a lovable eccentric."

But Tweedie protested. "Ec-centric, out of center, that just means out of the ordinary. If people would behave in ordinary, decent ways, there wouldn't *be* any animals to rescue."

Tweedie was ten the year of that pronouncement. Her father had recently decamped, gone to California to write film scripts. They had always called her Tweedie, a child's pronunciation of Sweetie, something Joseph had called Rebecca in those first good years. Her real name was Elizabeth.

Tweedie-Elizabeth was born in 1950. Rebecca married Joseph Gruber, the wildly successful novelist, three months earlier, in the middle of both her sophomore year and his survey of twentieth-century fiction, in which she took an incomplete. It would not have been ethical to compete for an A, she reasoned, even though she deserved one, while carrying his child. Rebecca heard that he now wore an earring. She hoped it was true.

"You didn't have to have me!" Tweedie, age twelve or thirteen, had cried with terrible prescience.

But Rebecca refused the bait. How could she, the woman in the middle, daughter and mother, possibly justify her choice to this furious adolescent? She had been determined to fasten Joseph to her, pin him down, make him serve as father and husband all in one.

What could she have said to Tweedie? *I wasn't pretty. I was almost fat.* Bryn Mawr was a cloister for bright girls like me, all of us fell in love with our professors, made them over into our images of Zeus, Apollo, whatever. I don't know how it happened, I'll never know . . . but he stood there facing the class with that way he had—has—of ramming his hands deep in his pockets, then rocking back and forth on the balls of his feet. He always wore clean tennis sneakers. His lectures were extemporaneous, brilliant, he never spoke from notes. The hour was over almost before it began. He was famous, a giant in that landscape. Of course I didn't know then he was mildly afflicted with satyriasis, I only knew I had been chosen! I was the luckiest girl in the world. And I didn't tell him I was pregnant until it was too late, really, to do anything about it.

"Your father," she called him to Tweedie, who screamed back, eyes screwed tight as if in pain, "Stop saying that! His name is Joseph Gruber."

Now, when Rebecca remembered him, she had to take little tucks and darts in the picture. Once he had been seamless, shining, perfect. Now he toed out like a duck as he walked. Under his lovely cleft chin another chin had formed. He was of only middling height, of only average athletic ability with his slight paunch, his sloping, almost-womanly shoulders. For ten years he had been the center of the universe around which she and Tweedie gladly spun, a parent to both of them, a friend, a conspirator.

Mama hadn't. Couldn't. Was walled off from Rebecca in mysterious ways. Clear, outspoken, competent Gussie, so full of fun and distances.

"I brought you up to be all the things women were not supposed to be," Gussie told her the night before her high school graduation. "To be strong and bold and full of adventure. To be forceful and innovative."

Rebecca, who was neither valedictorian nor class president, cheerleader nor Most Likely to Succeed, wanted the earth to open and receive her. She was nothing more than Honor Society, she was a signal failure, an experiment that never jelled.

Not even two years later, Rebecca and Joseph drove to the farm for Easter recess. Their marriage certificate, three days old, reposed in a file folder marked Personal.

Joseph went fishing. Rebecca faced Gussie across the big trestle table that had served for dining, mushroom identification, mail-sorting, and elbows-on discussions for as far back as she could remember.

"You must have been very angry with me not to have told me at Christmas," Gussie said, gesturing at the mound of Rebecca's belly, which Joseph's white shirttails did nothing to diminish. "Were you afraid I would try to talk you out of it?"

"No. I don't know, maybe. It's just what I wanted. Oh Mom, we're *married!* He's so wonderful! We're so happy!" And to her total surprise, Rebecca put her head down on the table and sobbed.

"I suppose I wasn't around enough," Gussie suggested. "I wasn't . . . tender enough . . . long enough."

"It's not in your nature to be tender," Rebecca said, blowing her nose. "With people, that is."

"You're right. I don't know what gets in the way. I wish I had held you more, cuddled you."

"Even though I was half an orphan."

"I'm sorry. I thought about your moral education and your intellect. It was all John Dewey and progressive education. I was too sorry for myself, Sweetydarl, long after your father died."

They stumbled awkwardly into each other's arms. Rebecca

could still feel that harsh and salty embrace. It was as close as they could ever come to saying *I love you.*

If Gussie had weathered the shock of Rebecca's pregnancy a bit grimly at first, she was weathering this one quite cheerfully. Her letters crossing the ocean to Tweedie contained dissertations on calcium and iron, emollients for the skin, and the magical properties of vitamin E oil.

To Rebecca and Milton, the once-young virologist who lived with Gussie, she only said once or twice, "I *do* wish this baby could have a father. It makes it so hard. I *do* wish, Rebecca, that our Tweedie were a little less . . . headstrong."

Milton made little murmurs of assent.

The ensuing silence acknowledged the way Tweedie was.

In mid-adolescence, Tweedie had made the leap from animal to human rights. In the ferment of the sixties, she collated and stapled, joined hands and sang, marched and sat in, and was arrested twice. Both times, because she was a juvenile, her case was continued with no finding. Once, she sat in at the Boston Navy Yard with Rebecca and twice she marched in Washington with Gussie. *Grandmother and Granddaughter Arrested at Pentagon* made headlines in the Springfield *Republican* and merited a feature article in the *Washington Post.*

Ten years later, armed with an advanced degree in international law from Georgetown, Tweedie landed a job with Horn Relief, a worldwide agency based in the Sudan. From headquarters in Khartoum, she lobbied desperately for volunteer doctors and nurses and drug supplies. In Juba, she structured food distribution and storage techniques. The

Japanese and Australians have been bulwarks in the acquisition and husbanding of water resources. Tweedie has attended conferences in Sydney and Nagoya dedicated to adapting modern technology for use in desert encampments.

Now she has friends in a dozen different embassies, and a few enemies as well. After several months of witnessing the hunger-bloated bellies of children, Tweedie no longer saw the starved and overloaded beasts of burden in the countryside. She hardly noticed the pariah dogs whipped away from cooking fires, or the gaunt mother cats scavenging in every settlement.

Two years ago she took a post with an inter-governmental agency called Migration Assistance Organization, pronounced Mayo, as if it were a binder for tuna or chicken salad. Headquartered in the heart of Europe, Mayo is dedicated to finding resettlement places for refugees and stateless persons, especially for the so-called hopeless cases. Tweedie has shucked the past and been reborn in her humanitarian zeal. She is a gifted administrator in a line of work that requires skillful dealing.

Rebecca remembers Tweedie describing a cocktail party in Islamabad attended by a well-known Ugandan, who in an earlier time supervised the torture of revolutionaries.

"He's a chameleon, he hangs on through every change of government. Now he's a bureaucrat again, he blocked the embarkation of one of our planeloads of refugees from their airport to a transfer point last week. There were 342 people on board, people who had just given up their housing—such as it was—their cooking pots—God! He kept them sitting on the tarmac for eighteen hours in the blazing heat, not knowing whether they would fly out of there or just get stuffed back into the cesspool of the tent city again. Only this time without identities."

"You know each other? I mean, you're personally acquainted?"

"Oh yes. He's very suave, would you believe, he has a degree from the Sorbonne. Anyway, he handled me three or four times . . ."

"Brushed against you? How?"

"Stroking my arm, my neck. Then managed to corner me between the hall and the stairway."

"What did you do?"

"Stepped on his instep very hard, with my high heel. Then said, *'O, je m'excuse, j'ai perdu mon équilibre.'* Walked away."

This was last Christmas on home leave. Tweedie is extremely loyal to family. Two weeks with Rebecca, two weeks with Gussie, a week in California with her father and his latest new family (Joseph has remarried three times), then she's off to Rome or Athens or Dakar to "visit a colleague." Of course there are lovers. Names are dropped and anecdotes told, but there is something brittle in the telling.

"How would you like to be my birth partner?" Tweedie had asked Rebecca in one of their weekly transatlantic phone conversations. Her voice always faded in and out, as though snippets of syllables had been detached from it along the underwater cable. "We could write a whole new chapter in the history of mother-daughter relations."

Rebecca, president of a small liberal arts college in northern Michigan, her head spinning from the request, riffled the pages of her calendar to cover her momentary vertigo. "When will this be, exactly? Or inexactly."

"January something. Around the tenth."

The scratch of a pen X-ing out a cluster of days. "Good

academic timing! I'd love to. I'm flattered that you asked me."

At the other end she could imagine Tweedie drawing a line through this item on her list. It was probably followed by Request Maternity Leave. Order Bassinet.

To be fair, that wasn't the first word of the impending baby. Tweedie had chosen to convey that news in a letter that contained all the appropriate clichés: "Something I've always wanted . . . very excited about . . . biological clock [she was thirty-six] . . . on the basis of good genes . . . has no wish to be acknowledged as father . . . promised not to divulge."

She had written Gussie at the same time, but far more frankly.

"You know how I feel about betraying confidences," Gussie said during Rebecca's weekend visit to the farmhouse. Milton had brought them both Bloody Marys and then gone tactfully off for a jog with the dogs. "But really, Rebecca, I don't like this . . . selectivity of Tweedie's. I think you need all the facts we can muster before you go off midwifing."

She unfolded the letter and passed it over.

"I don't know what you'll think of this piece of *extra vagance*, but I've decided it is now or never. I don't see why I should be cheated out of motherhood for want of a marriageable partner. The man I've chosen is an Indian diplomat, Oxford educated, gifted in languages. He speaks seven fluently and plays the sitar and the saxophone. Since I was but an impolitic dalliance, he is furious at my refusal to have an abortion. I am hoping for a little girl—I have no idea at all how to bring up a little boy—but whichever it is, I plan to bring it home during my four-month maternity leave for you to admire."

"Poor Tweedie," Rebecca said, "She must have had such high hopes."

"So you see why she couldn't bring herself to tell you."

Rebecca nodded, aware that tears were swimming in her eyes. She hoped they would get reabsorbed, she couldn't bear it if they fell, spattering her drink.

"Don't be hurt, Sweetydarl."

"Hard not to."

"I shouldn't have taken her from you every summer. It was wrong of me. Selfish. But I was lonely."

Rebecca wanted to cry out, But what about me? I was lonely too.

"Sweetydarl. I'm getting close to the end, you know. You're still in the middle."

"Meaning you're handing her back to me?"

"As if I could. As if anybody hands Tweedie."

They both reflected on this. Rebecca waited; was her mother about to say something more? There was something more, she was sure of it.

But Gussie, her conscience clear, had gotten up briskly. "Time to pick peas for supper."

After the plane lifted off from Kennedy, Rebecca ordered two vodka martinis. She had already been in transit most of the day, but the fund-raising, morale-building concerns of her job were not easily dispelled. How to keep up enrollments with a broadly based program aimed at married women in the area—ecology, Eastern philosophies, behavioral psychology, and poetry workshops—still ghosted her thoughts. The second cocktail went so quickly to her head that she gave in to the pleasant, mizzly sensation, cradled her head between the seatback and the cool window glass and let herself drift.

Of course what came up was Tweedie. Tweedie and Gussie, on either end of a seesaw. Rebecca as the fulcrum. Thirty-six years of this.

One of the ongoing mysteries of this triad was why the pensioned horses, the old foundered donkey, the fledgling birds saved alive with eyedropper and worm of hamburger, had never quite seized her conscience in the death grip that tightened on Tweedie. They had, after all, been subjected to almost identical proselytizing.

In a kitchen littered with fungi, wild grasses, and bits of birdshell, the child Rebecca had mastered the identification of a hundred specimens. The family cats slept on her bed. She fed the dogs, rode and cared for a retired police horse named King. But she was restless, anxious to break away. There was never a time—after the age of, say, ten—that she did not feel embarrassed by her mother's huge enthusiasms, her excesses. Do children ever understand how fame overtakes their parents? Just last year, during a month-long expedition in Denali, Augusta turned up a new moss of the tundra not yet taxonomized, but sure to be one of her major finds. And crowed unduly.

This women is eighty-five years old! Rebecca admonished herself. She is a living legend! Why can't you stop . . . blaming her? For loving Tweedie more than me? For taking Tweedie away from me?

Dinner arrived on its little plastic tray, a welcome diversion. She ordered a split of white wine and focused on hoping that Tweedie's baby would appear on schedule. She dreaded the prospect of waiting around for a week, God forbid, for two weeks, in attitudes of forced equanimity. They would cheer each other on, mother and daughter, while every neuron had already begun to jitter and twinge. She would aspire to an orderly calm for Tweedie's sake. Tweedie, fighting off the impulse to retreat into the solipsism of late pregnancy, would exhaust them both with little expeditions, projects, and bravados that both of them detested. Deferring to each other across the invisible wire that connected them for life.

Mr. Assounyub, the Afghan with impeccable manners, in detention in Papua, New Guinea, has written again. *My dear Madame.* Tweedie reads his jagged script on pale blue paper so thin that the whorls of her own fingertips shine through as she holds the page under the lamp. *Permit me once again to bring to the attention of your esteemed self my wretched circumstance.* But the page unfurls like a scroll in her lap; Mr. Assounyub's complaint grows longer and longer. It will take all morning to decipher this latest saga, and meanwhile his plane! His plane is being posted! She holds his expensive travel documents, his doctored passport in her hands, but they become a sparrow. She can feel its quick heart beating in her palm. Before she can open her fingers to release the bird, she wakes in the chill of January in her own bed.

Each time a jet takes off from the country's major airport, less than a kilometer away, the walls of her floor-through apartment in this converted farmhouse tremble. The wine glasses sing in the cupboard. Planes depart every minute and a half, streaking off to Bucharest and Bombay, Dakar, Damascus, New York. Although daylight only creeps onto the rime-coated pastures at 8 A.M., the planes begin to rise from the valley floor between two mountain ranges at six. By the time Tweedie leaves for the office, hundreds of people are halfway to Helsinki or Athens.

In this life Tweedie is called Elizabeth. She is a Protection Officer; she knows how to wheedle and bargain and even, from time to time, extort. Mr. Assounyub's hearing will take place today. If not the Dutch, then perhaps the Danes can be persuaded to take in this former student leader, whose English is eloquent and Victorian, and whose chief sin, ten years ago, was to lead a strike against the University administration. In Berkeley he would have been acclaimed a hero.

Fully awake now, getting up awkwardly, she hopes again that the baby will be early. Her mother is arriving this afternoon. If it turns out to be a long wait there will not be enough ways to fill the available time. Subjects are bound to come up, to be flung up heedlessly. Questions will be raised, problems for which there are no solutions. Tweedie remembers something the Deputy says: "There are no lasting solutions. Everything is *pro tem.*"

She and her mother are intimate without being confidential. They have lived together so long in their tandem singularity that they have learned, like yoked oxen, not to pull against each other. In fact, they make a conscious effort not to intrude on one another's private domains. This leaves long corridors of untenanted spaces between them, something they are both uneasy about. Even though their mutual sympathies, present if not vigorously articulated, bind them together as surely as the braids of a rope, Tweedie feels a little phobic flutter at the prospect of Rebecca's presence.

She stands barefoot in the kitchen, vaguely aware that something is out of plumb. Once again it rained during the night. Because her only windows at this end of the house are skylights as well, she cannot open them without incurring leaks. Now, as she empties the buckets and stacks them in the closet against the next rainy night, bending to put them in the corner, she feels the first squeeze of contraction rise across her belly, harden, then slip away.

Magically, she is already in labor as the plane bearing her mother across the ocean passes Gander and heads out over the water. It is a walking-around labor, possibly a false labor, possibly it is nothing at all. She nibbles on a banana and some *petits buerres* and does a load of laundry, balancing the basket on her hip as she crosses the courtyard to the communal laundry room.

The zeal to start out clean, she thinks. She showers, washes her hair, has two cups of tea. More contractions, mild enough to walk through. She is too restless to write letters, but puts Vivaldi on the record player and tries to plan a strategy for the four Sikhs stranded in a luxury hotel at the Tripoli airport, who arrived there via a hijacking in which they were taken hostage. But now it is hard to think clearly; this iron hand across the abdomen is the real thing. By prearrangement she calls her closest friend, a colleague at the office. Indeed, after Jenny arrives with her Jamaican backcountry wild talk, the contractions subside to mere twinges. There is much forced hilarity. Tweedie is surprised to discover that she is on the verge of tears.

Meanwhile, Rebecca's plane is approaching. Rebecca is bringing with her the little hooded towels, the vitamin E oil for the nipples of nursing mothers, and a convertible cradle from Sears Roebuck designed to hang from its own tripod, which has a crank attached to it. A few turns of the handle and the cradle will rock unattended for an hour. It has been an albatross for Rebecca to transport.

Jenny is waiting at the airport when Rebecca gruels through customs and is permitted to enter the public space. Her

English is crisply British, though her inflection lends it an exotic quality. The words appear to break open as she enunciates them. Later, reporting the rendezvous to Tweedie, Jenny says, "Indeed, we recognizèd one another at once."

By the time Rebecca enters the apartment, Tweedie's contractions are five minutes apart. She can still walk, talk through them. The doctor is called. He promises to come by within the hour, but that hour and most of the next pass before they hear him, audible a hundred meters away on his Mobecane. He balances his helmet upright on the kitchen table and, still in his leather jacket, pulls on a rubber glove to examine Tweedie casually on the living room sofa. She is already two centimeters dilated. Perhaps they should go. He must pay one more call, he will meet them shortly in hospital. His manner is distant, diffident, reminding Rebecca of an uneasy schoolboy.

A last look around. Rebecca takes a banana and a few cookies for sustenance, drops them in her shoulder bag, picks up Tweedie's overnight case, and they set off.

"Left here, then right at that church," Tweedie directs. "You go three cross streets and take another left, by that little *épicerie*, see?"

It is dusk. Peering down the unfamiliar streets, Rebecca tries to assemble landmarks to come home by. The little Volkswagen jiggles and spurts each time she shifts, she has not mastered the distances between gears yet. "Sorry, darlie," she murmurs. Receiving no answer, she reaches over to take Tweedie's hand and is surprised—no, unsurprised— by the fierceness of that grip. "You can do it. Tweedie, you're all right," she says, words older than time.

"You all right, though, Mom?" Tweedie manages. "Not such good timing, you must be . . . exhausted."

"Terrific timing! We'll have a whole two weeks on the

other side of the birth, much the best way," and then mercifully they are there.

Although English is her mother tongue, Tweedie will have this baby in her second or third language. She has gone conscientiously to all the meetings of the childbirth class in her sector, even the final practice ones when each of the other women had a husband for a partner and she had to make do with the instructor, a German-speaking midwife of truly imposing dimensions. Frau Lansdorf's thighs when she squatted to demonstrate an alternate pushing position loomed inside their leotard coverings as massive as old tree trunks. She looked as though she could deliver a baby with the direct dispatch of a hen laying an egg.

Tweedie had taken a stand early on about single parenting. She comported herself as if it were an ordinary happenstance, as if marriage were a quaint custom shortly to fall into disuse, like calling cards or the wearing of white gloves in the evening. And she had played this part so faithfully and with such granitic determination that she could no longer (she told herself) feel the bitter envy, the savage, corrosive longing to belong, the harsh inveighings of loneliness, or the slow clots of unsatisfied lust she had fought her way past six months ago. She would have this baby. She would have it in the prescribed manner and it would be hers in the way nothing else before had ever been wholly and singly hers. "A son is a son till he takes him a wife but a daughter's a daughter the rest of your life"; that was something Grammy James used to say approvingly of Rebecca, and of Rebecca and Tweedie, and by extension of women in general. The baby would be a girl.

Now the contractions are three minutes apart, they are serious contractions going somewhere, and she breathes as she has learned to breathe, riding the big wave up to the top on a series of puppy-like pants, then exhaling as it subsides, to coast for a blessed minute in the beautiful blue sky of painlessness.

Chiding herself, I must not think of these as pains! even as the first harsh moan bubbles out of her mouth. O God it was hard, what liars they all were with their bright talk of lollipops and tea, and cries out, O God! meanwhile clutching Rebecca's hand, mashing it into her own as she rises to the top and then ever so gradually slips down the other side.

When Tweedie is in labor, Rebecca becomes her. She too is feeling the balloon of contraction, how it hardens with a crust like a loaf of round bread, growing and growing. *"Inspirez, inspirez,"* the *sage-femme* urges, her practiced hands measuring the rise and fall. Four centimeters, six . . . Now Rebecca is lulling her daughter, using the yoga-drift, hypnotically soothing her to rest between rich, gripping seizures. "Go with it, go with it, lie back, drift as if you are lying on the sand in the sun." And indeed Tweedie closes her eyes, the frown lines ease, vanish, she seems almost to doze, then stiffens with the next big one.

Now she *is* Tweedie, but alone, terrified, taken, racked, and praying God O God, just let me get through this, I swear I'll never again, no never . . . and then the murdering oblivion of the scopolamine, followed by huge, wet cobwebs pressed over her face as she fought screaming to get free, *bastards, you bastards* and came to, afterwards, bruises on her shoulders and the insides of her upper arms from where they had held her down on the table, and two spidery hematomas inside her thighs from where they had forced them apart (she supposed; she was not there) at the moment when the head crowned.

And here in this room with white curtains and wallpaper flecked with bright dots, this room with its ordinary bed and pillows, a teapot on the table, a chair, a squatting stool, and behind a screen, discreetly, a delivery table, the backache takes hold of Tweedie, pressing, aching, pounding across the vulnerable small of the back, the lifting and holding arc of her body. Rebecca takes out her aloe cream and rubs, pressing down hard where Tweedie, in a passionate groan, directs. The other midwife, the one who speaks English with a rich New York accent (she worked for six years at Columbia Presbyterian), takes turns with her pressing, and the contractions still come and go. The mother enters the daughter and rises and falls with her as she has all her life, but before this, always in secret, at a remove. Now they are one woman in labor, passing the distended belly between them, puffing up the terrible mountain of rock, slipping half-conscious down the other side of it, filling their lungs at the bottom, making ready. *Ready.* Ready to push. *Now.*

"Mahvelous, mahvelous, dahling," croons the midwife. "I think we have this baby in five minutes now. And push! Push to the count of ten! Push not with the face, not with the neck, push from the chest. Push like the *caca.*"

"Much! easier!" Tweedie calls out, re-energized. But at the last, with all the bearing down, all the *poussez, poussez!* encouragements, the fetal heart wobbles and slows and the indifferent, silent, long-haired doctor, who arrived thirty minutes ago and has been standing at the window peering out as if awaiting a message, now squats to his work. He inserts the *ventouse* and sucks the baby's head to the mouth of the cave.

At that moment Rebecca re-enters her own body. She sees a creature come out. A large rat is backing out of the birth canal, the wet, matted hair rat-color and sparse. It is all a terrible mistake. Then the whole head emerges and she sees it has indeed a human face, still cowled in a marble-like material, something at once silken but mottled, like stone. The umbilicus, as thick as a grapevine and braided like the cord of a monk's robe, is wrapped tightly around the baby's neck. The baby holds it in one fist. The midwife quickly inserts a finger between the cord and the neck in order to loosen the noose, and the membrane breaks and the baby's face comes alive, gasping. One shoulder slips free, then the other, then the whole length of him—for it is a boy—slips free and howls in discomfort into the world. The doctor lifts him, floppy and bloody, to his mother's chest and he lies there, almost comforted, while the cord still pulses. Someone dims the lights, just as, with a snip, he is set free on his own support system. The other *sage-femme* takes him now, to suction his mouth and nose as he roars protests.

"Would you like to bathe him?" she asks Rebecca, who nods yes, and then he is in her hands, submerged in a warm bath, and he falls silent. This skill comes back unbidden. In minutes he is swaddled and dressed and put to his mother's breast. New as they both are, he manages to take hold and she to accept. He suckles a few minutes at each breast, a midwife on either side of Tweedie, like devout acolytes, and then lies calm and alert under his duvet on the lap of the grandmother who has also delivered him.

The midwives bring a feast of custard and tea and champagne and zwieback and they relive the birthing, like a sporting event, phase by phase, each fiercely proud of the other, and proudest of all of the little pale brown boy (they had both wanted a girl) who is neither exceptionally large nor exceptionally small, neither long nor short, who resembles all the other neonates and is their prize, their conspiracy.

•

Four days later, Tweedie and Rebecca sit on the floor of the living room with a bottle of Beaujolais and a full page of diagrams and instructions. They are assembling the Sears Roebuck cradle, which comes with pointed screws, end nuts, acorn push nuts, carriage bolts, knob, hanger wire, washers, and four rubber leg tips.

Tweedie reads: " 'A. Slide end cover into motor unit by straddling the inside end plate, as shown. B. Insert 2 top leg sections into motor unit as shown, and then line up the holes in the upper leg section with the holes in the end cover and inside end plate. Secure with two pointed screws.' "

An hour later they get to E. Rebecca is now reading: " 'Insert seat push rod into rear key hole of motor unit by alining push rod ear with keyhole slot.' Shouldn't that be aligning? And why key hole first, then keyhole, one word?"

Finally, a yellow slip in the bottom of the box. Rebecca again: " 'Once in a while we are less than perfect and one of our products reaches a customer with a problem or our instructions are not clear. Please use our toll-free number 800-' etc. etc." and they rock with laughter.

The baby is eight days old, vigorous, alert, and a poor sleeper. The mechanical cradle is something of a godsend, when all else fails. In the night Rebecca retrieves him once he is truly awake and squeaking. Sometimes she can forestall a feeding and spell Tweedie a little longer by walking the floor with him, a well-wrapped package, high on her shoulder. This too she has not forgotten. She and Tweedie are trying to discover the baby's natural schedule, but he is wildly erratic, sleeping only two hours between some feedings, then going more than six. Occasionally he is happy, a wide-awake little sailor rocking from side to side in the wind-up contraption.

Tweedie and Rebecca talk to Gussie every day, luxuriously long phone conversations. Gussie is failing, having little blackout episodes that she of course does not admit to, but Milton, her faithful companion, has called to report these mini-strokes. The vision in one eye has been affected, but her mind is perfectly clear.

"I meant to tell you this yesterday, Tweedie. The duckbill platypus has no nipples. Milk oozes through the pores of the skin of its abdomen, and the young ones simply suck up the droplets as they appear."

"That's fascinating," Tweedie says.

"Of course it's just garbage-pail information, but I thought you'd appreciate it. How is the vitamin E oil doing?"

"Just fine, Grammy. No problems nursing. The only problem is getting him to sleep."

"Swaddling. Tuck him up tight, he will feel more secure. In a litter the young always lie touching, you remember that? We poor humans are singular. No one should have to sleep alone."

Day ten. Rebecca and Tweedie are reading, on opposite sides of the living room, texts on nursing and child care. On opposite sides of the globe these last several months they had read texts on childbirth; they are staunch believers in book knowledge. How to make a solar heater, how to build a purple martin birdhouse, six steps to a slimmer you, it's all there. The British books are best, they agree; breezy, informative and non-condescending. The La Leche League is too evangelical.

The majestic baby, whose dark scrotum betrays the fact that he is of mixed blood (so the head nurse, a starchy nun, had announced), for the skin tone darkens only gradually, is sleeping fitfully, sucking the cuff of his sleeve. Sometimes he puts his whole fist in his mouth. He has not been circumcised, although Rebecca had promised Joseph that she would urge their daughter to arrange this little amenity. In this country, circumcision is thought to be a barbarism, medieval. Rebecca and Tweedie will conspire to convince Joseph that it was impossible to achieve, the baby's condition was not stable enough to permit it. It is dubious that this child will grow up to be the chief rabbi of Rome or Vienna, Rebecca reasons.

Tweedie is reading about wet-nursing in the eighteenth century. It was common practice for poor unwed mothers to put their babies out to baby farms, where they frequently sickened and died, and then to hire out as wet nurses to the wealthy. Often such a woman would substitute her own baby for the wealthy woman's. The heir would die at the baby farm and the wet nurse would bring up her own child in comfort. A great many plots in literature revolve around this switch—Gilbert and Sullivan's *Pinafore*, for one. Twain's *Pudd'nhead Wilson* for another.

It is the kind of subject Gussie would love to discuss. Gussie would know that wet-nursing never became deeply established in the United States. She would say, "American women were always too independent to take on *that* job for somebody else," and then add, "except maybe in the South. My own uncles," Gussie would say, "change of life babies, were suckled by the descendant of a wet-nurse slave."

But Gussie's life ends this same evening, which is predawn on the Continent. Milton the virologist calls to say that Augusta James died peacefully in her sleep. She left a will, she left notes and messages to them both. He sounds very composed, but sad.

"I want you to know, Milt, that Tweedie and I are deeply grateful to you," Rebecca tells him, but there is more. Gussie left her animals with explicit instructions as to their disposal. The old horses are to be euthanized, as is the donkey. Milton himself will take the dogs, he has grown quite fond of them and they know him.

Should Rebecca return immediately? It hardly seems necessary. They spend some time commiserating. They agree to hold a public memorial service for Gussie at a later date, when Tweedie comes to the States for her maternity leave. Perhaps they could establish a scholarship fund in her name.

The baby is not so fretful this day. He seems finally to be able to lie awake without making those grating, fussy noises that neither the mother nor the grandmother can bear. The fussiness, say the books, indicates an immature nervous system, a condition he will outgrow.

"I have to tell you something about Grammy James," Tweedie says. "It's something she wrote me a couple of months ago."

"After you told her you were pregnant?"

Tweedie nods. "It's the most astonishing thing, a confession, a document, actually. Wait, let me get it for you."

Rebecca sees it is indeed a document, several single-spaced pages typed on her mother's Smith Corona with the tail-letters—q's and y's—that always printed a little below the line they belonged on.

"When Grammy was seventeen," says Tweedie, shuffling the pages, "she had a mad, wonderful love affair with the guy who was the chief trainer for the Thoroughbred farm across from their property."

"The old Stoddard estate?"

"I guess so. It was 1917, the year of the first flu epidemic. She had just graduated from high school, a private day school, really." Now Tweedie is reading. " 'There was no question of an abortion, of course. In addition to the disgrace attendant on one, the illegal procedure, usually performed by a failed doctor or a veterinarian, was extremely dangerous. My parents were beside themselves with fury and terror. I had to be removed from the scene at once! So I was sent off to Indiana to live with some distant impecunious cousins, two dry sticks, staunch Methodists, who ran the local hardware emporium. I was alone in the house all day with two cats whom I observed very closely, keeping records of their sleep and awake times, and so on. Also, I studied Greek. After supper, as soon as it was too dark for my condition to be taken note of, I went for my daily long walk.' "

"God," Rebecca says.

"The day the baby was born he was put up for adoption and she never saw him again. Then she got the flu and she hoped she would die of it, romantically. 'Having lost my lover and given my child away,' she said, 'I was ready to lose my life.' She was so sick that all her hair fell out 'ignominiously.' "

"I think I always knew about this," Rebecca says slowly. "I mean, not the whole story, but I think I always knew there had been a great love when she was quite young, and that it ended badly. In my mind it had something to do with World War I, the influence of all those stories, I suppose."

"You mean about fiancés being killed at the Marne and the women vowing never to marry?"

"Something like that. They all became high school English teachers."

"But the way she described it," Tweedie says. "Listen to this: 'I must tell you, Tweedie, this grand passion was the sweetest interlude of my life. Even after almost seventy years, I have perfect recall for our feelings, our gaiety, indeed even our conversations. It was wonderful how he used to lift me up, his hands around my waist—I had a tiny waist, then—and twirl me around in the boxstall. "Augusta Wadsworth Kensington," he'd say, "second cousin twice removed of the poet! Watch her fly through the air." ' "

Rebecca is crying.

"Don't cry, Mom. Think how happy he made her. 'He taught me how to shake straw on a pitchfork—it's a fine art, to distribute it evenly—and we used to ride out together, galloping the jump course. Even though I was terrified of the drop jumps, I followed him over every one with perfect confidence.' "

"Can't you just see it, though," Rebecca says. "Packed off to cousins in the Middle West, undoubtedly paid to keep it quiet. Abandoned by those bitchy, upper-class parents with their expensive reputation. The groom was probably bought off, too. Banished to Virginia."

"Trainer," Tweedie corrects. "Actually, he went to Kentucky." They are both silent a minute. Rebecca blows her nose.

"They gave her chloroform," Tweedie says. "She described how they put a few drops on a handkerchief tied around her wrist and told her to sniff it when the pains got too bad. So she would sort of pass out and her arm would drop and then she'd come to and sniff again and pass out. Primitive but effective. The thing was, it's very bad for the baby."

"She never found out who adopted it?"

"She said she tried to trace him through the minister of the Methodist church in Leedsville. But I guess back then a natural mother had no rights. They could keep the records from you."

"Strange," says Rebecca. "Mom was so . . . indomitable. It seems to me that if she wanted to know badly enough, she'd have found out."

"Want to hear what she wrote at the end?" Tweedie asks. She has not known until just now that she would share this with Rebecca.

" 'And thus, Tweedie, while I cannot applaud your reliving my history, I am deeply happy to think that my genes are being handed on. Modified, broadened, no doubt improved upon. I know you will hold fast to your baby and that he will be a credit to us all.' "

The baby starts to squeak then and soon works up to full scale. Rebecca diapering him, Tweedie nursing him, separately and silently think how it all comes down to this moment. That the baby begins with Gussie.

JACK

Full moon in February casts extraordinary shadows on snow. Tree trunks and branches, fence posts and rails, all are doubled by moonlight so palely white that the illusion is of a landscape under water. At 4 A.M. Helen comes awake, pricked out of sleep by some sense of things askew. The house feels colder than warranted; prudence dictates that she go downstairs and check the woodstoves.

Russell, who tended the stoves so professionally, sizing up the stack of split logs and choosing two that nestled inside for a perfect fit, died early last winter. She got through the rest of that season the hard way—day by day and nights of bitter tears. This year, things are going a bit easier. She no longer obsessionally thinks of mingling her ashes with his, for instance. She is resigned, a little better than resigned, to going on without him.

They always both said they wanted their ashes to sweeten the farthest field, and he got his wish. Helen isn't sure their two grown sons will be faithful to hers; they may have something else in mind. A religious service with flowers. That prospect horrifies her.

Once up, she glances by habit out the bedroom window

at the paddock. There he is, a gaunt ghost horse, an Ichabod Crane-carrier of a horse, hanging his head over the top rail of the gate, facing downhill as if awaiting the Messiah. She is not at all surprised to see him. There was no latch Jack could not unseat with hours of patient effort. She and Russ used to joke about teaching Jack to untie their shoelaces; it would save all that bending down.

Jack's presence echoes something she was working on in the dream that jolted her awake. Something Russell was doing, freshly glimpsed as in real life, a secret event tearing past her, as elusive as a coyote she might catch sight of out of the corner of her eye. She feels she is living a double life, going on with the one they shared the long slow years of his cured cancer and then his new cancer and its remission, and the final recurrence. Days, she tends the farm, reduced now to three broodmares and a crop of youngsters. Nights, she rejoins Russ in a shadowy space full of bizarre events. There are ocean liners and snowmobiles in it. Planes take off for wild destinations. The grown sons frequently appear as children again, and horses long gone reappear as weanlings. Rampant and unpredictable as they are, Helen welcomes these dreams. But what was the one now eluding her?

Jack stands motionless in the spectral light. The temperature hovers near zero, but he appears oblivious to it, breathing out little frost-puffs that hang in the air like nimbuses by his shaggy, oversize head. As Helen watches, prickly with cold and premonition, he turns toward the house and lifts his gaze to the blind windows as if he could feel her line of sight interlock with his. After a long moment of attention, he turns back to continue his downhill vigil.

They are on the verge of a true exchange, that haunted moment when their eyes meet. She watches for a long time as he stands guard at the gate facing the serpentine road that winds down to the valley. Perhaps he is there not to stare down, but to invite up, or in. Perhaps something is about to be born.

When she dreams Russ back (it happens less frequently now), she feels pregnant with his presence. The first time, he sat bolt upright in his coffin (there hadn't been a coffin, his remains were cremated) and said, "Boo! I was only fooling!" Later, he called her on the phone but was cagey as to his whereabouts. Even inside the dream she knew she couldn't return the call. Lately, he came and went like the coyote's handsome brush, barely but thrillingly experienced. She hated waking up, knowing he had been there but unable to remember the context.

How she and Russ felt about Jack says something about how they felt about each other. They were bonded, that's a word animal people use, Helen says to herself, to express the rapport they've developed with their dogs or cats or horses. You don't go around loosely saying you love your horse. It's okay to love your dog and it's almost okay with cats, but horses are too big, too dangerous, you might say too sexual.

She and Russ belonged to a generation that didn't verbalize affection in public. They used to say they were dinosaurs, so long married as to be an embarrassment to their kids, whose playmates all had multi-parents, stepfathers, half brothers, four sets of grandparents. So they put a lot of tenderness into the barnyard, side by side wheeling sawdust or shavings, lifting hay bales. As if in search of sainthood, she and Russ anointed themselves daily hauling water, mucking stalls, paring hoof abscesses till they bled, poulticing sore ligaments, and keeping up a soothing banter with their herd of home-raised Standardbreds.

Helen and Russ met half a century ago, give or take a couple of years, in Providence, Rhode Island, when her

Wellesley College swim team lost the last meet of the season to Pembroke. Russell, who had hitchhiked down from Boston, hopped on their bus for a free ride back. Although he was still in uniform, the war was over and the army was about to muster him out.

In the Oxford Grille in Cambridge the next night, over his beer and her beer which she did not drink but ceded to him, Helen found out Russell had majored in chemistry at Cornell; was shy a couple of credits of an advanced degree; loved motorcycles and horses about equally.

Back then he had been pursuing a diver on the team named Pat Thornbury, but his feeling was not reciprocated. In fact, when Pat saw him on the bus that day she turned to the other squad members and made a little moue of deprecation for the benefit of the girls. They called themselves girls; it had not yet occurred to them to do otherwise. Favoring Veronica Lake hairdos angled over one eye, they were gorgeous well-fed girls in sloppy joe sweaters that hung low and loose over their plaid skirts, the hems of which brushed their thick white ankle socks.

Helen was a freestyle swimmer, best at long distances. The 200-meter was her event. She swam for Wellesley because it was free, required no outlay for equipment, and balanced her fierce dedication to the classics, which she was later destined to teach to a broad mix of indifferent and enthusiastic high school students. Her passion for horses, developed in early childhood, had to wait almost two decades for gratification.

Russ's passion for her—it took her a long time to forgive him for choosing her as second-best—was not immediately evident. It bloomed sturdily, though, like an antique rose. By Christmas they were engaged and the following June they married, which was the way, Helen reflected, their entire

generation had responded. If you survived the war, you were
programmed to sign the contract and procreate.

Their first child was born ten months later, the second,
eighteen months after that. Because the babies came so close
together and because they prided themselves on being in
the avant-garde of child-rearing, parenting for them was a
fifty-fifty affair. Helen now thinks it prepared them for these
last twenty years of heavy horsekeeping. She wonders if they
were slightly worse than average parents. Awfully absorbed
in each other, it is possible that they stinted the little boys.
Whom she loves and resents in their adult phase, in about
equal measure.

Russ had a good job as a research chemist with a large
pharmaceutical house, but it didn't last, nor did the next
one. By then, Helen had found a terrific situation teaching
Latin part time in a private girls' school. It wasn't that Russ
ever exactly lost a job; it was more that the job lost him, lost
his attention, his respect, his desire. He moonlighted on the
side in a variety of small businesses, but nothing quite
scratched the itch to be free.

They bought an old farm in western Massachusetts on
their eighteenth anniversary. Old farms could still be had
back then for the back taxes and a little something to sweeten
the deal. Helen moved out there for the summer with Nick
and Donnie. Before the chimneys were pointed she had
acquired a bay mare for herself, with an elderly companion
horse the kids could ride. Russ drove out on weekends, and
while he complained a lot about the mosquitoes, which were
fierce, his romance with horses burst into bloom.

He and Helen explored the countryside, mostly at a sedate
trot, with a few gentle canters thrown in. Russ was always a
tactful rider and handler. He never tried to muscle a horse,
and he turned out to have reservoirs of patience with them.

He and Helen talked about starting over, maybe getting into breeding trotters for the nearby track.

About that time, he started losing his voice and then regaining it in little episodes of what he called bronchitis, although he rarely coughed. It was nothing, he assured Helen, his father at about this age had had the same thing. If it persisted, he said, sure, he'd see a doctor.

When Donnie graduated from high school (Nick waiting in the wings, just a year behind), Russ was so hoarse he could hardly congratulate his firstborn. They all made spirited jokes about Russ's speechlessness, but Helen, in a moment of blinding clarity, foresaw the truth. Six weeks later the surgeon removed his voicebox and told them how lucky Russ was. The cancer had not yet spread. Months of chemo and radiation therapy ensued; months more while Russ learned to make approximate sounds without his larynx. He was clean. He had been a heavy smoker and a moderate drinker since his teens, but stopped smoking and went on the wagon without any histrionics. In three months' time, he and Helen had burned all their urban bridges behind them.

Jack came to them only a few years later by default; his owners could not keep him at home. Stabled in an indifferently fenced pasture, it was no trick at all for him to break out whenever wanderlust overtook him. One strand of electric wire? He rolled under it. Sliding post-and-rail? He inserted his draft-horse-size head between the middle and top sliders and used his shoulders to work the board loose. Thin boards he knocked down, turning around and taking careful aim. Thick ones he chewed to the desired thinness.

A careful fellow, once out his hoofprints attested that he always trudged along the shoulder of the busy country road. But his continual bustications said clearly that he could not

live alone. Helen and Russ took him in because no one else
wanted him. Homely and smart—particularly adept at lifting knitted caps off human heads—he served as surrogate
uncle to the annual foals, sensible trail horse to accompany
each flighty youngster as it arrived at driving age, and alpha
horse for the herd.

Why, then, Helen asks herself as she crawls back between
the covers, has he left his mares inside tonight?

After that, she sleeps fitfully and awakens to the flaming
sky of a winter sunrise. Jack is no longer there. Possibly he
was never there. The paddock and fields beyond are iced
over with old snow crust, an empty landscape. Possibly,
Helen thinks, I dreamed the whole episode.

She dresses and stamps out to the barn to feed. Jack stands
dozing in his stall, its door hospitably open. No sign he had
meandered by moonlight, except that the insulating cover of
the watering trough in the alleyway has been nudged to one
side. He had helped himself to a drink. By the rational light
of morning he appears well fed, tending toward hay belly.
His expression is serene, even self-satisfied.

The impatient yearlings begin to set up a ruckus. The
little bay mare bobs her head as she always does, awaiting
her feed. The two big mares whicker rustily, as if unused to
communicating. The barn cats appear purring, insinuating
themselves under her feet. There is half a mouse corpse at
the threshold to the grain room. It is a perfectly average
beginning to the day.

Even so, a sense of things unanswered haunts her all
morning. At noon the sun slips behind a cloud bank. The
wind dies, the air grows heavy with moisture. A weather
breeder, no mistake.

In waning daylight the first snow squalls blow in. By late
afternoon the flakes have thickened, the wind slams doors

in the treetops. Closing up for the night, Helen wedges a whittled peg into Jack's door latch to hold the bolt in place. Just in case.

Don't worry, she dreams he tells her that night, enunciating carefully in a perfect, accentless English. *We'll have 122 inches by morning.*

Inside the dream, she never wonders where he learned to talk. She thinks, on waking to light snowfall, how marvelous the illogic of dreams is. She is careful not to mention this episode to Donnie, who calls from the city for a little phone chat. He's heard she has a fresh foot of snow on the ground, right? A little less than a foot, she tells him, meanwhile thinking, *122 inches.* Grateful for his attention, Helen is wary, however. She doesn't want to hear again how she should give up this place, sell out, travel, find a nice apartment "closer in." She especially doesn't want a lecture on how arduous even the narrowest snow paths are for someone her age, the skinny trails she clears from house to barn, barn to manure pile. Her shoulders ache from the effort.

To Nick, who calls later that evening, she rhapsodizes about the fresh snow, about how snug the farmhouse feels, how well the young stock are doing, which one is going to the old trainer in March, and so on. Nick, at least, is a little bit horsey. And he is fond of Jack. Helen is careful to mention an old volleyball that turned up in the paddock while she was shoveling, and to omit the dream.

People who put words in the mouths of animals must be primitives, wild eccentrics, or going round the bend, right?

Helen and Jack expect to have several more years together. Jack is aging. Helen can see it in his gradually deepening swayback. He is having a little trouble now chomping down his hay pile, but his eye is bright, his sense of humor (today he is enjoying batting the caved-in volleyball round the paddock with two yearlings) intact. If he starts to lose teeth, there is always beet pulp, Helen tells him. You can last forever on beet pulp and hot bran mash. Tea and toast for you, he says. And prunes.

This is not a dream but rather the tone of voice two old friends take in conversation. And Russell is always with them, sharing the banter, the snow depth, the wind chill factor, the flaming, stubborn determination to keep fast and remember.

THE CASSANDRA EFFECT

"The stirrup came late to the Western world," was the phrase Alicia Loomis had just written when she smelled it again in her carrel, the slight, intrusive redolence of horse. Head bent over the page, she pinched her thin nose shut and held her breath for a long minute. Sometimes, as with the hiccups, that helped. Then, determined to complete the thought, she scribbled, "although the Chertomlyk vase of the fourth century, B.C., is often alluded to as possible evidence that the Scythians possessed this knowledge."

Don't panic, she told herself. It might be real this time. It might be something in here that you wore two days ago riding with Paul. But what? The car coat Alicia always reserved for the five-minute walk to Firestone from her narrow brown apartment on Witherspoon Street. And there were her Princeton gloves. And the scarf, a patch of color, not needed this early April day.

Something could have hung next to these clothes in the closet, then. Don't panic! Maybe your riding boots got closed in by mistake. Maybe you forgot to leave them out in the back hall last time. Maybe it's not the same as when Pa died.

Everything depended on this thesis. She needed to get it puffed at the MLA, get it published, maybe even made into a coffee-table book with illustrations from the Bayeux tapestries and illuminated manuscripts.

The department professed to be enthusiastic about Alicia's topic. And why not? It didn't impinge on any of the tenured professors' specialties. It didn't even come close to the usual offerings. It was fresh, it afforded a new approach to old questions: The Effect of Changing Styles in Equitation on Warfare in the Chivalric World.

She loved what she was doing, scribbling away in the cubicle the library had allotted her. But really, what right did she have? Alicia could barely drag herself out to peace rallies, she who was a veteran of the civil rights marches. Now when she went she skulked on the fringes, like a CIA agent.

In other parts of the world this winter of '67–'68 women were out scrounging roots and grasses to boil. Babies were quietly dying in Africa, American GIs were dangling Vietnamese out of helicopters. All the news reports of torture and mutilation hammered her down even tighter in her carrel. "What am I doing this for?" she complained intermittently to Paul. "Who needs another thesis in medieval history?"

"To get your ticket punched," he'd say. "To have a marketable skill."

"But once I'm marketable, I'll have to move on, find a teaching job."

"I'll miss you."

And he would, she realized. But the pleasant interlude would fade, be subsumed, eventually forgotten. He did not speak in the voice of a man with only one phone call; with bail or without, Paul would get by.

But would she? One more year and she'd be thirty-five; a very late bloomer. The face that looked back at her out of the mirror was pleasantly freckled, moderately pretty. Thin nose, high cheekbones, lips that had been described as bee-stung. A little too sensual, Alicia always thought. She had spent her adolescence trying to diminish their effect with makeup. Her auburn hair still naturally wavy and thick. Average figure, average height, a pleasing enough arrangement.

I'm old enough to be your father, they always said, the kinds of men who found Alicia attractive. Or the kinds of men Alicia responded to, drawn as inexorably to the Older Man as iron filings to the demonstration magnet. It was partly to escape one with a wife and teenage children that she had left Manhattan and a job in publishing to go back to gradu-ate school. That, and a terrible restlessness she felt in the city, a claustrophobia that nagged her not only in elevators and crowded subway cars, but made her ears ring in sealed glass office buildings.

And then her mother died and left her a small inheri-tance, enough to get by on if she lived frugally. After filling all the History Department graduate-level requirements, she managed to wring a niggardly grant from the Gossheuven Foundation for Medieval Studies to support her dissertation.

When the smell started coming back, however, she was terrified. Somewhere Alicia had read that olfactory sensa-tions are frequently the sign of a silent tumor. At the Health Service they ran her through a standard physical. Head-aches? Periods of tunnel vision? A ringing in the ears? Out-patient tests, including an electroencephalogram, turned up nothing.

It was much the same in the Princeton Hospital. Alicia lay back as the radioactive dye was injected in her vein.

The flushed feeling that overtook her, a mysterious inner warmth, was not uncomfortable. She half dozed, troubled even here by the faintest tinge of horse smell.

No lesions. No tumor of the olfactory nerve. Health Service suggested counseling, that her problem was psychogenic. They offered a list of psychiatrists and psychologists approved by the medical staff. It began with a Dr. Bernard Adelman and ran through Heinz Volkemar. There was one female name; it had been typed in at the bottom after the list was alphabetized.

Wilhelmina Koning saw her patients in an attic room overlooking the back lots of two other mildly seedy Victorian houses on Remington Street. It was a brisk ten-minute walk from Alicia's apartment into a part of Princeton where she was unlikely to encounter a colleague. Alicia tramped up the added-on outside staircase every Thursday at ten. She wondered if Dr. Koning had any other patients; there was never any evidence that other hands had rummaged through the musty pile of *National Geographics* on the table. Sometimes there was the comforting racket of children rising from the floor beneath. The Other Koning—this was how Alicia described the arrangements amusingly to Paul—was also a Dr., a Ph.D. in mathematics, recently acquired. He had been a minister who lost his faith.

"Or found it," Paul mused. "In numbers."

"Yes. Well, now he teaches calculus at the Camden campus of Rutgers."

"Banished to the provinces but longing to get to New Brunswick, right? But what's *she* like?"

"I don't really know. Very low-key, kind. Somewhere in her forties, has this perfectly straight-cut hair, like a bronze helmet."

"It's a national style, sweetie. Called a Dutch bob."

"No, it's very unusual," Alicia insisted, "especially with her eyes. She's got these big hazel, almost green eyes."

"Sounds like some transference has taken place already," Paul said.

"Oh, well. Transference." Alicia made a face.

"So. Is he Dutch too?"

"Definitely. They were childhood sweethearts. Her father was killed in the Resistance. When she was a teenager she went around with a razor blade hidden in her palm and sat next to German soldiers on trams so she could slice the buttons right off the front of an officer's overcoat. 'He was somewhat intoxicated,' she said."

"Boy, Alicia. That's more personal interchange than I ever had in six years on the couch." Paul made it sound like a triumph.

"This is different, this is therapy," Alicia reminded him. "Wilhelmina says we have to come to trust each other."

They hadn't talked much about the smell yet. Alicia alluded to it as "my symptom" and Billie—she was more comfortable with Billie than Wilhelmina, she explained—called it "your olfactory hallucination." It was like an enlarged breast node, Alicia thought. Some days she could palpate it easily and some days she had to root around to find it, but they both knew it was there somewhere, lurking, waiting to expand.

Right now, Billie was still setting the stage, asking interested questions about Alicia's relationship with Paul, with the department chairman, with her former lover, her dead parents, gathering other biographical data. And wonder of wonders, she seemed genuinely interested in the thesis.

When people at cocktail parties asked Alicia what she was writing about, she tried to explain. "The development of the longbow was a Welsh invention that spread to Europe around the time of the Battle of Crécy in 1346. It changed the whole methodology of war."

"Really?" someone could usually be counted on to comment. "Really, Alicia. How?"

"Well, for one thing, arrows shot from the longbow were so lethal that armor was invented to protect the rider. And then they saw they had to protect the horse, too. Naturally, they had to breed bigger and heavier horses to carry all this ponderous stuff. These gigantic horses were so clumsy in all that boiler plate that the warriors had to get off them to fight. And fighting hand-to-hand altered the whole code of sportsmanship."

By now she had lost most of her audience. Nevertheless, as the first dissertation student in twenty years to present a topic in her field without Christ symbology embedded in it, the department thought her promising.

Alicia didn't have any real friends in Princeton. Women graduate students were a rarity, although a British woman was writing a philosophy dissertation about the legacy of Aquinas and the Schoolmen in Schopenhauer. Partying was pretty elaborate in the Ivy tradition and she was too shy to seek out invitations. It didn't matter. She had little time for socializing between the lavish half-days she spent riding with Paul and the painstaking hours here in the library.

She cleared a little space on the table and wrote, "On a Korean water jug dating from the latter part of the fifth century a pair of egg-shaped stirrups is clearly discernible. Their use hereafter can be traced moving rapidly eastward into China, westward across Siberia and Russia into the domain of the Holy Roman Empire."

Outside her library window the forsythia and quince were loosening their hold. Bits of petals fell, were lifted, and sailed off in the light wind. Dogwood was coming on. The azaleas had begun to redden, the daffodils were in bloom.

God. Even without breathing through her nose, it was no longer a whiff. Now the entire carrel smelled of horse, an odor of ripe manure and apple, tinged with neat's-foot oil, sweat, and dander. The day her father died, an end-of summer day, the same overwhelming perfume.

As a child limited to once-a-week riding lessons on tired school horses, Alicia used to keep her jodhpurs in the bottom drawer of her bureau. Every night she went down on her knees and opened that drawer for a few restorative inhalations before hopping into bed. She prayed every night for some mysterious happening, something unforeseen and magical that would catapult her and her parents out of Philadelphia and into the countryside. Anywhere where she could have a horse of her own. And then, when she was eleven, that simple and uncomplicated wish was granted in the ugliest possible way.

Her father, it seemed, had defalcated. That was the term they used when they ousted him as comptroller for a variety of city agencies. Alicia came to understand that the term was a shade less baldly accusatory than *embezzled*. Gerald Loomis didn't go to jail for steadily accumulating and then covering his gambling debts by juggling the books. Several city officials said he deserved to. But in view of his long service, etcetera. The war had just ended in Europe, the public mood was one of general easing.

The Loomises moved from the city to Marshfield, a fairly elegant community in exurbia, but with a right and wrong side of the highway. Just after Alicia's eleventh birthday they were loosely installed with all their worldly possessions in a drafty frame house set down on two acres of leased-out cornfields. It overlooked the turnpike and reverberated all night from the succession of semis roaring past. Behind the house stood a barn in reasonable condition. It had a stall for Alicia's dream horse, and two other stalls that could be rented out to boarders.

In fairy tales the exorbitant wishes, when they are granted, bring with them other sorrows. It was true in Alicia's case too. Up until then she had had an average childhood, though lonely, not unduly oppressed by thought or opinion. Now she had to face some terrible awarenesses: That the hopes of adults could be dashed and their spirits could be broken. That people who appeared to have a comfortable, non-violent marriage could harbor huge red angers. Even worse, that a man and a woman could continue to share a house, a child, a bed as lovelessly as her two cats, Blondie and Skeezix, shared the same litter box, ate out of adjoining bowls, took up positions on the same windowsill, but elaborately ignored each other day by day. When she first discovered this parallel, she was appalled. Gradually she got used to it; nothing much had changed. At least there was no hissing or spitting.

Horses, on the other hand, were without guile. You knew where you stood with them, you had only to look at their ears. They had no unfulfilled aspirations. They were creatures of habit and loved a daily routine. The real estate broker who sold Gerald Loomis the house had two horses, big raw-boned dapple grays, that he and his wife boarded some distance away. The Loomis barn was more convenient to the state forest and certainly cheaper. A deal was struck. The animals hadn't been in the barn more than a week when a little brown mare named Easy Money arrived. She had been

too small to race well. Alicia's father had acquired her, he
winked, in a swap. She never learned for what.

What you feel about your first horse, Alicia once tried to
explain to her Manhattan lover, what you feel is unmatched
by any other experience in your life. "Oh, I know it's supposed to be power, mastery, sexual expression, but that's so
easy. So pat. A horse of your own . . ."—she twirled the
spaghetti expertly on her fork, its tines snugged in the bowl
of a spoon—"when you're twelve or thirteen and you haven't
got a single other friend. . . ."

He murmured appropriately, this father of three daughters. None of whom, miraculously, was pressing for a horse
of her own.

Alicia told Wally all this in a ratty West Side restaurant.
They had drained the first bottle of Chianti almost before
their dinner came and were working on a second.

"They're so damn spooky," he said. "You can't trust them,
you never can tell which way they're going to jump."

"Coming from a trade-books editor with two glitzy horse
books on his Christmas list," Alicia remembered saying,
"that's practically treason."

The spaghetti went down like worms. It was November.
A cold rain slanted into the canyons of Manhattan. Every
time the steamy front door of the Trattoria Aldo was opened,
Wally looked up furtively.

It was always terrible when Alicia and Wally tried to meet
in the city. But the spring and summer before when they
had marched shoulder to shoulder with activist nuns and
priests and hordes of college students had been almost the
happiest time in Alicia's life. She and Wally had flown to

Detroit and to Boston together. The camaraderie and the singing, the sense of belonging, were like a huge sporting event.

On a flight to Atlanta where they first met, there was time to develop the intimacy that overtakes strangers buckled side by side, slicing their Salisbury steaks with plastic knives. Wally's house specialized in spy novels, stories of international intrigue, native-grown homicides with interesting case histories, Alicia's in scholarly historical texts. He was so improbable a character in this setting, so kindly, so thoughtful, even dry, behind his rimless glasses that Alicia's heart lurched. She loved the little hesitation in his voice each time he spoke; a pause that was not quite a stutter, but a catch, as though he was holding something back. She could not have said why she was so beguiled. Certainly she was lonely, and more than that, apprehensive. She was going to the rally, she told herself, as an observer.

That night he had stopped by her room in the Sheraton to offer her a placard and an armband that would identify her as part of the same group with which he was marching. At least that way, he said, they would be in the same bloc in case there was trouble. She had just gotten out of the shower when he knocked at her door. She remembered how she had held her bathrobe closed at the neck, embarrassed by how girlish and frilly it was. Somehow the message was conveyed and read. He groaned, burying his face in the cleft of the damp polka-dot pink wrapper. He was twenty years older than Alicia, he loved his wife who was obese and kind to the children and didn't, he said, especially care for the physical side of marriage.

The whole spring and summer they romped in air-conditioned hotel and motel rooms across the Southland. Alicia, moreover, was swollen with the rectitude of their cause. Hadn't

Jack Kennedy said that we must meet this moral issue? "This is the land of the free . . . it is a time to act!" God, how he stirred people. A president with sex appeal. More than sex appeal—true charisma. Not since Gandhi, people said. Not since FDR. Magnificent.

Ten days after their awkward Chianti-blurred supper in Manhattan, Kennedy was assassinated. Possibly the world had not before witnessed such patriotic grief. Certainly, the nation had not mourned a loss like this one since Lincoln's murder. "The last leader our nation had believed in, the last father-son-husband figure to us all," one commentator wrote. People everywhere felt a helpless fury. Strangers wept openly, patting each other, on street corners. A black cab driver in New York City said, "It was the first time in my life I cried with white people."

Alicia could never forget the funeral procession, the horse-drawn caisson as it turned toward the Rotunda of the Capitol, the traditional riderless horse behind, led in hand with a pair of highly polished boots turned backward in the anchored stirrups. She would take that beautiful sad sight with her forever, and the way the horse had jigged and skittered from side to side, neither quite in nor out of control. Like a tethered soul breaking loose, she thought, she who had no faith and wanted none of its consolations.

Nothing was the same after that in the civil rights movement. Oh, people still marched, linked hands, and sang. People still cared, but without the old passion. Camelot had ended. What Kennedy's death did to Wally was devastating. Stricken, he confessed to his wife that he had been unfaithful in Atlanta and Birmingham, Jackson, Detroit, and Boston. Stricken, he had confessed to Alicia that he had betrayed their relationship. From time to time she saw him in midtown restaurants, where editors take their authors to cosset them or thrash out contracts with their agents. He was older, drier, with pink rims around his eyes. She told herself that she felt nothing, nothing at all, she could hardly remember how her heart had lurched that first day. And how could it have lurched over this soulless male who found horses unbeautiful, did not respond to their magnetism? But the truth was, if she allowed it, she could rerun every motel scene, every city, every side order of french fries or onion rings they had shared in their mini-history.

In his new life in the country, Alicia's father had made some astonishing changes. He raised guinea hens and started writing pulp thrillers which he sold for modest sums to paperback houses called Launcelot Press and Weatherwave Books. The poultry were capable of the most amazing range of sounds, purring and gabbling all at once. Alicia loved watching them bob about, wearing their little forehead daggers. The eggs that they laid were little bigger than marbles. It took a dozen to make an omelet.

Alicia's father's presence around the barn delighted her. He had this funny way of referring to himself in the third person as the Pa-Man. Years later, as a college sophomore, when Alicia learned that it had been the family nickname for Katherine Mansfield's father, the pang of recognition almost broke her heart for the second time. Mostly she called him Pa, but late afternoons when he came around to watch her haul water to the stalls and give the alleyway a final raking, she sometimes called him softly, Pa-Man, as in: *Now, my Pa-Man, if you don't mind. It's time.* For she always backed out raking. She loved the pristine look the wood shavings had, all untrodden. Her mother felt that way about a clean oven, but it was twenty years before Alicia was willing to connect the two passions.

Alicia and her father didn't talk much. He told her he came at feeding time because he loved to listen to the rhythm of such serious chewing. That was a side of him, Alicia thought with satisfaction, that her mother never knew. Her father's larcenies didn't diminish him for her. His gambling obsession seemed to her to be something like Easy Money's terror of crinkly plastic, something she couldn't help. She thought to herself that she loved them both not less but more on that account.

Once they were settled in Marshfield, Alicia's mother seldom went out of doors. She was like an early Christian martyr caged between the wrong end of town and the whooshing turnpike. The state forest at the bottom of the cornfields held no fascination for her. Even when the realtor and his fluffy wife came out on weekends to ride their matched grays, she could hardly be induced to stand on the porch and watch them canter off. Keeping horses made about as much sense to her as keeping rhinoceri. They were nearsighted—didn't everything they looked at appear seven times larger than normal?—and stupid, full of danger. One of these days, she predicted, Alicia would really get hurt.

The house itself was pretty down at the heels. Brown stains had invaded the wallpaper of all six rooms. Windows stuck and had to be jimmied open, leaving ugly gouges in the windowsills. Everything needed refinishing. The faucets leaked and occasionally a buried pipe burst. Alicia's mother scrubbed and mopped up and even repainted a couple of rooms, but her heart wasn't in it.

Thinking how shamefully she had treated her mother combined with the now-vivid horse smell in the alcove. It was making her dizzy. The aroma of horse cloyed, it invited nostalgia of self-blame. She had perfect recall for her adolescent cruelties, how she had held aloof from helping with groceries or laundry, tiptoeing past the kitchen as if it were a sickbed. She had let it be known haughtily that running the barn required infinitely more skill than keeping house. She was, after all, earning money. She would be happy to pay board if that was what was wanted. Her mother, provoked into it, slapped her across the mouth with a dishcloth. It was a muslin dishcloth outlined with big basting stitches in red and blue thread. It was wet and nasty and Alicia told herself she had richly deserved it.

When she turned thirteen, a weekend job opened up at the elegant horse center from which her boarders had removed their horses two years ago. In good weather she rode Easy Money over the connecting fields two miles and stabled her while she mucked out. Nine box stalls on one side of the aisle, nine on the other. If the weather was very bad, her father drove her there in the aging Pontiac. Instead of money she was paid in private dressage lessons from Major Moldau. At first she was so shy in his presence that she trembled in the saddle, meanwhile praying that he wouldn't notice. Possibly he thought she had some deteriorating disease or possibly he was kinder than she imagined a former major in the Hungarian Cavalry could be. Under his calm tutelage Easy Money learned shoulders-in and turns on the forehand and haunches. Alicia learned to carry herself well back in the saddle, balancing evenly on both sitting bones, to come squarely into the halt. How easy that sounded, how difficult to attain! She fell rapturously in love with the Major, who once patted her on the thigh after she had ridden a decent first-level dressage test. She would have mucked a hundred stalls for his praise.

Four years later, at Mt. Holyoke, it was a native Virginian, a screamer as opposed to the whispering Hungarian. No transference there. Since she was a scholarship student on a tight budget, Alicia worked in the college stables along with two other young women. Riding lessons were available to students from other colleges in the area. One evening a week, Alicia taught a class of four beginners, among them, Dino di Rossi, a dark, skinny Amherst junior, a true Roman. His father was one of the captains of industry who had risen, as Dino put it, "from the ashes of Italy's defeat at the hands of the Allies."

Dino frequently sounded like that. He had no sense whatever of the clichéd phrase. He was majoring in economics, part of the process of grooming him to manage an automobile plant in northern Italy when he graduated, and he drove around the valley in a little Fiat Spider his father had sent over to alleviate his homesickness. He was said to be writing a novel in his spare time.

Alicia fell in love with Dino there in the dusty arena as he went round and round on a patient elderly gelding named Horace. She fell in love with the way he worked so hard at learning the correct position, establishing just the right amount of tension on the reins, following, always following with elbows and arms so that good old Horace trusted him and came right up on the bit. The way he cared, never catching his horse in the mouth. He didn't nag her, like the others: "When can we canter, Alicia? But when do we go over some jumps?" He rode to develop *sprezzatura*. That became their code word. A careful nonchalance that comes with good balance, *sprezzatura!* Remembering Dino made Alicia feel old and used up, full of self-pity. She grabbed her coat and stumbled out of the reeking cubicle into the sunshine.

What did it mean, the smell coming back? She shook

herself. Sternly, saying, look here, you're all right. Billie says you're not going to have a nervous breakdown. You're too well grounded for that.

Along Nassau Street, the shops were already displaying the trappings of summer. Bathing suits, brightly colored sandals with woven rope edges floated tantalizingly behind the big windows. Alicia sniffed experimentally, but out here there was only the slightly vinegary taint of car exhaust. In her head she was running through that whole summer and the disaster that followed.

Dino found them an apartment in the back wing of a farm-house in Sunderland. Money flowed unstintingly from Rome. Alicia told her parents that she was living at Happy Acres, the day camp where she was in charge of the riding program. She didn't like lying to them. She felt she could have told her father she was living with Dino, but he would have been unhappy about it. She couldn't bear to contribute further to the little hump of misery he carried on his back. And she could never have told her mother, not back then. Her mother already had enough treasured grievances without Alicia's providing more.

The only times she and her mother did something together were at Christmas and Easter, when they put in an appear-ance at church. On these occasions, Alicia took her moth-er's arm as they walked well down the aisle toward the nave. Her mother wanted to be seen here, normalized and Chris-tian. It was little enough to do. Alicia could take no credit for so small a gesture.

While she stood in the middle of the riding ring and had the little girls go in circles around her on those poor tatter-demalion horses that camps lease for their summer programs, Dino planted a garden. The eggplant crop failed, the peppers were a disappointment, but oh! the tomatoes, and oh! the zucchini.

They stirred the same saucepot with their matching wooden spoons in the little Pullman kitchen, bumping hips as they urged each other to taste and see. In bed they bumped hips too, for it was not quite a double bed. It seemed there was never a moment they were not wrapped around each other, even the hottest, most humid nights of early August. Alicia prayed that their summer would never end, inventing elaborate fantasies in which she found kind foster homes for all the spiritless, melancholy horses of Happy Acres, and constructed a paradisiacal scenario for Dino and herself. In it they lived happily ever after with gardeners and chauffeurs and a governess for their dark, skinny children. She even invented a cottage on the grounds for her parents when they came to visit. The fantasy hung there as ripe as the one eggplant that had fruited, oval and purple, in their vegetable patch.

An intermittent insomnia seized Alicia toward the end of that August. She would come awake at 3 or 4 A.M. aware of a barnyard smell in the room. Their apartment overlooked a cow pasture. The nearest horse was miles away at Happy Acres, but Alicia could have sworn that the faint aroma teasing her awake those nights was that of her own barn back in Marshfield. Dino humored her when she mentioned it, attributing the smell to a dream she had suppressed. For hadn't he a hundred dreams of home, all these years coming and going? And wasn't Easy Money home in the barn, hadn't Alicia had to choose this summer between him and the mare?

Gerald Loomis shot himself in the mouth on Labor Day. He sat down in one of the empty stalls still bedded with wood shavings, put the Luger, his World War II souvenir, in his mouth, and pulled the trigger. Of course he had gone on gambling secretly. He had sold the down-at-the-heels house, the barn, the two acres of cornfields to cover his more serious debts, and then he had put a bullet through his brain.

After her father's suicide, Dino took the part of the bereaved brother, standing between Alicia and her mother, holding each of their elbows during the graveside rites. Alicia wasn't sure that her mother even knew Dino was there at the time. The doctor had given her enough tranquilizers to make her a mere spectator at the burial. It was days before her face got over feeling numb. Days before she could do any of her proper grief-work, as she called it, making it sound to Alicia like a take-home exam.

At Christmas Dino was summoned home. His mother had leukemia, the prognosis was uncertain. She was dangerously ill, she was hospitalized, then at home, then readmitted to Sancta Maria. She underwent a course of chemotherapy, she had four transfusions. Even Dino, who was an atheist, went to church every morning to pray for her.

As long as it appeared that his mother was dying, Alicia wrote Dino daily. She kept up, not a barrage, but a steady flow of sympathy. She had lost a parent, he seemed about to lose a parent. She hoped it would be resolved quickly; otherwise, she feared that the family would close around him as the sea around a young whale.

And then miraculously his mother began to recover. She was able to gain some weight, her hair regrew—it had all fallen out during the chemotherapy—she was in remission. But the threat of recurrence held Dino in place. He wrote less often. The letters dried up like unused garlic cloves. He entered the family business, he put away his novel. *But next summer, Cia, I will come back to the States to see you.*

Somehow Alicia limped through the semester with a string

of charitable B-minuses. By spring she was less woolly, she could focus again, speak up in class. Blake revived her; they were reading *Song of Innocence* in her English lit course. Still, that whole year she could not look back on the season with Dino, the toy housekeeping, the lighthearted lovemaking without experiencing a physical sensation of sinking down, being drawn into the earth. She could still see the cluster of grapes carved on the headboard of that old oak bed. She could still hear the rusty-hinge cry of the red-winged blackbirds opening those hot summer mornings.

Paul was waiting in the Periodicals Room, his topcoat neatly folded in an adjoining chair, his Irish tweed cap on top of it. Next to the cap, a splash of chrome yellow, half a dozen daffodils furled in florist's paper. His own daffodils, thousands of them naturalized on all three sides of the huge flagstone terrace in Busby Township, were already past the peak of bloom. Alicia knew at once where these had come from. She had passed them earlier in a pail of water at the feet of the paraplegic who sold candies and sundries from his wheelchair on Nassau Street. Paul couldn't walk by that orange-slickered figure, or, for that matter, flowers past their prime.

Twice a week Paul collected Alicia from Firestone and carried her off to ride with him along the hushed, sandy trails of the Pine Barrens, where enormous heaps of rusted cars rose like dinosaur hulks in the scrub growth and clusters of deer, hardly larger than dogs, scattered at the horses' approach.

Paul was half English, half American. In profile he reminded Alicia of a falcon, except that his nose was balanced by a strong chin. Crusader-blue eyes, she thought.

But the mouth was Gallic and sensual. A handsome face, half ruined. It seemed always at war with itself, almost as if he had suffered a stroke and determinedly recovered most of his muscle control. His blond hair had gone gray in the bleached, somewhat waxy way that fair hair ages. In Alicia's opinion he wore it trimmed too short, rather like a Prussian officer, accentuating the slightly reptilian loose flesh of his neck.

He had of course graduated from Princeton. After the war— World War II, that is, he would always insist, half mockingly—he had taken his advanced degree at Harvard as one of Talcott Parsons' disciples in sociology. From what Alicia could see, he lived on unearned income and connections. An amateur botanist, he had written a small book on wildflowers, illustrated with his own meticulous line drawings. He was a migratory-bird counter for the Audubon Society, a personal friend of Cleveland Amory, a dedicated anti-vivisectionist, a soft touch for Spay-a-Cat collections and dog pound emergency funds.

Harley Newcomb, chairman of the History Department and one of Paul's oldest friends, had introduced Alicia to him. Paul needed someone to ride with him on a regular basis. He had tried a number of local youngsters but they were not dependable, or too noisy, or careless around the stable.

"He's a typical fussy bachelor, even though he's been married," Harley defined him. "The thing is, he's obsessed with horses. He took on this jittery Thoroughbred his vet was going to have to put down, and nursed it along. It was a racehorse, cracked its front leg in its first start. Now, this crazy beast is sound enough to ride, but he's a menace."

"What way a menace? Rears? Runs away?"

"As I understand it, mostly he balks at things. Paul says

he won't go on the trails alone. Anyway, there's this perfectly sensible other horse that's not getting any use, the one
he'd like you to ride. I must say, Alicia," Harley beamed
with paternal pride, "he was fascinated with the notion of
your dissertation. I think the two of you will hit it off."

So it had been arranged. In fact they *had* hit it off. Alicia
was grateful for the twice-weekly diversion. The Thoroughbred Balthasar was beautiful. Alicia immediately understood Paul's attachment to him despite the nappiness, the
shying, the jigging in place. Once this horse had been a
prime athlete, bred to carry a tough little man for short bursts
of enormous speed. Now he was asked to go calmly at the
trot in the company of dilettantes, the hysterical whippets at
his side. In his limited view, this was clearly unspeakable.

Paul had taken several falls from Balthasar but always, it
seemed, he as rider had been at fault. Inattentive when some
grouse flew up alongside, he had been unceremoniously tossed
into a thicket of blackberries. On another occasion he had
started to dismount to tighten the girth when a dog spooked
the horse. Caught with his toe in the iron he had been dragged
several yards before he could twist free. Once when they
were overtaken by a logging truck that blasted its horn, Balthasar had literally leaped into a ditch with Paul. The horse
was unscathed but Paul had broken his collarbone.

There was a considerable edge, then, to each of their excur-
sions. "Another adventure," Paul would say, smiling his
thin-lipped smile as they mounted. Alicia, at ease on Paul's
gentle bay mare, could think of no appropriate rejoinder but
she rode the mare as close to Balthasar as she dared to give
the horse some feeling of security.

When they came back from their rides and were finished

cooling out their horses, Paul made fruity gin drinks to salute the sunset. If it was too chilly to sit on the west-facing terrace, they drew chairs up at the glassed-in end of the kitchen and waited for the deer to arrive.

"Here they come!" Paul whispered, tugging at Alicia's sleeve. "You get first looks." He handed her the binoculars.

In twos, in threes, in groups of five or more they came gliding out of the thin woodlands to browse in the rye fields, moving birdlike and silent, scattering and regrouping. Four bucks, a dozen does, several weanlings. Clearly this was the high point of the day for Paul. He alternately sipped his drink and studied his deer through the glasses. Alicia sipped her drink and saddle-soaped whatever piece of tack she had selected that day to clean.

"I don't understand how you could let it go like this," she grumbled, scraping a year's accumulated sweat and grime from the cheekpieces of Balthasar's bridle with a table knife, then lathering the leather with glycerine soap. The warm flexibility of cleaned leather aroused her.

"Listen, dear heart, before I met you *nothing* ever got cleaned."

"I can see that. What did you do when it got so stiff you couldn't work the buckles?"

"Threw it out. Bought new stuff at that tack shop in Princeton, the place you say is way overpriced."

Alicia was silent.

"Does that shock you?"

"Since you ask. It's *scandalous*."

"Not so scandalous in the grand scheme of things," Paul murmured and rose to renew his drink.

At this moment, the discrepancy between the landscape with deer and the little interior on Witherspoon Street was

so great that Alicia felt as if she had wandered onto the set
of an expensive Broadway production.

After the dark had enclosed his deer, his view, his king-
dom, Paul would investigate their supper options. Usually
his housekeeper had left a casserole, a baked chicken, her
own special noodle pudding. Occasionally Paul had some
other engagement, but for the most part the Wednesday and
Sunday afternoon rides developed into full-scale evenings.
Sometimes he drove Alicia back after the eleven o'clock
news. Many nights she stayed in the guest suite. If Paul had
an early flight out of Newark or Philadelphia, they got up
together. Usually they'd confer in the kitchen, in the half
light.

"I'll run the dogs first," Paul would say.

"I'll just go and do the horses, then," Alicia would respond.

By the time she had fed and watered, turned them out,
and mucked stalls, Paul would be jogging back up the
driveway surrounded by his ecstatic whippets. There was
time for a quick cup of coffee before they set out for Princeton. Paul would drop her off at Firestone or her apartment
and then head for the airport.

In November Paul revealed that he had a sister in New
York, he was going there for Thanksgiving. For Christmas
he would fly to Arizona. He always had Christmas with his
ex-wife, they were good friends. He didn't trust his housekeeper, though. When he was away he suspected that she
took home the chickens she was supposed to cook and feed
to the whippets, substituting dry kibble. Would Alicia like
to come and stay over the holidays, just to keep an eye on
things?

They were not yet lovers. Alicia wondered if it would come
to pass. He was in the habit of kissing her nicely but negli-

gently as they walked back up from the stables to the kitchen door. She came to understand that the kiss said, *There! Another outing on Balthasar and still alive and whole!* He always bent to help her out of her boots before he worked his own loose with the bootjack. He was jealous of the fact that one of the dogs, the bitch named Isadora, preferred her to him and always lay with her sparrow-like head in Alicia's lap. No matter. This was the Looking Glass, she had walked right through the mirror and now stood on the other side.

To realize that Paul was older than her father would have been now, had he not put the gun in his mouth, did this dampen or enhance the pleasure she took in their time together? She tried to think how ingratiating, how deferential, how altogether cowed her mother would have been in this echoing mansion with its slate floors, twisted iron statues, huge modern paintings that were slashes of red and yellow against crusted, dead-white canvases.

"But are you comfortable there?" Billie asked her. "You are at home in it, what you call the mansion?"

"I've gotten used to it. I don't feel like an interloper, if that's what you mean."

"Not what I mean. What you interpret. You must learn to listen to yourself, hear what you say about your mother. Do you project some of your own feelings onto her?"

"Dino was rich too," Alicia said slowly. "I would have lived in a castle. A villa, at least."

"And your father with his gambling, do you see? The classic fantasy of the gambler, it is?"

"To strike it rich. Live like a king. 'If wishes were horses . . .' "

"What is that," Billie asked. "That last part?"

"Oh, it's a fragment from a nursery rhyme: 'If wishes were horses, then beggars would ride.' "

"And there was your father wishing always for the fast horse. Do you sense any connection with your symptom?"

Alicia did not. Billie sighed. Downstairs a child's voice whined on the ragged edge of tears. The hour ended.

It snowed only fitfully that winter. There was scarcely a Wednesday or Sunday that they did not ride out together. Balthasar was calmer. They allowed themselves some brash uphill gallops, with only a few bucks at the outset. On this enchanted schedule Alicia carried out her research.

The dissertation went well. Alicia was particularly taken with the difference in equitation between the Frankish knights at the close of the eleventh century and their opponents, the Seljuk Turks. The latter were small men, invariably mounted on little Arabian mares. They rode short-stirruped so that they could draw their bows or slash with curved scimitars. The charging Franks, riding straight-legged, bowled them over. But often the European horses, almost all of them big stallions, went over to the enemy.

"It's a wonderful story," Paul said. They were trimming bridle paths and fetlocks. Balthasar, for all his jitters, was calm about the clippers, but the mare was edgy. She needed Alicia's practiced soothing. "How did I ever get this done without you?"

Praise, but only perfunctory embraces. Had he been celibate since the divorce? Did he prefer men?

Was Alicia falling in love with him? Sometimes, back in the Witherspoon apartment, soaking in the too-short tub, she allowed herself to daydream. She is wearing a peach-colored nightgown, she knocks at his door just after he has put out the light (for they read in their separate bedrooms the times she stays over). She invents something urgent.

Smoke. Yes, she smells smoke, and one of the dogs smells it, too. She hears one scratching and whining. They go down together to the kitchen to investigate. And then, after there's nothing . . . she frowns. He still shows no inclination? Well, then, she twists her ankle, falls to the floor, she cannot walk. Will he carry her upstairs?

"I'm a bit early," Paul said, holding the daffodils out to her. "But it's such a beautiful day, I thought we could have an extra-long hack."

"Perfect! I'm ready for one. And what a nice thing to do." She took the flowers and they walked down the corridor together to her carrel to collect her scarf and gloves.

Alicia sniffed tentatively. The air still announced the presence of horse. "Smell anything?"

He pretended to bury his nose in her hair. "Dr. Somebody's peppermint castille?"

"No. You don't smell anything . . . strange?"

"Am I supposed to detect some scholarly aroma, a zephyr from the Middle Ages?"

And so she shrugged it off.

On the drive to his estate bordering the Barrens, Paul was in a buoyant mood. Lyndon Johnson, his bête noire, had declared he would not run again, thereby enhancing Bobby Kennedy's chances.

"I thought you were clean for Gene."

"Alicia, McCarthy doesn't stand a chance. He's too inaccessible."

"Robert Lowell likes him."

"Lowell's a poet, not a politician."

"I thought you didn't think Bobby had the intellectual prowess."

"Is that what I said?"

"Intellectual balls, to quote you exactly."

"Let's just say I was a bit hasty."

They crossed the barnyard and entered the stable together. Paul put Balthasar on the crossties and began grooming him. Alicia brushed the mare in her stall and then came out to fetch her tack.

"Want to ride the Big B today?"

She was a little taken aback. He had never offered to swap horses before. "Love to. Think I can handle him?"

Paul cinched the saddle and threaded the reins through the rings of the running martingale. "If we can get you up on him."

"I've ridden big horses before. Just give me a leg up, will you?"

He cupped his fingers for her left knee and she vaulted into the saddle. Balthasar immediately plunged left, then right, wheeled, and reared as high as the restraining straps would allow. Instinctively Alicia dug her heels into his sides to drive him forward and down, then faced him at the paddock fence. For one wild moment the horse thought about hurdling it, then came to a halt, quivering.

"Jesus, Paul!"

He gave her a quick sidewise grin. She could see the sunlight glint off his front teeth. "Hadn't even got your stirrup yet, had you? Anyway, you did fine."

"Sure as God made little apples he knows someone new is up," Alicia said as they jogged across the stubbled field. "Who says Thoroughbreds are all stupid?"

"I never thought so. But he's learned his lesson," Paul said appeasingly.

"Like hell he has. I don't know why you keep him. Really, Paul, he's totally unpredictable."

"Totally. That's the attraction. Look at him! God, he's gorgeous. I'd forgotten what aesthetic pleasure it is to see him under saddle. God, look at that stride, that shoulder! Doesn't he just flow like melted butter?"

"More like molten lava," she said.

Balthasar balked at the highway. He resisted every effort to get him to cross the asphalt, even following the good mare. It was the same road he crossed twice a week to reach the woodland trails of the Barrens. More rearing, wheeling, snorting his fear snort. Backing away, dangerously close to the ditch.

"Maybe you'd better get off and lead him."

"If I get off and lead him once, he'll make me get off and lead him every time." Alicia suddenly turned him and jabbed him sharply backward. In three wide strides he had backed across the dreaded ribbon. She struck off at a brisk trot down the sandy track.

"Well ridden," said Paul, amused, coming alongside. "I'm sorry he's so awful today."

"Liar. You love it."

"Well, it would be terrible for my image if he went better for you, wouldn't it?"

It was a long hack in bright sunshine dappled here and there by taller growths of pines. Along the creek the willows had come into leaf and the path was littered with spent catkins. They went miles farther than usual. Balthasar improved with the workout. She was able finally to relax and enjoy his smooth action. Coming back across the highway the horse dropped his nose and moved forward as calmly as an old school plug.

"No dragons going home," Paul noted.

"I'd turn him and make him go across again but I don't want to crowd my luck."

"Anyway, it's late. It'll be dark before we get over the hill to the cornfield."

It was fully dark before they finished cooling out. Once the animals were fed and settled, Alicia and Paul walked in companionable silence up to the house. Paul stopped on the terrace and turning her toward him gave Alicia her ritual hug and kiss. This time it was something more than a dry, propitiatory act. But did she have to put her life on the line to arouse him?

During supper they listened to some new Schubert recordings. Afterward Paul sat, clipboard propped against the arm of his Eames chair, making notes for a tactical session the next day in Washington. Despite all his reservations about Bobby Kennedy, he had signed on. Now he was drawing up both sides of the domestic issues for the Indiana primary campaign.

Alicia thumbed through Paul's supply of magazines, trying to pull abreast of the bad news in the *Atlantic, Harper's,* and *The Nation.* Fighting in the Saigon area had intensified. In Tennessee the sanitation workers' strike was shaping up as a major civil rights struggle. Nelson Rockefeller would not run for a place on the Republican ticket.

The smell was coming back. It had something to do with sitting quietly; it had something uncanny to do with current events. She got up restlessly, walked across the room into the kitchen and stood at the glassed-in end, staring out into blackness. The bitch Isadora came and nestled her pointed nose in Alicia's palm. Behind her she heard Paul move, click on the TV for the late news.

Martin Luther King had been assassinated. The cities were going wild. Rioting in Memphis, Washington, Chicago. It was Walpurgisnacht, a night of truncheons and tear gas. The authorities had called out the dogs, the horses. Looters streaked past, bent double under console TV sets, even mattresses. Even, improbable! two men carting off a refrigerator. Alicia watched glass shatter, blood run in the false color of television. She shivered.

"Jesus, Jesus, Jesus." Paul paced, pounding one fist into the other palm. "Jesus, I knew this was coming."

Hours later, after Paul had made half a dozen phone calls, they sat quietly together with brandies. Alicia poured out the story of her first premonitory smell of horse. She wept again for her father. She confessed how the smell had come back today and how terrifying it was to be a Cassandra. They made a false start up the stairs, then came together on the living room couch. The whippets, closed in the kitchen, whimpered and scrabbled at the door with their nails. The leather upholstery was cold on Alicia's back.

"I didn't think you knew how to cuddle," she said to him afterward. They nestled together in Paul's bed as the sky lightened.

"I don't, really. I haven't had much practice."

"You're doing fine." She sniffed the air to locate her olfactory symptom. It was still there.

"Maybe you're right, Leesh. Maybe it's all linked to your father's suicide. And maybe in some way King's murder brought all of that back to you. But you have to stop socializing with your therapist and get down to the hard part. You should start seeing her more often. Promise me, first thing tomorrow—"

"Today."

"Jesus, today."

The Cassandra effect, Alicia now called it.

"Do you smell it now?" Billie asked.

"No. Not in here."

"Do you smell it out of doors?" She was crisply professional.

"No. Mostly it's worse when I'm alone. In the library, in my study alcove."

"Tell me about the first time."

Alicia described the late summer days with Dino. She tried to recapture the enchanted-cottage atmosphere of the farmhouse, the extreme happiness that had fluttered under her breastbone like a live thing.

"Would you say you were both somewhat manic?"

"I suppose. The mild mania of first love. But I knew it was over when he went home. With all his promises, all his fantasies about next summer, next year, next Christmas, I knew."

"Did you feel rejected? Did you feel he had treated you badly?"

"I don't think I was able to feel . . . anything, really. What happened was a long siege of no-feeling. When I finally began to snap out of it I wouldn't let myself dream any more dreams about living happily ever after. When he married his beautiful Emiliana I cabled my congratulations, I was determined to behave correctly."

"And you think to behave correctly is to repress your feelings?" Billie's voice was uninflected but Alicia read the reproach in it.

"Correct starchy behavior," Alicia said, "is to send a cable on your former lover's wedding day. Every Christmas you get an elaborate religious card featuring golden halos. And every year after the first one, you also get a birth announcement."

Billie murmured a question.

"It was a girl. Isn't it funny? Dino couldn't make a boy. I

never wanted a boy. One or two baby girls, that would have been wonderful. So he and Emiliana had five little girls in a row."

"And each time he wrote to you?"

"Oh, yes. He wrote as if we were old school chums, old locker-room buddies. He sent all these proud-father snapshots."

"And did you have the horse smell then?"

"No. Not between that first time and a few months ago."

"The smell you notice in the library, is it the same?"

"Yes. It's the same, except now it's not so . . . pleasing. Now it's too strong, it invades everything."

"It takes over?"

"Exactly."

"And that first time?"

"The first time, with Dino, just before my father killed himself, I don't know . . . it was there, all right. But it wasn't overpowering. I could deal with it, I could almost make it go away by refusing to smell it and by Dino being so rational about it."

"And this time?"

"It was much stronger. That's what's so terrible. Exactly the same premonition and then it came true. It's a Cassandra thing, it comes back before a terrible event. Before a death."

Billie wrote in an upright black script, words Alicia could not decipher upside down. She had never taken notes before. Then she put down her pen, pushed the paper away in a gesture that said, There! No more preliminaries.

The three-times-a-week sessions cut into Alicia's working time. Her dissertation faltered; it was harder to concentrate. She felt ghosted by a hundred new childhood memories. But when she brought them up, Billie sat like the neutral observer of a family quarrel.

"The time Ma slapped me across the mouth with a dishrag," Alicia said. "I remember so clearly how I walked away. I wanted to scream, punch, fall down on the floor in hysterics, but most of all I wanted her not to know that I cared."

"Mm." That was Billie's signal. It meant *go on*.

"I walked out of the kitchen and I ran down to the barn. It was pouring rain, I put on my oilskin pants and poncho top and I took down Easy Money's old turnout halter and snapped two rope lead shanks on it—I wasn't going to ruin my good leather saddle and bridle. Then I hauled the poor dear out of her nice dry stall and climbed on her from the fence rail and rode off into the woods. I didn't have any idea about where we were going, just out of *there*. In the back of my mind I guess I wanted to punish my mother."

Here Billie was roused to nod yes.

"It was just getting dark. I was awfully cold and scared, shaking, I don't know how long we stumbled around in the state forest in the rain. My father had gone off somewhere that afternoon and evening—I think it was Daylight Saving Time by then—I wanted to stay away long enough to be missed, to scare everybody into being nice to me. But when I got back and dried Easy off and put her up again with some hay, nobody had even noticed I'd left. I remember thinking I could have been killed and no one would have noticed probably until the next day."

"And then they would be sorry?" Billie smiled.

"Very." Alicia managed a matching smile.

On another occasion Alicia remembered studying Family Units in third or fourth grade. "It turned out that I was the only only-child in the whole class. I remember Mrs. Serota commenting on it in a tone of wonderment or disapproval, I couldn't quite tell which, and how I confronted my parents with it at dinner. 'One of you was quite enough,' my mother said. And my father laughed a little embarrassed laugh, as if I might ask something about sex next. I felt humiliated. Obviously I had been such a disappointment to my mother that she didn't want any others like me."

Once, Alicia remembered a lighthearted detail. She patiently picked all the pimientos out of the olives in an olive jar and repacked the olives in the same neat rows. It seemed to her that this guilty procedure stretched over a long period of time before she was caught. Incredibly, her mother laughed; she was not punished. The next time they went to the grocery store her mother bought an entire jar of pimientos and gave it to Alicia for her own.

One good detail! While it didn't balance the unhappy ones, it counted for something, Alicia thought. People grow and change, she exhorted herself.

Peace talks opened in Paris, but the fighting in Vietnam did not abate. Body counts invaded Alicia's consciousness. *Life* magazine did a feature article on the uses of torture to extract information from captive guerrillas. Wet towels were used to suffocate the victim. Electric shocks were applied to his genitals. What did it mean, that men could do this to other men? And women to women. What did Billie think, she who had escaped the Holocaust? For wasn't this another?

But Billie was cagey. "What do *you* think it means?"

"I think it means we are capable of infinite depravity."

Billie chuckled. "You sound like a Dutch Reformed minister."

Spring was almost impossible to bear. Paul was gone on

frequent occasions. Alicia tended the dogs and the horses. The housekeeper came in days, grumbling over the mud, over the boiled chickens, over Paul's mysterious ways. Alicia suffered the magnolias' fulsome bloom. The dogwood, the azaleas, the cherry trees came into season, then ebbed. Alicia sat on the terrace with Paul's binoculars to watch his deer rummaging in the rye field at dusk. Now the Cassandra effect accompanied her everywhere. She lived in a state of suspended terror, awaiting another death. The air in her carrel was overpoweringly horse. Even Billie's comfortably cluttered attic room smelled increasingly of it. Only out of doors could she escape her symptom.

On Monday-Wednesday-Friday Alicia climbed those outside stairs to revisit her father's suicide. Nightly she redreamed surreal versions of it. The more freely she talked about that time in her life the sharper the horse smell became. Billie assured her that was to be expected. Resistance, resistance. Together they trod the squashy ground of Alicia's memories.

"What about your mother, did you ever smell the horses when your mother was dying?"

Why didn't she? Why not? When, exactly, had she known her mother was dangerously ill? The diabetes had gone on forever but had seemed less severe after the Pa-Man's death. Alicia realized she had almost forgotten her mother's disease. There were never cookies or sweets in the house. Sugar was evil, it rotted your teeth even while you lingered over the forbidden chocolate bar. Her mother was always painfully thin, Alicia could not remember any of her indulgences.

"Her most sensual moment was to make herself a cup of strong tea. I remember her little sigh of satisfaction, sitting at the kitchen table late in the afternoon. I don't think I noticed that she . . . wasn't herself. Weaker. Shooting more insulin. I never knew she had hypertension until the stroke, I'm not even sure that *she* knew. She wasn't the sort of person who went to doctors if she could help it, she didn't trust them. She didn't really trust anybody."

"Did she trust you?"

"We never . . . she wouldn't have asked me . . . the truth is, we were always two strangers. We were polite and distant, we shared the same bathroom, we had the same last name, the world called us a mother and a daughter. Trust? I was the last person my mother would have trusted. I couldn't do anything right in her eyes. And knowing that, I didn't even try. We didn't know each other. We didn't *want* to."

"That is very sad," Billie said, shaking her head so that her neat, straight hair flew from side to side. A value judgment, it startled Alicia. How was she supposed to feel, for God's sake?

"Isn't it?" she agreed neutrally.

"And the stroke, how did that make you feel?"

"Oh God. I don't know. Numb. I didn't feel anything. It happened when I was just getting started at Dutton, I had three books to edit and I was worried I wouldn't be able to get through them if I had to run back and forth to Philadelphia every two days. And then she died the very next week, she did me the kindness . . . of not lingering."

"And were you sad then?" Billie sounded hopeful.

"For a long time I didn't feel anything. I'd think about how I ought to call her up, you know, on a Sunday morning, and then I'd remember. Maybe . . . maybe I felt relief. That it was over."

"What kind of relief? How did it feel?"

"That she couldn't blame me any more. For the way my father was, for the way I was. For hiding chocolate bars. For loving horses when she hated them." Tears rolled down Alicia's cheeks. Tears wetted her neck and soaked the front of her blouse.

They were both silent. "Does it surprise you," Billie said finally, proffering the box of tissues, "Does it surprise you to find you are grieving for your mother?"

What surprised Alicia was that there were so many tears. "How long will this go on?" she sobbed session after session. "God, I hate this! I don't want to do this any more."

"Where does it hurt you?"

"Everywhere! Nowhere! It doesn't hurt, it's just so awful. I *hate* crying. I *hate* the way my head fills up, my throat aches. And I can't breathe, that's the worst part! I can't *smell* anything. . . ."

Billie was nodding emphatically.

"I did say that, didn't I," Alicia said slowly. "That's incredible, isn't it." She was silent for so long that Billie finally urged her forward.

"Try to say what you are thinking. Put it into words."

"I was thinking how desperately I want . . . I want you to hold me."

"And that is very hard to say?"

"It's . . . very hard. I mean, it doesn't matter how much you read about transference and the primal scene and Oedipus, it's all only words until you go through it."

Billie smiled at her. Nodded, smiled, rocked. "I think that's a good stopping place for today."

Paul came back from Nebraska just long enough, as he put it, to get some laid-back California clothes. Then he would be off for the Democratic primary in that state. They managed one ride together before he repacked.

"He's a lot calmer," Paul said, puzzled, taking Balthasar over the in-and-out jump at the bottom of the cornfield. "Usually he bucks like hell when he lands. What's your secret, Leesh?"

"I've been working him on the longe line every night, under full tack."

"Full tack? Side reins?"

"Ten minutes each way of the ring. He's learned all the voice commands. He really wants to please, Paul."

They cantered soundlessly along the sandy path. When they pulled up Paul said, "You know? I think I liked him better the other way."

Alicia was furious. "Fine. You can always ride him bareback for kicks. Why don't you take him out in just a halter, you know, the way the kids do with their bareback ponies, with two lead shanks snapped on for reins?"

"My, aren't we testy! You'll have to teach me how to longe him."

"Gladly."

What she realized now was how much *she* had to learn. Like Balthasar, she was enjoying the process, even though it caused her anguish. She and Billie were working a fine jigsaw puzzle, one crafted out of good wood with elaborately shaped little pieces. It would be a long time before Alicia could step back and see the whole picture with foreground and sky and figures in the middle distance. But every session there were memories that interlocked and led to others.

She was so absorbed by the development that it was almost a relief when Paul left again.

Alicia was getting used to the routine, the clamorous presence of the dogs, the comfortable evenings with books, magazines, the television if she chose to turn it on. The

Cassandra effect was fading. She could hardly detect its presence any more. The dissertation was almost finished.

But she was chronically sad; never before had she been so melancholy. She had a lot of grieving to catch up with, Billie pointed out.

In a few more weeks she would be finished with her thesis, she could begin to plan for the future. She thought she would go to the MLA meetings in Chicago, she thought she would apply for a teaching job in the Middle West, make a fresh start. "Maybe it will be some place where I can have a horse of my own again."

"I have no doubt," Billie said. "The nurturer in you is always going to need a horse of her own."

Before she locked up for the night Alicia went outside to check on the horses. They were grazing in the far field, slow-moving shapes silhouetted against the darker line of hedgerow. She slept fitfully; in her dream the barn had caught fire. Her father ran here and there with a bucket of water. Over and over her mother rang a bell.

Knowing it was Paul she lifted the receiver.

"Alicia?"

"Are you all right? What time is it?"

"It's Bobby," he said, and his voice broke. "They shot him. I didn't want you to find out from anyone else."

"Oh my God. God. Is he . . . ?"

"He won't survive. They got him in the head."

She had never heard Paul cry before, she would not have thought he was capable of it. It was thrilling and terrifying all at once, as if an uncrackable code had yielded its secret.

They talked for an hour across the distance. Alicia reached

out and pulled a blanket from the bed and draped herself in it, as if at a campfire. Paul sounded calmer now, more in control. She was quaking still, even inside the blanket. But before they ritualized their goodbyes, before they spoke the sane arrangements for Paul's return, the hour of his arrival in Newark, providing he could get a flight, Alicia realized she had not been forewarned by the Cassandra effect.

She settled the receiver into its cradle and sniffed cautiously. Nothing. She drew in a deep breath. The air held the tantalizing aroma of full summer. Fresh-cut grass with the tang of rain. Nothing more.

BUMMERS

It's the middle of February, 20 degrees Fahrenheit, and some clean wet snow is falling on the scuffed stained snow of the sheep pasture.

Ariella and Dirk Envers are supposed to be cleaning the sheep shed. None of their own ewes are due until March but Bonnie, their mother, is hoping to pick up a couple of bummers this month. She's a weaver and a vegetarian. When she culls their flock in the spring, though, she sends the unwanted ram lambs and the used-up ewes off to market.

Ariella hates her calling it *market* when it means to be killed. Hung up on a meat hook for the blood to all run out. That's where her last year's ram lamb Mocha went. Also, Ariella hates her name, she plans to change it to Anne as in Anne of Green Gables when she comes of age. Of age in this state (Massachusetts) is eighteen, light-years away, as far as Ariella is concerned. She will be twelve next week.

Dirk, who is eight and small for his age and legally blind besides, is chipping away at the frozen sheep shit with a garden trowel. Tears are running down his face, melding with snot. He hates this job, he hates Bonnie even if she is his mother, and besides being multiply handicapped he is clinically depressed.

When she saw the word written on his school record Ariella thought it was *multiply*, as in addition and subtraction. Dirk is an albino, he was born without any pigmentation and he can't ever be out in the sun without tons of sunscreen slathered on him. He is so nearsighted that in order to read he has to hold the book right under his nose. But there's nothing the matter with his brain; in fact, he is *smart*. He reads a lot of the same books Ariella reads, even parts of *Animal Farm*, but nobody knows this except the two of them. There's a little bit of palsy in his left leg from being oxygen deprived while he was getting born. Bonnie calls it a hitch in his gitalong, as if he were somebody's pony.

She says it's all right for Dirk to hate her out loud and Ariella can, too, anytime she wants. She understands why they call her Bonnie instead of Mother. She says hating your mother is a way to defend yourself against admitting how much you love her and want to keep her around. She knows this because she used to hate her own mother behind her back and after her mother died she felt horrible. Bereft. That's a word Ariella loves.

It's lousy the way Bonnie is always cheerful and wears her black hair in one big braid down her back while Ariella's blond mane has to be cut every few weeks to keep it in a Dutch bob. Bonnie is 4-H leader of the sheep club and room mother of Dirk's third-grade class and she says Dirk will grow out of his sadness. Look at all the sadnesses she's had to grow out of, beginning with her husband's desertion.

So there isn't any father (this contributes to Dirk's depression, in the words of the school psychologist) though there was one once, named Peter. Ariella thinks that Bonnie and

Peter did drugs together a lot and that he went off to fry his brain alone when Bonnie quit.

They must have been on drugs to give her and Dirk their ridiculous hippie names even though the whole hippie thing was over with long ago. They should have stopped being hippies before they had us, is what Ariella thinks. Maybe Dirk's palsy came from drugs. Maybe hating Bonnie behind her back came from drugs, too, and not from loving her too much to admit.

While they're chipping and raking out soiled bedding they can hear their mother singing away out front. She's stacking firewood the Baptist church delivered in a big dump truck last week, just slid out yards of split logs into a pile and drove off. Bonnie jokes that she's a Baptist-agnostic, but four cords of oak are worth getting saved once a year. They have two woodstoves and the house is always toasty warm.

They inherited this house from Peter's family, who called it a camp and used it weekends and for a couple of weeks in the summer. It has no indoor plumbing, something Ariella is careful not to bring up at school or 4-H meetings. She never really minded until a couple of years ago, as if it were perfectly normal to have to put ashes on the icy path to the outhouse or pee in a chamberpot in the kitchen in the middle of the night. For b.m.'s you went outside no matter what, that was a house rule. They have a cold-water tap in the kitchen sink and there is always hot water in the kettle on the woodstove. But when Ariella visits other houses, she spends a long time in the bathroom gravely memorizing the configuration of tub and shower, toilet and basin. A mirror over the sink with fluorescent lights would be neat. Pale yellow tile on the walls and dove gray ones on the floor, that's what she plans to have in her house. Plus a big glass jar of bubble bath crystals.

Any minute now she is going to get her first period and then she'll be trundling to the outhouse a zillion times a day to check if her napkin is all bloodied. Her best friend Maggie, whose mother is a state senator, has already begun to menstruate. Men-stru-ate, three syllables. Maggie's mother said when she was a girl they called it flying the red flag. Bonnie snorted when Ariella told her this. She said where she came from they called it getting the curse.

Ariella still finds it hard to believe that everybody female over the age of twelve bleeds once a month, they keep it such a secret. One of these days she's going to get up the courage to ask Mrs. Arkwright, who is Maggie's mother's mother, what they called it when she was a girl. Even though Mrs. Arkwright is old enough to be their great-grandmother, she insists that Ariella and Dirk call her Helen, which is her first name.

Ariella and Dirk spend a lot of time with Mrs. Upright, that's how Bonnie refers to her, which Ariella thinks is plain ordinary jealousy. She is a fixture in Dorcasville, says Bonnie, who grew up in New Jersey herself and would give anything not to be known as a former flatlander. Helen was born in the house she lives in and she plans to die there. She has Welsh ponies that are the great-great-great-great-grandchildren of ponies she started out with; ponies with little pointy ears and bright Arab-like eyes. She used to go to shows with them and she still drives them around in pairs sometimes.

Moreover, she has an ambitious vegetable garden (for no good reason, says Bonnie, who has a good-sized one of her own) and she pays Ariella to help in it. Dirk mostly watches because he doesn't see well enough to plant the feathery little seeds of parsnips and the microdots of lettuce. Helen always has something for him to do, though. He brushes the patient ponies and he washes Helen's show cart, a phaeton.

Ariella is mortified when she discovers how it is spelled. She's been seeing it in her mind as *fayton*.

Your mother is pretty terrific, Helen tells Ariella. You should be proud of how self-sufficient she is. This is in response to a discussion of bummers, which are newborn lambs the ewes can't or won't nurse. Ariella really wants one because she has heard that a bottle lamb is much easier to train than one raised with its mother. Last year, in 4-H— it stands for Health, Head, Heart, Hands—the visiting county agent told Ariella that she was going to have to walk Mocha a mile a day for a whole month to get him trim enough to take to the 4-H show.

Look at it this way, Bonnie said. Be glad you live on a dirt road and have some place *to* walk him. What if you lived downtown, on Center Street?

What Ariella said in reply to that was predictable.

I don't want to hear another word about bathrooms, Bonnie told her. And you can stop mooning about your long-lost father, too. He was only good for one thing, like a borrowed ram.

Ariella's first class, Fitting and Showmanship, was the one she worried about most. Mocha not only had to be svelte and spotless for it but his fleece had to be exactly half an inch long. All over. That in itself demanded some heroic labors, mostly on Bonnie's part, as she wielded the shears. He had to stand quietly in his halter and lead line, squared up on his recently bootblacked hooves.

His performance was respectable enough for Ariella to go on to 4-H sheep camp for a whole week of ovine education. While she was there enjoying the communal bathroom with four sinks, three toilets, and two showers, she allowed herself to be homesick for her mother a couple of times. Also, she thought about her father. She didn't have a single living memory of him, only of the way his barn jacket smelled. (It still hung on a hook by the back door.) She thought that Bonnie's hating Peter was probably a way of defending herself against loving him too much. Maybe she smelled his jacket, too.

Once the sheep pen is decent, Ariella gets Dirk to help her wrestle a bag of shavings onto the toboggan. Together they pull it to the shed and tear the kraft paper open. They make two more trips before Bonnie is satisfied. By then, the new snow has magically whitened the smudged pasture.

Last year, Ariella's other lambs were named Cocoa and Butter Pecan. One of the other girls in 4-H, the granddaughter of a dairy farmer, was a bit cannier. She's been naming her lambs after states. So far, Wyoming and Mississippi have made it to the big time. Her best friend Maggie has lambs called Marigold, Petunia, and Violet. Bonnie tells Ariella that she may be painting herself into a nomenclatural corner.

They are just sitting down to Bonnie's vegetable lasagna (Ariella's secret favorite) when the phone rings. It's Lila Anderson, on the far side of Dorcasville, a call Bonnie has been expecting. One of her aged ewes, a Cheviot, has a newborn she can't nurse, born this morning. They've milked out the colostrum, if Bonnie wants her. It's snowing pretty good so they'd like to bring her up right away.

The lamb, a tiny, pure white female, arrives in a laundry basket. For Ariella it's love at first sight. Bonnie's already set up Dirk's old playpen in the kitchen and the kids line it with newspapers. Vanilla settles in, greedily empties a two-ounce bottle of colostrum, and falls asleep. In exchange, Lila, who is also a weaver, takes one of Bonnie's ewes, the one with the silvery brown fleece she's had her eye on.

For unfathomable reasons as attributable to sunspots as

to stock market conditions, this is going to be a big year for bummers. Not an hour later, the phone rings again. Gertie, the Delbert Lords' prize black ewe, the one who had mastitis last year and now has only one usable teat, has just delivered triplets. One is a little ewe lamb, very weak. There won't be enough colostrum for three, but Rebecca Lord has a pint she froze last week, when one of her ewes had a stillbirth. Just their luck, she says, to have the births so far apart. Otherwise she might've tricked Beulah, mother of the lost lamb, into taking on two of these. She's dried up now, though.

Their nearest neighbors, the Lords run about sixty head on their farm, which is a mile up the road, uphill all the way. In order to take advantage of the Easter market they breed early and lamb early. They are kind but unsentimental about losers and winners. It is decided to leave the weakling on the mother; Bonnie drives the sometimes unreliable old Ford pickup up to the Lords' place to collect the two black ram lambs. One she will give back when it's ready to run with the flock. The other, she'll get to keep. Dirk goes with Bonnie and Ariella elects to stay home with Vanilla.

What should only be a twenty-minute trip—ten up, ten back—stretches into an hour. Ariella is not going to worry. It's probably the truck, she tells herself, and it turns out she's right. Delbert drives Bonnie and Dirk and the two bummers back down the hill in his Bronco. Even so, he barely makes it into the turnaround.

Looks like it's turning into a good nor'easter, kids. No school tomorrow.

He ought to know; he drives the school bus on their route. Bonnie says she won't be needing the pickup in this weather anyway and they all joke a little about being snowbound.

The wind picks up not long after the three lambs are snugly

packed in the playpen. Bonnie pops some popcorn, since there won't be any school tomorrow. She mixes up a batch of lamb milk replacer and goes out to pull down some more hay for their flock, securely penned in their shed. And while she is out, the power fails.

Resourceful Ariella opens the woodstove box just enough so she can see across the room. She fetches the emergency candles from the shelf by the window and is just tilting one into the flame to light the wick when Bonnie comes back in.

That is goddamn dangerous, Ariella. She uses her totally uninflected I-could-kill-you-for-that tone.

I didn't know where the matches were.

For future reference, they are *in. this. drawer.* Then she relents and says in a normal tone, Always strike away from yourself.

The wind is a presence now, wailing around the corners of the house and slamming doors in the treetops. All three lambs start in at once. Vanilla is so much smaller than the coal-black woollies (Ariella has already named them Coffee and Chocolate but can't yet tell them apart) that she is getting squashed. It is decided to swivel the couch around to block off the kitchen and then liberate two lambs at a time. They skid around on the linoleum, dodging chairs. It's better than television, a regular baaing convention.

Almost happy, Dirk falls asleep on the couch watching. Ariella and Bonnie set up the Scrabble board at the kitchen table. By the light of two candles and an old kerosene lamp they each draw seven letters. Straining up the grade toward them they can hear the lovely grating music of the plow.

They must be expecting a good one if they're clearing in the middle of the storm. Else it's the Jack Daniels I gave Rusty for Christmas.

Ariella goes to the window to watch as the grader lumbers

into the turnaround, its flashing lights rotating as it negoti-
ates the tight space. The sliding will be terrific tomorrow!
She and Bonnie listen to the machine's slow retreat. Ariella
feels a little twinge of regret. For one sunlit moment, while
the plow headlights slanted in their windows, she could belong
to the world outside. She turns back to the game. Bonnie
has made *quest* on a double word score.

Afterward, no one will be able to say how it happened. A
candle fell to the floor; a lamb bumped the table and the
lamp fell into the playpen; guttering wax dripped unnoticed
and eventually ignited the newspaper. The kitchen is aflame
in an instant and then the couch is engulfed. Dirk is
screaming, Bonnie snatches him up in her arms, flings open
the kitchen door and rolls with him in the snow.

Ariella finds that her mind has divided from her body. It
is hurling directives from somewhere else, somewhere up
high. Her body grabs jackets off their hooks by the door and
heaves them outside. Somehow her hands find her boots and
Vanilla at the same time. Going out, she throws the lamb
ahead of her, clear of the doorway.

Dirk is sobbing Mommy Mommy Mommy and Bonnie is
cradling him, kissing him, weeping tears onto his uncovered
head. One whole side of him is badly burned. Oh Dirky,
darly Dirky, Bonnie is rocking and rocking him, it is all
happening in slow motion, the house lit from inside now like
a Halloween pumpkin.

Ariella is somebody else. She is in charge. She guides
Bonnie to the sheep shed, thrusts her inside, rushes back to
capture soaked and shivering Vanilla who is lying inert on
the snow. Finds the jackets and hands them in through the
sheep pen door. Stay in here, Mommy. You'll be warm
enough. Vanilla too. I'm going for help.

It's only a mile, she keeps telling herself as she strikes

out through the now unfamiliar cottony landscape. Her feet trot up the roadway where it was plowed, stumbling here and there where the wind has mounded drifts. This is the mile you walked with Mocha. They killed him. The other two lambs are all burned up by now. It's only a mile.

At some point she becomes aware of the jacket she has pulled on, a foreign jacket that hangs down to her knees. Her father's abandoned jacket with its adored smell. My father was just a borrowed ram. My mother is Bonnie, my Mommy. Poor Dirky, poor Mommy.

Delbert Lord is plowing his barn driveway. As he backs out and half turns to make a wider sweep, his headlights pick up Ariella. She is bathed again in false sunlight; as he stoops over her she whimpers, Fire.

Dirk is coming home tomorrow from the hospital in Pittsfield. Home, for the three of them for the time being, is with Helen Arkwright, whom Bonnie is now calling Helen. Vanilla is off her night feedings, thank goodness, and has her own stall in the pony barn. One of the black ram lamb bummers lived, no one can figure out how. Delbert says the other one asphyxiated right off and didn't feel himself burn up. Delbert told Bonnie that the saved lamb can belong to Dirk, if he wants it. Ariella doesn't know whether the survivor is Chocolate or Coffee, so they're going to let Dirk decide what to call it. It's still in a playpen in the back hall, but will be ready to move to the barn in another day or so.

During his two weeks in the children's ward Dirk has grown progressively more cheerful. The doctors say there isn't going to be any appreciable scarring. *Appreciable*, a word Ariella collects. Was it being with other suffering kids that turned him around? Was it nearly dying in a fire that leveled his home? Or, as Bonnie insists, was he simply out-growing his melancholy on his own schedule?

Ariella now calls Bonnie Mother. It's a formal word and feels rusty in her mouth, but they are both getting used to it. Her period has still not arrived. She did ask Helen, though. Helen says in her day they called it falling off the roof. Ariella thinks she would like to invent a new figure of speech. She will call it catching your bummer. She will rush out to meet it.

HEY DUDE

Gusty winds and strong rain have been scouring Pickaway County all day. The roads are slick with fallen leaves; dead branches lie scattered everywhere. It is late Friday afternoon when Abigail Haines backs out of the driveway in her Volvo station wagon—the Beast, Bret calls it—to go pick up her grandson. And that is when the dying sentinel maple at the corner of the barn crashes down on the car roof.

The reasons Abigail drives a Volvo wagon she cannot afford are: (1) She can haul hay, grain, dog and cat kibble in it; (2) five adolescent boys of diverse dimensions can crowd into the back along with Bret to be conveyed to soccer practice; and (3) her four dogs can go along with her if she feels like taking them. Sometimes taking them is easier than rounding them all up and luring them into the house.

Bret has been hers to raise since he was four and still wet the bed. Hers since anything red was a source of danger and had to be neutralized by walking backward until he could touch something black. Since the whole year, in first grade, that he insisted on wearing his next-day school clothes to bed the night before.

Years ago, Abigail Farnsworth roamed this community, a jaunty rebel with long auburn hair down to her buttocks. Fresh out of St. Ann's prep school she married the local garage attendant (the marriage was annulled), moved in with a dog handler, traveled all over the country with him training and showing German shepherds, and fell in love with the breed.

The Korean War ended, people began to buy art treasures, fancy ponies, protective dogs. But it was time for Abigail and her handler to part amicably. In Lovetburg she acquired her first two Connemara ponies and met and married Thomas (Bud) Haines Jr., of equal rank and station. He taught biology at the Fraxton School, a coed progressive institution the Farnsworths had always shunned, and she taught equestrian skills painstakingly learned at St. Ann's.

A controlled alcoholic, Bud was capable of keeping his sunny side up to the world. Abigail finally, acrimoniously, got pregnant; she had not really wanted a baby. From a childhood full of laundresses and maids, gardeners, stablehands, and cooks she found herself upper middle class and land poor, breeding lovely Connemaras she and Bud had to scramble to feed.

Her lawyer father had loved Dickens, books with good leather bindings, shad roe at the Oriole Club. A man who never cleaned his own tack, he rode for thirty consecutive years with the Fraxton Hunt. Her mother never went into the city without her hat and gloves. She was famous for her candelabra and dinner parties.

By the time that Nan was born, the ashes of both of Abigail's parents sat in urns on the mantelpiece of Five Maples Farm. The hunter hacks were gone, supplanted by Abigail's Connemaras, and several German shepherds had the run of the place. Bud came and went at will. He hadn't longed for fatherhood, although a son would have pleased him. When Nan entered first grade he and Abigail agreed to an emancipating divorce.

Still with her are four dogs she thinks of as family members. Morris is a grizzled fifteen; his son, Archer, is only a little younger. Sweetie Pie, a runty little bitch Abigail keeps out of pure contrary affection, was adopted from the pound the day she was to be euthanized. Lacey, the final one, is Abigail's last link to Nan, her disappeared druggie daughter. Nan has been gone for ten years, going on eleven; Lacey was hers.

Several cats police the barn, as do unnumbered bantams. Abigail likes the companionable gabble of them underfoot. Also, they clean up any dribbled oats.

Not that the ten Connemaras dribble much. The market for these large ponies used to be extraordinary. Abigail could count on a well-broke four-year-old to fetch $30,000 or $40,000. Off it would go with a fat little rich girl astride to sweep all the pony classes at Covington. Nowadays it is hard to sell any of them for $5000. But every April Abigail goes on breeding her pony mares to Cuchulain, her Connemara stallion. It is what she knows how to do, and besides, she could not live without it. By which she means the whole process—the standing at stud in the spring, the ultrasounding of the mares to see if they have "caught," the eleven-month wait for foals to be born, with all the white nights that entails for Abigail when their due dates approach, those first glorious days of new foals staggering around their mothers, the lovely summer months with mares and their sucklings decorating the pastures. The cycle, that's the attraction. Abigail says that's how she knows she's alive.

•

The demise of the tree, the biggest one of the five that line the approach to Five Maples Farm, happens in slow motion. First there is a *whoosh*, like a jet plane taking off, then a crack, which Abigail experiences as the sensation, under local anesthesia, of a wisdom tooth being extracted. Then a roar of freight trains, followed by the silence of a vacuum. She hardly notices the actual impact of the tree trunk because she is suddenly blind and deaf. Her head hurts. Has she fractured her skull?

It takes her a few minutes to realize that she isn't actually sightless. She can still hear, but all that foliage draped across the windshield and both sides has totally enclosed the car. How like a bird, Abigail thinks dreamily, wrapped in maple branches. It's her head *and* neck now, aching away. And something else is nibbling at the edges of her consciousness.

Bret, her grandson. She'll be late picking him up at dancing class. Bret takes modern dance on Fridays and is gorgeous at it, supple, ravishingly loose-limbed, he's going to make a career of dance if he doesn't permanently maim himself skateboarding with his rowdy friends. In the hope of supervising this latter activity, Abigail has permitted a skateboard ramp in the upstairs of the barn. Down below, the ponies have grown inured to the hideous racket; none of them skitters at the after-school crashes and thumps any more.

Fridays, right after class, she and Bret always go to McDonald's for the standard fare and after that, with split-second timing, they dash to Columbus for their tandem weekly sessions with Dr. Popkin. Once a month they meet with him together, like a couple whose marital discords he must adjudicate. Abigail refers to him as Dr. Popup. Bret, at the psychiatrist's insistence, calls him Matt. The idea is to defuse the threatening authoritative father role and substitute that of an older brother. Dr. Popkin was the school counselor's idea a year ago, when it was feared that Bret, always borderline hyperactive, was approaching meltdown.

Abigail appreciates the Popup input, as she thinks of it; she can use the moral support. Bret resents everything these days; of course he's entitled, with an absentee mother and an unknown father. There's a certain opprobrium that attaches to a teenage boy who has to live with an old crone grandmother. At least to a white boy in an upper-middle-class suburb, Abigail amends. Right now she wishes she had a cigarette, although she hasn't smoked for ten years. If she could just light up, lean back, take a deep drag, it would ease the pain.

She has had Bret through chicken pox and a broken leg the summer he fell off the barn roof chasing a kite, temper tantrums that verged on convulsions, which she aborted by throwing cold water in his face (considerable retrospective disapproval voiced here by Popup), failing grades, a touch of sleepwalking, pimples, showers of such dimensions they depleted the hot-water supply, and now girls.

Very aggressive girls, in Abigail's opinion, though she prides herself on her open mind. They phone him early and late, their mothers ferry him around to parties on weekends. She is touched to learn in one of Bret's unguarded moments that Spin the Bottle is still a popular option. Though where the hormonal flush will lead them she shudders to think. Bret is already lobbying for a learner's permit a year down the road. So far she has managed to stall him on grounds that he must pull all of his grades up to B's and do his evening barn chores cheerfully and regularly, rather than in the current sporadic and angry mode.

Nan at least had loved the dogs and ponies. Bret has Nan's blue eyes and ever so slightly beaky nose, an appealing combination. He is tall and skinny with freckled arms and promising shoulders. His manner is deliciously offhand, which tantalizes the girls. The offhandedness carries over to chores but Abigail can be quite grimly insistent. Also insistent about his language. She fines him 50 cents every time he calls her Hey Dude, she will not have it. Yo Bro is the same.

Grandmère, he says, for revenge. It's probably the only thing that took in French I. She can't imagine how he will turn out.

Sometimes Abigail takes the Cointreau bottle and a crystal cordial glass left over from her earlier life upstairs with her and sits watching late-night television, cradling Nan's graduation picture in her free hand. She talks to it silently, feeling the liqueur loosen her joints, feeling her elbows flap. Nan was doing drugs even then. *I can stop any time I want,* she told Abigail. The same furious way she used to declaim to babysitters: *You're not the boss of me!* The same outrage displayed by the ten-year-old Nan, left behind at a fence, screaming as she jumped to her feet, *Get me a new pony! This one's no good!*

At first there were postcards from Nan from New Mexico, Arizona, then northern California, as she meandered from commune to rehabilitation center to ashram. Then even the Christmas and birthday cards ceased. Abigail hired a private eye who tracked her to a sheep farm in Oregon. From the dips and pauses in their one phone conversation, Abigail deduced that the old Nan had vanished, leaving only this pathetic burnout. She surfaced once more in Santa Cruz, where her stay was brief and unsatisfactory (this from a priest working with street people), then fled to Mexico to avoid arrest on a drug rap. Abigail wonders every day if Nan is still alive. Chances are fifty-fifty, she thinks.

"Don't worry," Bret said, six months into the Popup regime. "I know my mother did drugs. I think she's probably dead by now. Of an overdose, I mean. So don't worry, I'm not a user and I don't plan to be."

"Maybe she's not dead," Abigail said. "Maybe one of these days we're in for a happy surprise."

"Don't get your hopes up, Grandmère."

Whenever they speak of her Bret always uses the past tense; Abigail fights to retain the present. She tries to foster the idea of Nan as mother, she encourages Bret to raise up his memories but for the most part it's a game he will not play. "I remember the dogs got fed before I did," is the kind of thing he will say. "I remember she screamed at me a lot."

"She sang to you," Abigail says. "She has a very sweet voice, she sang you all sorts of lullabies, real ones and nonsense ones."

"Maybe she did. Maybe she had her good moments. The thing is, I only remember . . . little rotten details."

"You hate her for leaving you," Abigail says. That's a very Popup remark.

"I used to hate her. But now she's dead and gone there's nothing left to hate."

It is very dark inside the Volvo. Little rotten details, Abigail is thinking. Bret knows how to get to her. The knife pain is spreading now, down from the top of her head into her neck, down into her spine as well. The wind seems to have let up, though. It's hard to tell; everything is muffled by the downed tree. Very cautiously she experiments with moving. The head pain is constant; stretching side to side doesn't seem to influence it. The left front door handle is jammed. Inch by inch Abigail attains the far handle. Inoperable. Damn! The top story of the maple has swallowed up the entire car, a whale taking down Jonah.

Some way to climb into the back? God, how to? The roof pleats under her fingertips as she gropes, wincing, for a body-size space. Then begins the perilous ascent over the front seat through a crawl space barely wide enough to admit her shoulders. It's like giving birth; no, *she* is being born through this jagged metal birth canal.

At one point Abigail slips into a dream state. Nan is there, and an old boyfriend whose name Abigail has forgotten. To her horror he is doing a line while Bret watches. "Now you try it," he instructs the boy. "Keep the straw up straight and just sniff slow and easy." Abigail reaches up to knock the mirror out of his hands and comes to, shivering.

The same agonizing struggle to try the back doors. No luck. But wait! There's a crack of gray, a different darkness, a milkier film, along the tailgate. The impact of the tree must have sprung the snap lock. Someone screams with pain as Abigail forces the back window up and rolls herself out.

What comforts her is knowing the ponies are all fed and in their proper turnouts for the night. The dogs, too, fed and housed; Morris, who is now frequently incontinent, is locked in his safari cage and Archer lies alongside him in another one. The other two have the run of the house but by now, Abigail knows, they are sleeping on the living room sofa. She thinks how cozy it would be to curl up there between them and just gradually drip dry, she hasn't the strength to bathe and clean up.

But the next time she comes to she's inside a ring of light.
One of the faces peering down at her is Bret's. After waiting
half an hour for his always punctual grandmother, he called
the house. When there was no answer but his own smart-
alecky voice (*Hi! This is Morris, Archer, Sweetie Pie, and
Lacey. We're too busy eating the cats right now to talk, but
you can leave your message at the sound of the beep*), he had
the good sense to call the police.

Such as they are, Abigail thinks. Sam Holt, still an awkward boy in his uniform but with boots now and a gun, used
to clean stalls for her. She tries to say his name but has only
a vague croak.

"Don't try to talk," several voices say in chorus. "Lie
still, don't talk."

"Ms. Haines? We've got a stretcher here. We're taking
you in for x-rays."

"Not a chance," she says, and this time her voice works.
"Just get me into the house, Sam. Let me get into some dry
clothes."

Sam insists. "It's my duty as a police officer and a par-
amedic."

"Read me my rights, Sam. The right to stay home, the
right to have a quiet concussion, the right not to have any
health insurance [she doesn't]. I'm conscious, I have my
rights."

"You're bleeding."

She puts her hand up to her head. "Just a nick," she says
but doubts it.

"At least let me take you to Doc Harrel's?"

Red Harrel, a hometown boy, briefly her lover forty years
ago. Made good in Cleveland tending strokes and heart
attacks, now retired to a quiet family practice.

"Abby Farnsworth! You fall off your horse this hour of night?"

Whistling through his teeth he neatly shaves a strip on either side of the gash and takes seven stitches. He doesn't discuss x-rays with Abigail; he knows better, but gives her some codeine and strict messages about staying off her feet for twenty-four hours.

"Wake her every two hours," he tells Bret. "Set your alarm and wake her every two hours all night. Just be sure she can be roused so we know the concussion isn't a fracture. If you can't wake her up, don't waste time. Call me."

"I'll be roused," Abigail promises them. But she dozes off in the front seat of the cruiser before Sam pulls into her driveway. "It's just the codeine," she assures Bret. "This isn't any worse than half a dozen other tumbles I've taken in my life."

The two of them get her inside, up the stairs and onto her bed. She insists she can manage the rest on her own. Bret leaves, then pads back in.

"Gamma?"

"Mm."

"I've got my alarm set for midnight, I just wanted to warn you."

"Mm. Fine."

"Want me to take the dogs out?"

"That would be nice," she manages to say, then sinks down.

Bret is here again. She is sure it is part of the same conversation but he's bending over her, shaking her gingerly. "Dude, hey Dude, come on. Wake up."

"I'm awake, lovey."

"You okay?"

Her head is pounding but the rest of her seems to be working. "Mm. Fine."

"Okay. See you at two, Dude."

"Fifty cents, Dude," she says, and drops off at once.

THE MATCH

At first he mistook her for a lost child. Watching the tassel of her knitted cap bob up over the granite ledges as she made her way toward him he gradually revised his image. Even as he was being discovered he could see this was a young woman, slightly built, moving awkwardly across the uneven terrain. Unused, he thought contemptuously, to woods walking. As she came up to him, a little out of breath from the climb, he saw she was no longer young although her face had weathered well with smile crinkles at the corners of her generous mouth. It was the snub nose that helped him mistake her for a child.

His one outing of the season when only antlered deer could be taken, he was none too pleased to be walked up to. From where he crouched on his stand he had an almost unbroken view across the glade and partway down the ledges. A providential dusting of fresh snow had fallen overnight powdering the rocks and pine duff. His own footsteps now barely showed; he had been careful to skirt the clearing and climb to his stand as economically as possible. Now he was ready, as ready as any cougar might have been fifty, a hundred years ago, for the big cats knew how to wait to pounce.

The tree stand was traditionally, not technically, his. The property belonged to an out-of-state flatlander named Walter Chester who had bought up huge tracts during the recession and was still holding them, doubtless waiting for the market to improve. By now he had probably forgotten he owned this east-facing slope of Grimes Peak.

The small person had reached the foot of the tree and called up to him. "Why are you doing this?"

"What are you doing out here? Who are you?"

"I live down there." She gestured behind her. "I'm trying to find out why you're doing this, what the purpose of it is."

"Jesus!" He replaced his rifle in the sling and clambered down from the platform. "The purpose is to take a deer, lady. It's hunting season, didn't you know that? Here's my license."

"Of course I know that. I mean, why are you hunting? Why do you want to kill a deer?"

He was baffled but only for a minute. "What are you, one of those animal rights nuts? Don't you know the deer would starve if we didn't thin the herd every fall? Or you, you bleeding heart, would you rather see them starve to death?"

"There's no real scientific evidence for that, you know. It's just a line the gun lobby puts out for propaganda. If the deer weren't hunted to death they wouldn't reproduce so heavily and the population would level off."

"Lady, that's just about the dumbest crock of . . . oh hell. I'm not gonna stand here arguing with you. Just turn around and go back the way you came. You've already ruined the morning for me and prob'ly the afternoon, too."

"Do you do it for food? Do you like to eat deer?"

He didn't especially like venison steak. Ground up it made a passable hamburg and doctored, an even better sausage.

But he wasn't crazy about the taste of it straight. He gave most of it away.

"It's none of your damn business if I eat it or stuff it. Now get outta here before you get shot at."

She was persistent. "Does Mr. Chester know you're here?"

"This land's not posted. Chester knows better than to post his land. And besides, he probably doesn't even know where his property lines are."

"What does that mean, 'he knows better'?"

"Lotta things happen on posted land. Soreheads'll chop down trees, shoot up signs. One time a bunch of guys sank a rowboat just by plugging it with shells over on Nonesuch Pond. Absentee landowner puts up all those No Hunting signs, he's just asking for trouble."

"It just so happens Walter Chester is a friend of my family's. He'll be interested to hear this. I'm renting the caretaker cottage from him."

"Wonderful." Wes picked up his 30.30 and began sighting along it.

He was determined not to say another word. Sure enough, she turned around and started back toward the ledges. Even in the presence of a raised rifle she walked like a proud cat, never hurrying.

Wes had hunted this area ever since he was old enough to carry a gun. At first he went out with his father, a man not in the habit of saying much, and he watched and crouched beside him and tried not to hiccup or scratch himself. His father brought down a deer every year but one and that one was a hard winter with deep snows. The deer all yarded up in cutover lots lower down the mountain and it was more like shooting fish in a barrel than a man stalking deer with his rifle and his wiles. He didn't even buy a license that year.

Well, the old man was seven years dead. Wes's sister had left Liston five years ago to marry the music and arts teacher in the next town. There were no other siblings. Wes had an ever-changing population of strays, lost or abandoned dogs he had taken in, black and tan, spotted and splotched damaged dogs that were his family. Everybody in Liston knew he was a sucker for dogs. Also cats, but he was not passionate about cats. They didn't meet you halfway.

Like most people in his part of the country, he was respectful of bears. He believed every bear story he heard. He honored coyotes too, for their quick wits. Maybe they brought down a lamb or two, but mostly they preyed on mice and moles. They ate berries, fish. Once he'd watched a coyote casually stalking grasshoppers and catching them in his mouth in mid-jump. Porcupines were vermin in his book, along with woodchucks; skunk didn't rate much higher. You could club a porcupine, just step on his tail and clonk him with a two-by-four. Wes had pulled enough quills out of enough dogs to whet his appetite for finishing off any porcupines he came across.

If questioned, he would have said he loved deer, loved their secretive presence, the sense of a whole herd of them fanning out, even as he hunted. Loved finding the flattened wallows where they had bedded down. In tall grasses you could spy out a group, four or five all traveling together, lying down together. Lots of times in late summer he'd put up a doe and her fawn, faced them across a clearing, the fawn's tawny spots making it almost invisible in the dappled sunlight. It was something to see.

The day was ruined, he was sure of it. That woman's footprints were visible little ovals laid out like a lure bisecting the glade he had been at such pains not to sully. Her odor was in them and worse, the scent of her perfume, her hair

spray, whatever foreign smells she carried. These would linger for hours. He felt violated by the encounter, unnerved
to have his rights questioned, his compact with the land cast
in doubt.

He knew those crazies were out there, he had read about
them picketing experimental labs—and here he had felt a
warm onrush of sympathy thinking of dogs held prisoner in
metal cages, tortured and then sacrificed for the advance-
ment of medical science. He had read with an almost glut-
tonous fury about rabbits having their eyelids sewn open to
permit technicians to test for allergic reactions to drugs and
even to various cosmetics.

But he had never connected these protests to deer season.
Or bird season, for that matter. Though he didn't care for
duck, from time to time he hunted grouse and bagged his
limit. They made a good small meal, legal and plentiful in
October. Kinder, he thought, than supermarket chicken which
he privately called concentration-camp chicken, knowing
the conditions under which they were raised. Why are you
doing this? he kept mimicking her lilting treble calling up
to him. Cute little open-faced thing, she'd gotten to him.
Yeah, Wes, why the fuck?

As it turned out, he got an eight-point buck late that
afternoon, not more than thirty minutes before sunset. Wes
was honorable about hunting hours and leery, too, of being
caught in the woods at twilight. Eighty percent of all hunting
accidents happen just at sunrise or when the light is fading;
he remembered reading that. It was fully dark by the time
he got the buck field-dressed and dragged it, leaving a trail
of red on the snow, out to his pickup. Grunting from the
effort, he loaded it into the back; he'd take it to Deveraux's
Hardware, the official inspection station, in the morning.

He would have to admit he delayed getting into town till

midmorning in hopes there'd be people around to admire his take, and he was right. It was a bright crisp day for getting errands done; half the town crowded up to the scales where his buck broke 180 pounds, not quite a record. Dev measured, inspected, then tagged it as it hung swaying a little in death, its glazed eyes open. Several little boys daringly poked and stroked its hide. The wispy woman from the woods, coming out of the store with a package under her arm, locked eyes with him as he glanced around. He looked away first.

Since it was the first Saturday of the month, he stuck around for the EMT drill, which was held at noon in the firehouse, preceded by pizzas and followed by beer and horseshoe pitching, if the weather allowed. Wes had been a member of the emergency medical team and the volunteer fire department ever since he came of age twenty years ago. Joining up was part of turning twenty-one in Liston; he had never questioned it. It said you were a responsible citizen; if not a family man, at least not a hell-raiser.

He was married, briefly, that same year of his majority. In Liston, New Hampshire, you pretty much married your high school sweetheart. His, Mary Ellen Dowd, had gone to college out of state, which was in itself unusual. Wes had signed on at the telephone company with his dad right after high school. Most of his work was laying out new lines, which suited him. He guessed he knew every back road in Liston County by heart. He knew where the wild daylilies flowered and which pond's spring peepers gave earliest voice. Often he could take his latest rescued dogs with him. Desk work was a disaster he chose to avoid whenever possible but Mary Ellen thought he ought to take an administrative job and try to get ahead.

She didn't care for the way he hung out with his rowdy

buddies late at the firehouse or went off to the tavern on the highway with them for a few beers. Wives traditionally raised these objections and husbands good-humoredly placated them with white lies and excuses, but in Wes and Mary Ellen's case, things escalated into pitched battles.

Wes wasn't a fighter by nature. He was a low-key guy, kept his own counsel. He treated women carefully, pretty much watched his language around them, never raised his hand to one. Not like men he knew who just lost it when they drank. Beat up their women, then played this game of a thousand sorries after. Flowers and all that, courting them all over again.

They actually got along a lot better after the divorce. Mary Ellen met an aspiring lawyer down in Concord and eventually they married and started a family. She and Wes still exchanged Christmas cards and every once in a while he'd run into her when she came back to Liston to visit her folks.

Bachelorhood suited him. But he wasn't a recluse. He bought a pre-cut log cabin and assembled it over the summer months on a five-acre lot that bordered the federal wetlands. His nearest neighbor was a mile in any direction. Every June he threw a big bash for summer solstice with kegs of beer and loudspeakers blasting rock music well into the night. And every Sunday after Thanksgiving he spread a buffet with venison meatballs and red wine. Everybody came.

The women really let down their hair at Wes's parties. People paired off in the goddamnedest combinations; he was always a little obscurely ashamed the next day reviewing these events. He wasn't in the habit of sleeping around though it sometimes happened. He didn't really want a steady woman, a fact that was generally known in town. Mostly he stayed home and talked to his dogs and watched cable TV, which came in at a discount rate on the telephone lines.

Right into December, Wes was out on the Grimes Peak Road overseeing the installation of nine new poles. The Liston phone company was converting some of its old lines that zigzagged through woods on right-of-ways to less maintenance-dependent lines along the roads. The men were hurrying to get poles into the ground before a hard freeze closed them down for the winter.

Going in and out the one-lane road twice or even three times a day Wes couldn't avoid meeting his little woods walker. He had since learned her name was Julia and she was a "fiber artist." "What the hell is a fiber artist?" he had asked Perry Damon, his informant.

"You know. She does things with wool," leaving him with a vague image out of his grade school history book of a woman carding and spinning fleece.

And then he saw an exhibit of her work at the Liston Christmas Fair: felted mittens and berets tarted up with embroidery, some loose-woven throws with knotted fringes, and something that looked like a rug but was meant to hang on a wall, with interlocking animals woven into it. "A tapestry," he was told. The price tag was $1200, which guaranteed that he wasn't going to buy it. He went back a couple of times just to look at it, to study the stylized animals that seemed to be dancing in tandem around the edges. They were a puzzling procession: What looked like an oversized mouse was linked to a cat, in turn hanging on to a dog that seemed to be chasing a pig. At the front of the little parade, a child. The pattern repeated all the way around. He marveled at the intricate design, the way the colors shaded into one another. He could see she really was an artist.

The morning of December 10 when her car overtook him on the Grimes Peak Road he wasn't sure how to act, so he nodded and lifted one hand in terse acknowledgment. By the time she came back from town, though, the backhoe was planted across the road and she had to stop. It was obvious to both of them that a brief chat was in order. She initiated it.

"Well, I see you got your deer after all."

"Yup."

"Is it good?"

"Don't know. I sent it over to the Chesley Home."

"What's that?"

"State home for folks that can't live on their own any more."

"So what are you eating?"

"Oh, lots of things. I got some brook trout still in the freezer from last spring."

But then the backhoe finished maneuvering. She bumped the Nova out of neutral and into drive and was gone.

"Hope she isn't planning to drive that hunk of junk all winter," he said to no one in particular.

She was gone over Christmas and most of January. He knew this in the way that small-town news travels. Jimbo Flood, Liston's one plumber, had been called to come out and drain the pipes. He would go back and restart the system on the 20th. He'd had to build a helluva roaring fire just to warm the place up before he dared prime the pump.

Wes didn't have any official reason to run out the Grimes Peak Road but toward the end of January he told himself it might be good to see how the poles were setting up now that there was two feet of snow on the ground. He had heard the sound of wheels futilely spinning, wearing away rubber, before he even got to where the road bends and begins to climb. Her Nova was wedged sideways on a slick patch. There was a sand barrel a little farther on; he had a shovel in the truck so it didn't take long to free her.

"You'd best get some grain bags full of sand or even a couple of concrete blocks to carry in the trunk of this thing. Road's gonna get lots trickier than this."

"Thanks. Hey, I wanted to say I'm sorry about . . . that day up there." She gestured behind herself in the direction of the ledges. "This isn't an apology or anything, I still don't believe in hunting, but I'm sorry I spoiled your day."

"S'okay. Now it's none of my business but if you're thinking about staying all winter you oughta get rid of that Nova and pick yourself out something more suitable. Something with a stick shift and four-wheel drive. Automatics are no damned good on these hills."

"I might stay." She turned a smile on him so vulnerable and radiant that he felt heat rush to his face. She held out her hand. "Julia Mather. Soon to be Julia Hesselstrom again."

"Wesley Kingsley. Never been anything else." He smiled back. They shook gloved hands and exhaled little ghost puffs.

"I might stay," she repeated. "I have a little money. My kids are grown and gone. One's in law school, the other's a painter, she's in California."

He was frankly stunned. "You don't look old enough to have grown kids."

She made a little face that said she had heard that before. "You?"

"Oh, I'm just a fixture. Born and raised here, work for the telephone company. Had a wife once, long time ago."

They didn't exactly run out of things to say. It was as if, Wes thought afterward, they had both arrived at a crossroad, a four-way stop, and neither was certain who should go first. He thought she could have invited him back for a cup of coffee or to see her work. He thought she thought he might refuse or he might make a pass at her or God knows. He thought he should have mentioned the tapestry, he could have asked her to explain it. He found he couldn't imagine her life, he didn't have enough to go on.

Ten days later his beeper went off just as he was sitting down to his supper. He stashed his plate on top of the fridge where the dogs couldn't get it, shut the cats into the back hall, jammed his feet into his boots, and took off, licensed dome light twirling, for the fire station.

"Fire at the old Chester place," Perry told him.

"How bad?"

"Can't tell. Pumper's already out and so's the ladder truck."

"It'll be a bitch if we have to pump in this weather." He wondered who had turned in the alarm. She must be out there; nobody else would have seen a fire till the place burned down to the ground.

"You better believe. Guess we'll go in your truck," Perry said. "Mine's skippin' again."

"Points?"

"Prob'ly."

By the time they got there they were superfluous.

"Chimney fire!" Perry spat his quid out the truck window, half in disgust, half in relief.

Ray Jenkins and Charlie Santos had hauled the steaming woodstove out of the cottage. It sat on the satiny snow crust like a surprised black bear.

Inside, the stovepipe dangled from the chimney flue, its elbow bent at an improbable angle. Windows had been opened to dissipate the smoke. It was almost as cold in as out of doors. Julia Mather stood in the middle of a group of volunteers. She looked pale and a little scared; they always did, after the crisis was over. He hoped she wasn't going to faint.

Apparently she had let the stove go out during the warm afternoon, then attempted to start a fire when she got back from her errands. Cold stoves are stubborn starters. When the fire didn't catch promptly she added several wads of newspaper imperfectly crumpled. These ignited all at once, lodged in the pipe cutting off air flow, and a severe downdraft sucked the rest of the papers into a fiery mass. Clouds of smoke billowed back into the room, a familiar scenario. At that point she panicked and dialed 3434.

". . . dizzy," he heard her say.

"Get a blanket, somebody," he said, shouldering his way into the group. "Charlie, see if you can heat up some water, she needs some hot tea or something."

It was an electric stove. While they waited for the teakettle to hiss, Wes opened several cupboards in search of a tea bag.

"What's this stuff?" He dangled a square packet with foreign symbols on it.

"Miso," she said. She was now sitting at the table wrapped in a rose-colored comforter and she was still shaking.

"Whaddya do with it?"

"Drink it. It's like soup."

"Smells like a goddamn Chinese restaurant. You got some coffee somewhere?"

"No."

"Tea?"

"Any whiskey?" Ray asked.

"Whiskey's the worst thing in the world for shock," Wes told him.

"There's some chamomile tea over there, on the left." She gestured above the stove.

"Jesus, not that sissy stuff," Ray muttered to Perry.

"I'm sorry," she said. "I don't keep any stimulants around."

Wes didn't like the looks of her lips. They were still a pinched lavender. Little spasms of shivers were coursing through her body, making her teeth chatter. There was something appealing about her, even desirable. He wondered about the stimulants remark. Was she a former alcoholic? He stirred the miso and handed her the mug.

Within an hour the squad had cleaned creosote out of her stovepipe and chimney flue. Wes himself clambered up on the roof and shone his company flashlight down to check for any obstructions. Charlie and Ray carried the stove back in, with rather more grunts than were required. They reattached the pipe, leveled the stove, relaid a fire, and got a good blaze going. They instructed her in the care and feeding of woodstoves in general, airtight cast-iron ones in particular.

"You guys go ahead," Wes said. "I'm gonna stay awhile and put up a good pile of kindling so we don't have to come back out here again."

They shuffled around a bit as they were leaving. Perry gave Wes a broad wink. "Don't wear out that little hatchet."

Since there was nothing else, he fixed Julia a second cup of miso; himself, chamomile. "Where's your milk? You run out?"

"I don't use milk. I'm a vegan."

"What's that?"

"Someone who only eats plants."

"You mean like a vegetarian? They eat milk and eggs and things."

"Ovo-lactarian vegetarians do. Vegans don't."

"Judas Priest. No wonder you're such a slip of a thing. Whaddya live on?"

"Fruits, vegetables, nuts, whole grains. Lots of soybean products."

"You mean like tofu?"

"Tofu is one item. There's also soy cheese, even soy ice cream."

He grimaced.

"Want some peanut butter cookies to go with the tea?"

"Criminy, you mean you eat cookies?"

"Well, I don't have two heads, Wesley. I was stupid about the stove, I don't eat meat or dairy products, but I do have a life."

"Yea-zoo, I didn't mean you didn't, I just . . . ."

"Well, you act like you think I live in a cocoon. I've been around, I've been arrested five times, I've gone to jail."

"Arrested? What for?"

"Criminal trespass. Theft. Destruction of government property. Disorderly conduct. Resisting an officer." She ticked them off on her fingers.

"Come on, Julia, don't bullshit me. Theft of what?"

"Theft of cats, for one. We broke into a lab at Preston University and stole six cats they'd been injecting with various paralyzing agents, cats that were going to be 'harvested'—that's the euphemism they use for killing them."

"Oh, that's it. Animal rights, I remember reading something about it in the paper. Oh yeah, it fits."

"You think I'm crazy."

"I think you're crazy but I respect it, you know? I gotta respect you for living what you believe. You steal anything else?"

"Mink. Primates. Dogs, most of them family pets that were picked up on the streets and sold to biomedical labs."

"Jesus H Christ." Wes was amazed. She looked like a perfectly ordinary person, definitely not the warrior type.

"You have any pets?"

"Dogs. Five of them right now. Summer people drop them off in my driveway when they're sick a them. Some go to the pound, some I keep. I try to keep the puppies, give them a good start."

She winced.

"See, people don't have respect for animals, they treat them like a Nintendo game or something. See, if you needed to take out a license to have a dog or a cat, there wouldn't be so much . . . abandonment."

"Five dogs. I never would have guessed it."

"Couple a cats too." He said it modestly, aware he had just won a hundred brownie points.

"Be careful. Next thing you know, you'll be joining our group."

"What's it called?"

"AA. *Animals All.* Our slogan is: A rat is a cat is a dog is a pig is a boy."

"I get it. Is that what you put in the border around your tapestry?"

She looked pleased. "You saw that?"

"Saw the whole exhibit. You're the first artist I ever knew close up."

"Thank you for telling me."

He closed his hand over hers, felt her stubby, tough fingers. She did not pull back.

He stopped by the next day with a pickup truckload of split hardwood from his own pile.

"You shouldn't have done that."

"You've only got a cord, cord and a half out there. It can get a whole lot colder than this here. You better believe."

"I've got backup electric heat. I don't like to use it much, it's so expensive."

"Well, this'll hold you for a bit." He hesitated. "You gonna ask me in?"

"Certainly."

He ended up staying for lunch, which was surprisingly normal. Vegetable soup, homemade bread, apples and cookies.

"I don't s'pose you'd come over for supper one night? Meet my dogs?"

"I'd love to," she said, not missing a beat. She bestowed that smile on him and this time he felt the flush begin in his groin.

"Another thing. You can call me Wes."

"My friends call me Jules. My fellow thieves call me J.J."

"You're lucky to have two names. I'm just plain Wes to friend and foe."

It snowed steadily Thursday, the day she was to come over. He didn't trust the Nova so he went to fetch her himself. Driving back, he tried to explain about the snow, how it lifted everyone's spirits, how it was good for the pastures—"poor man's fertilizer, they call it"—good for insulating the ground, wells, houses. Good for horses' and cows' hooves, for the skiers, for replenishing the reservoirs.

"Why, that's practically a prayer, Wes," she said, embarrassing him.

He knew she was an animal nut but he wasn't prepared for the reception his dogs gave her. It was downright eerie the way they howled and fussed and rolled over on their backs to have their bellies scratched.

He had given the meal much thought, not wanting to contravene her code. He fixed a pasta sauce laced with plenty of garlic and mushrooms and he put a dish of Parmesan cheese on the table, which he sprinkled liberally over his portion. She passed it by. He'd bought an apple pie from Ella's, an authentic local bakery. He topped his with vanilla ice cream. She had peppermint tea while he doused his coffee with cream. The dogs lolled under the table. Not one growled or snapped at another. The cats sat on top of the refrigerator, the Maine coon cat with the torn ear kept his yellow eyes fixed on Julia while his bushy tail hung down, forming a plume.

"So you don't drink coffee or tea or beer or wine?"

"I'm a recovering alcoholic."

"That's what I guessed. Well, you came to the right place. So's half this town."

"I went off the deep end a few years back, after the really bad arrest. I couldn't sleep so I started pouring myself nightcaps and then I found I couldn't stop."

"What bad arrest?"

"Oh, this was in Michigan the night we broke into the university."

"You broke in?"

"You always try to commit your sabotage at night. We destroyed their files on mink research, they claimed it was thirty years' worth."

"You just ripped up the papers?"

She laughed. "No, better than that. We set them on fire. But three of us were caught and the cops were really brutal."

"You take the cake," Wes said. He couldn't picture her in that environment.

"I don't like to talk about it. They hog-tied me, if you know what that is."

He nodded.

"And two of them beat me up on the way to jail, ruptured my spleen."

"Jesus. These were men beating on you?"

"State troopers. Good old boys."

Wes made some commiserating sounds.

"The thing is, they'd been staking out the lab for weeks, waiting for something to happen."

"But what I don't get is, why do you want to put yourself on the line like that? When you know people are gonna jump you for it?"

"Wes, I've cared about these things all my life. I care that people still club baby seals for their fur. That fishermen cut the fins off shark for Chinese restaurants and then toss them back in the ocean to die. I've been there, it's so ugly. Even rats. I'm not fond of rats, but if you've ever seen them trained with electric shocks to run a maze. . ."

"So now you're out of jail and on your own?"

"Well, first I had a sort of breakdown. Too much pressure from all sides. I pretty much got out of the movement . . ."

"The animal rights movement?"

"The activist, confrontational part. Then I joined the other AA—"

"Alcoholics?"

"Right. I went to meetings every week for about a year. And now I just try to stay clean."

She got up then and started clearing the table.

"I'll wash," Wes said. "You can dry if you want."

The last cup was in her hand when he came up behind her, lifted the hair on her neck, and asked, "Would you get mad if I kissed you?"

She turned to face him. "Where is this going?"

"It isn't going anywhere you don't want it to go."

"Wes. It's been four years since I've kissed a man."

"Well, let's not wait any longer then, okay?"

She opened her arms and took him in.

Fitted against him he smelled her hair, unperfumed but faintly minty. Her mouth opened under his as she kissed him back. He ran his hands down her sides and cupped her to him as he grew hard. But the dogs went wild, scrabbling to get between them.

"You see who they prefer," Julia said. "Now I'm an interloper."

"Don't be too sure. I could be the one they want to drive off."

After some order had been restored Wes suggested they retreat upstairs.

"It's cozy up here under the eaves," she said in his monastic bedroom. "Toasty warm."

"Warm air rises," he said, and facing each other they began to undress like two teenagers at a strip poker game. At that moment his beeper went off.

"Shit!" He rebuttoned his shirt.

She pulled her sweater back over her head.

"I've gotta go, I can't not go, you know?"

"I know."

Her tone was so level that he couldn't tell how she meant it. Was she disappointed or relieved?

"You stay here, Jules. Maybe it won't take long. We get a lot of emergency calls that don't amount to anything this time of year." He swiped his lips across hers, then leapt down the stairs.

Jimbo Flood's parents' dairy barn had burned down. Out of thirty head of cattle they'd only been able to save sixteen. It was the worst disaster in Liston since the 1962 hurricane. There'd been a rash of electrical fires then as the winds brought down power lines, poles, transformers, or so the old-timers said. This fire was electrical, too; a defective cooler had shorted out.

Wes could still smell the charred timbers, hear the live cows moaning for the others as they milled around directionless. His ribs were bruised from the jostling he took as he and Charlie raced into the barn, hooting and shoving, shooing cow after cow into the open. He didn't feel the kicks so much, it was their sheer weight pressing on him. The cows' lowing in terror like the rising of a terrible wind was a sound he hoped never to hear again.

He and the others struggled to round them up, driving them through stinging sleet into the open pasture where all they could do was huddle like football players. It was pitiful. Even though there was a stand of pines at one end of the pasture, the Floods would probably lose some more before they could arrange to get the survivors trucked to neighboring farms.

It was well after midnight when he returned bruised and bone-weary and caked with soot and mud. She had left the outside light on. The dogs, accustomed to the sound of his truck, whined a little but didn't bark.

He tiptoed upstairs. Jules was asleep in his bed, in his flannel pajamas. He took a long hot shower, rooted around in his bureau for another pair, and slipped in beside her.

She woke long enough to identify him. "Wes?"

"Shh. It's 2 A.M. I'll tell you in the morning." He curled around her and spoon-fashion they slept.

When he woke, her side of the bed was empty but the imprint of her body was still there. He could hear her downstairs talking softly to the dogs. The storm had cleared. A brisk wind now whipped up great froths of snow and swirled them into the trees so that it looked like a fresh snowfall was under way. March had come in like a lion, all right.

"There you are. I made you some coffee."

He took the cup with a little salute, then sat down facing her to tell about the fire.

"God. Those poor people! And the cows, cows are so afraid of fire."

"All animals are. Don't know how many'll pull through." He was secretly pleased that her first response was sympathy for the humans.

"You must be beat. And hungry. Maybe we can have some oatmeal?"

"Listen to me, Jules. That's the first time I've spent a whole night with a woman in umpteen years."

"Really? How'd you like it?"

"Don't know. I fell asleep so fast I didn't have a chance to . . . appreciate it. I'd like to try again."

"Before breakfast?"

"Before breakfast."

"You'll be late for work."

"I'll call in sick."

As they started up the stairs together she said, "Where's your beeper?"

"In the truck. I'm not taking any more chances."

Word got out around Liston that Wes was keeping company with the lady who almost burned the Chester place down. Although he suffered the ribbing good-naturedly, he didn't volunteer any information about Julia. What they did or said, where they went or spent the night was their own affair. Mostly she stayed over in the cabin. Five dogs were like having children all over again, she said. Days, he went to work and she to her studio in the caretaker's cottage. Her work was going well. She said she had started a new tapestry, this time with cows in it. The Floods sold off the survivors. They were putting the farm up for sale and moving to Florida.

"With the rest of the snowbirds," Wes said, disapproving. Julia said how sad it was to see good people leaving the land. Although she didn't approve of keeping dairy cows.

"Well, what about raising sheep? What about the ram lambs, you can't use but one or two for breeding. If you don't sell them for meat you've got to castrate them. What about that?"

"I know. But shearing their wool once a year feels different to me from keeping cows, breeding them for calves in order to rob the milk. And those little vealers raised in slatted cages in the dark, not even able to turn around, that has to be the cruelest practice."

"I agree with you there. Round here, though, people raise them on grass, mostly they don't pen them up."

"So it's a short happy life. But what right do we have to do it?"

Silence was Wes's first reflex. He rooted around warily for something to say. "Thing is, I wish you didn't care so much."

"I know. I went overboard once. I'm learning not to obsess."

"How do you do that?"

"I use up some of it in my weaving."

"And the rest?"

"I do this with it." She pounced on him, tickling him in the armpits until, howling *I give up!* he caught her in a bear hug.

With something close to sorrow he saw that he had fallen in love with her. To him she was a small mysterious goddess whose values often struck him as bizarre. He saw he was ready to spend the rest of his life unraveling the mystery.

Fitted together like spoons they would drop wordlessly into sleep. One night he would awaken inside her dream and then he would know the world that she knew.

Little by little Wes gathered that there had been a major nervous collapse. Not one big dramatic moment the way it happens on TV and you see the person led away drooping between two starched attendants. Jules's had been a sort of gradual decline. Of not wanting to get up in the morning and then not wanting to eat and on top of that, more vodka downed earlier and earlier until evening had backed up into afternoon. She told him that her marriage had begun to come apart well before her breakdown. Her causes sat down with them at breakfast, crawled into bed with them at night, breathing between them in the king-size bed.

He understood that she was trying to warn him. "I don't scare easy," he told her.

In mid-April he rototilled a space for her garden and watched as she plotted what to plant where. Because the garden was so close to the cottage he didn't suggest fencing it. He didn't count on the lawless ways of several generations of rabbits and woodchucks that had laid uninterrupted claim to that space. All the lettuce went down in one night and about half the peas were nipped off at ground level.

Shooting was out of the question. Gas bombs in the chuck holes were vetoed, too. His Jules was a vegan without a garden. But the Swiss chard pulled through and, cunningly wrapped in hardware cloth, several broccoli seedlings thrived.

He didn't taunt her with questions about how the vegetables she bought at the grocery store were raised. Those acres and acres of soybean fields must have harbored thousands of rabbit nests. Farmers learn how to be ruthless. Did she make the connection on her own?

Black flies, that terrible scourge of the north country, came on schedule. It was mid-May.

"They'll go as soon as the mosquitoes get here." Wes bought her an Adirondacks hat to wear out of doors, a skull-cap with netting that hung down long enough to be tucked in a shirt.

"God. I never thought I'd pray for mosquitoes." She pulled out a packet of seeds and studied the instructions on the back.

"Jules, it's too early for squash."

"Too early? It's got to be eighty degrees today."

"And tomorrow it could frost. You've got to wait till the oak leaves are the size of a mouse's ear."

She looked up at the bare branches. "A mouse's ear? What kind of scientific measurement is that?"

She wouldn't come to his June solstice party. It had nothing to do with meeting his old friends. No, it wasn't the rock music. Or the beer. She was around people who drank all the time and she hadn't succumbed.

"Well, what is it?"

"Nothing. I just don't . . . do parties."

"What about gallery openings?"

"That's business, not pleasure."

"Jules, it would mean a lot to me."

She looked stricken. "I can't do it, Wes. I . . . have to go to New York that week."

Sometimes she came sharply into focus for him, like a painting done with a child's primary colors, the outline inked in with a thick black pen. All summer it was the plight of the dolphins and killer whales. It was the relentless navy teaching dolphins to defuse bombs in the harbor. Teaching them to pick up objects off the ocean floor. Forcing them to dive deeper and deeper, beyond their range. Teaching them to recognize mock-enemy frogmen underwater. Several dolphins had died of mysterious ailments.

She drove down to Connecticut to observe the protests, although she swore she wouldn't take an active part. "Never mind the issue of capturing them, taking them prisoner. Just ask yourself, what right do we have to make animals fight our wars?"

"Even if it saves lives?"

"It's a moral issue, Wes."

"Promise me you won't get mixed up in this?"

It was one of the July dog days. He had taken the afternoon off. They were lying side by side on a mangy strip of beach at the local lake. Her neat, compact body bound in two strips of cloth lay so close to his gangly freckled one and yet not touching; he could not stand the hunger he felt. "Marry me, Jules."

"You want to marry me to save me? God, Wes, what can I say? I'm not sure we're a good match. I'm not sure we're any match at all."

"We're a perfect match. And if you don't get in the water this minute and start swimming I'm going to fuck you here right in front of the good citizens of Liston."

Over the late summer while the squash prospered and a few beans began to climb the tepee he set up for her, he felt her distancing herself from him. She was inundated with visitors—sunshine patriots, she called them, but he suspected they were her fellow conspirators—and after they left she was frequently too tired to come for supper. Even his vegetarian pizza couldn't tempt her.

At the end of August, a gallery in Soho sold her new tapestry. She called him with the news; she was bringing supper.

"Ta-da!" Out of one brown bag she took four zucchini. "Home grown." Out of another, some strange-looking yellow things that she identified as chanterelles.

"You mean they're wild mushrooms? How do you know they're not poisonous?"

"Trust me."

He had to admit it was a wonderful if poisonous stir-fry. "Marry me, Jules, just in case. We can die happy."

It was an ardent night. Afterwards, they slept as soundly as exhausted athletes. She tickled him awake before the sun came up and inveigled him into making love again and then she left him to get an early start on the long drive to New York City.

"You're wearing a groove in the thruway," he told her, hugging her close at the door of her car. He who had never seen Manhattan, who had only been to Boston once and chose not to go back again.

"I'll be back in a week. I'll call you."

After six days he ran up the Grimes Peak Road to check on the garden for her, although he was damned if he was going to pull any weeds. Her mailbox at the end of the long driveway was stuffed full to overflowing. He gathered up the newspapers and fliers, rifled through the letters—nothing personal, just various agency pleas for contributions—then left the stack inside her screened porch.

What was he looking for? A love letter? Some clue as to her whereabouts?

On a hunch he shaded his eyes and peered into the living room / kitchen. It looked just as he remembered it, only much tidier. None of her papers, tools, utensils, not even a wilted floral arrangement; she was forever picking wildflowers and assembling sprawling bouquets of the commonest weeds. To Jules, goldenrod was parlor worthy.

From this angle he couldn't see into the workroom but he knew how to get inside without picking any locks. Around back he shouldered open the bathroom window Jules had slipped through one night when she forgot and locked her key ring inside.

The studio was bare. Her loom, her spinning wheel, all the paraphernalia for her felting were gone. The wall hangings, the assorted mittens and slippers, belts and berets were gone. He couldn't take it all in. She must have spent days packing up, patiently breaking the loom down in order to crowd it into her car. He knew before he entered the bedroom that it too would be swept clean.

There was a note on the bureau with some folded-over bills, weighted down by a key.

"Eventually you'll figure this out, dear dear Wes. I didn't have the courage to tell you face-to-face. My life in Liston was too lovely and a lot of its loveliness was your fault. Meanwhile, my guilt just grew and grew. I've gone back undercover so it's no use looking for me. Just know I will never forget what we had together.

your J.J.

P.S. Here's $30 for Jim Flood. Please ask him to come up and drain the system and leave the key under the 2nd brick on the R out front (that's where Mr. Chester hides it)."

It was a week before he contacted Jimbo. He couldn't face the enormity of her absence. And then, one night, making his solitary supper, moving among and talking to his dogs, he thought of Ray Waterman, the tamed, reduced Iroquois who taught music in the Liston primary school forty years ago. Every fall Ray was persuaded to open the music program with a war dance. Decked out in feathers and beads and poster paint, this grown man stomped across the stage and shook his rattles as accompaniment to a high, nasal keening that sent shivers coursing down young spines. Every boy in the class elected to study drums. The girls got penny whistles and triangles and were known as the rhythm section.

They only got to see Ray Waterman once a year in his Indian regalia. The rest of the time he stood at the blackboard in shirt and tie demonstrating half and whole notes on the treble clef.

Jules, he thought, was like that. What he had seen was the tamed Jules. The true terrorist self, J.J., had never surfaced in his presence. He could only guess at its nature.

The hardest thing for Wes was having to face the hopeful excited millings about of his dogs day after day when he drove into the yard. It was clear they had not forgotten. He wondered how long it would take to dim their expectations. As long as her scent lingered, he guessed.

Early in November he took in a soaked mongrel pup not more than three months old. Perry had found it being swept downriver. He named it Jay and let it share his bed until he could get it socialized with the others.

When hunting season opened on the second Saturday of the month, Wes was ready. He rose early, put on his orange cap and vest, loaded his rifle and sling into the pickup, and drove out the Grimes Peak Road. The sun was just coming up as he started scaling the ledges that led to his tree stand in the glen. It was a flaming sunrise, unusual for autumn. As he climbed up over the granite outcroppings the sun's rays blurred his vision, bringing tears to his eyes, but he was back in his own skin.

FLOTATION DEVICES

From the outset, the all-day snorkel boat trip looked a bit tacky. The line of tourists queueing up to board was long. Three dozen in all, young, tanned, and athletic looking, being handed aboard negligently by two languorous types in charge. One was a native of Minor Island and proprietary about his vessel (no shoes on board). His assistant, a lanky Louisianan with a broad Delta accent, wore a silver ring on the third toe of his left foot. The three women friends, Laney, Anna, and Maureen, divested of their shoes, which were added to the broad assortment of others' sneakers and espadrilles, hightops and sandals stuffed into canvas bags and stowed in the bow, scaled the ladder to the abbreviated upper deck in full sun.

Not their first choice, Laney remarked, but the lower deck, shaded and with cushioned seats, was packed tight. She suspects that the boat's legal limit had been exceeded but decides not to mention it. A little flicker of disappointment came and went on her still-handsome face—steep stairs were not easy, given the arthritis in her hip joints.

Practical Anna unzipped the duffel and handed round the T-shirts and cotton pants they had been advised to pack. It is odd that Anna, with her carefree, bohemian past, has in middle age become the list-maker and straw boss.

Maureen pulled on her ancient jeans. She feels a rush of affection for the worn, faded cotton. It denotes a day at home, off campus, release time. As others in some ancient religious ceremony had once anointed themselves with holy oil, each of them applied sunblock 15. Anything over 15, according to a dermatologist colleague of Laney's, is a waste.

While the boat was still at its moorings the heat was oppressive, seeping into what Maureen called their aging pores. Finally the engine coughed and turned over and soon the stiff breeze of passage mitigated the fierce rays of the sun.

Laney is a gynecologist, Anna an artist. They first met twenty years ago at the Donner Trail Ranch, where each was being processed for a divorce, and they have vacationed together annually ever since. Pummeled by Chinese masseurs in Beijing, feted in Abruzzi after Laney extemporaneously delivered a client's newborn infant on newspapers spread on the floor of the cafe, adored in Arizona where Anna's Tempe exhibit of big-breasted clay goddesses was hailed as a political statement, they are a study in harmony.

Laney is in her sixties, Anna not far behind. Like college roommates, they tell each other their dreams at breakfast. They compare wardrobes and figure faults, they inspect their old love affairs as scrupulously as botanists peering into the blush-colored thickets of pistils and stamens. Both are women who have surmounted all manner of crises to arrive at their careers.

Laney was thirty-five when she entered med school—battered her way in, she likes to say. In her forties, a respected gynecologist who pioneered *in vitro* fertilization, she became an activist. Almost once a week you could read her expert testimony in the *Times* in court cases involving rape, abortion, and wife-beating, as it was then known. She has a file of hate mail from anti-choice fanatics—she refuses to call them pro-lifers—and has had to resort to an unlisted phone number to keep their verbal assaults at bay.

Anna often remarks how spectacularly successful Laney is at separating her private life from her public one. It's something she's always had trouble with.

Anna, who began life in a staid midwestern Lutheran farm family, number three in a cluster of six siblings, is a blithe spirit. She can live out of her helmet, she says, and means helmet, not hat, wearing one shoulder bag and carrying a canvas duffel into battle. Traveling light disencumbers her vision, but she is never without a little sketchpad and some smudgy stumps of pencil. Shapes are what she is after, shapes and textures, ideas that can translate months and even years after into great stone figures. If you study Anna, who is short and square, you begin to see that she would have an up-close blocky vision of the world and that she would need to write it large in the massy sculptures she creates.

Maureen is Anna's friend and contemporary from long ago, from the days when Anna was still married to Bart, who is now dying of AIDS. Back then, Bart and Anna and Maureen went skiing together almost every weekend, along with David, who had been Maureen's childhood sweetheart and became her spouse. Back then, Maureen's Ph.D. in Comp Lit was still fresh and virtually useless. Now she is well published; long married and five years widowed, the mother of two grown sons, she has an endowed chair, and when she looks in the mirror she has to admit it: Her face is falling in. Her dead husband, an architect of modest but impeccable reputation, taught in the same university. It was a peaceful life. Some might have called it monotonous. The civil rights movement, the Vietnam War, and their implacable hatred of Richard Nixon gave it some color.

By the time David died of a blood disease he had lived with for ten years, the two children were married and living on opposite coasts. Maureen had a year of insomnia, an intense, intractable sleeplessness she got through in David's woodworking shop. Midnight to dawn in his basement room she planed, routed, sanded, glued, and clamped, next to his radio tuned to a twenty-four-hour classical music station. Now she sleeps lightly, but goes to bed at eleven like an obedient child. Here on the Island she has been sleeping, as she puts it, like a stone.

Laney and Maureen have never met before this rendezvous on Minor Island. Anna in a sense is their Virgil, she knows the names and locations of every beach, including the nudist one. She knows the way down to the sinister strand that once belonged to the Mellons and where a lesser relative committed suicide by leaping from a tower of obsidian onto the rocks below. She knows how to get to the dark lagoon dotted with great egg-shaped volcanic extrusions, a brilliant patch of fine sand favored by islanders and accessible only by goat path. She knows which vegetable stand has the freshest—or the least dubiously unfresh—fruits and veggies and where to buy antacid or paper towels when the island's supply mysteriously vanishes. She further knows exactly how many gallons of water remain in the cistern of their borrowed house and how many minutes make an unacceptably long shower. "We never flush for Number One" is the island motto; rain water is its only potable source.

The owners of the house—a pair of pediatricians from Washington, D.C.—are patrons of Anna's. This is her seventh invitation to their hideaway perched on an outcropping overlooking the Caribbean. She knows the names and destinations of the cruise boats that anchor below the deck in the twilight and steam off around the point at dawn. She alone pilots the little Jeep that comes with the house along the treacherously narrow roads on Minor, only occasionally forgetting to drive on the left.

Today's view from the narrow balcony of the snorkel boat was its sublimely unchanging paradisiacal self. Hummocks of outlying mountains on offshore islets lay ahead, dots and dashes of sailboats between them. The water, which Anna characterized as falling between sea-foam green and Gauguinesque turquoise, shimmered and glinted in the full sun. The boat's motor thrummed a hypnotic sexual rhythm.

"What a great idea this was," Maureen said, and Laney murmured appreciatively. They still defer to each other a little warily, these two; sharing Anna, after all, could have created some problems but none has arisen so far.

Anna the organizer leaned back and smiled. "This is only the beginning, ladies. Wait and see."

By ten o'clock they were so ravenous that they had devoured all the turkey sandwiches and drunk half the water in their pre-frozen water bottles. At that point the intercom sputtered and coughed; the tour leader, whose name was Barnaby, came on with a hearty hallo. He pointed out Turtle Cay, Finnegan's Leap, and Copenhagen Point on the left, on the right, and dead ahead. Next came a casual lecture on how to adjust your mask and snorkel.

Maureen found his Island accent all but impenetrable. "Chaucer is easy compared to this. I only get about every third word."

Anna interpreted. "He says nobody allowed off dis boat widdout wearen dis flotation device." By standing up and craning forward, they could see a limp yellow gadget shaped like a long bib dangling from his hand. "Apparently there's a button you press and a tube you blow into," Anna explained. "Then it inflates."

For Laney this was comforting news. Neither she nor Maureen had ever snorkeled before yesterday when in the dark lagoon, floating over angelfish and silver fry, they had practiced with rented equipment; sometimes Laney's mouthpiece seemed to leak and she came up choking on a mouthful of salty water. Rather than complain, she solved the problem by taking the whole bite plate inside her mouth and clamping her teeth on the tubing. This morning her jaw was a little sore from stretching to accommodate the foreign mouthpiece.

Maureen had felt more than a little claustrophobic face-down, even in the shallows, but she forced herself to breathe normally by focusing on the coral sea fans and the little yellow-striped sergeant-major fish that burst in and out of her line of vision. Suddenly she drifted over a pale green turtle as big as a toilet seat and rose up sputtering her astonishment. Luckily, she could put her feet down on sand as he zoomed away.

Toward noon they arrived at their first snorkel site, in shallow water just off Copenhagen Point. The sea was pellucid and flat. Barnaby cut the motor; his assistant, Ronnie, set two anchors.

"Perfect conditions!" Anna enthused. One by one the passengers sat down on the flat stern of the boat, rinsed their masks, spat into them, and smeared the spit around with a judicious forefinger. The women smoothed the hair back from their temples and foreheads so the mask would seal. Some people began by donning their fins, others the yellow flotation vests.

Everyone seemed tremendously competent. In ones and twos they bobbled off into the transparent water and spread out like mini-submarines. A little tentatively, Maureen and Laney followed Anna into the water. Last off the boat, they straggled after the others.

Barnaby, wearing what looked like a rubberized sweater and carrying a red buoy, led the expedition. His odd covey trailed him, arms at rest by their sides like unused tentacles, buttocks bobbing above water like floating apples as they propelled themselves with little thrusts of their fins. A husband-and-wife pair stayed close on his heels, she with one hand tucked in the waistband of her mate's trunks. Another couple had lashed themselves together with a plastic line that had round bobbers attached. Clearly, staying together was a good idea. When Anna moved up with the main group, Laney and Maureen lagged, torn between wanting proximity to the boat and a desire to see what there was to see.

After about ten minutes of fanning and drifting, the main party turned in a general semicircle and splashed back raggedly.

"Barracuda!" Anna told them, spitting out her mouthpiece to say the word. Some snorkelers had begun to actually swim, using strong overarm strokes, back to the boat. It was a purposeful if not hasty retreat.

"Nothen to be skeered of," Barnaby scolded them after everyone had flapped up the ladder and regrouped. "Barracuda never bite you less you dead or dyen. Dey has to be blood in dee water."

"The book said never to invade a barracuda's resting place," Laney pronounced. She had been browsing the night before through the usual literature of place that accumulates in a vacation house. "In the presence of fresh blood, the barracuda will come out to investigate."

"And after conducting a cursory investigation," Maureen offered, "he takes a trial mouthful."

Laney thinks how refreshing Maureen is, so wryly good-humored. She has observed that women can do this for each other easily, more easily than men. Less at stake, she thinks. We are allowed to be afraid of barracudas.

"But did you see that school of creole wrasse?" Anna asked them. "The little blue and purple fish, about fifty of them, swimming in a sort of vee?"

Laney and Maureen had to admit that they hadn't. Once the boat was under way again, they were happy to cover up again against the sun and breeze. Anna dredged up a package of cookies she had been saving, and there were three pears left.

Maureen loves pears. She wishes Anna had packed more than three. How like Anna, actually, always even-handed and always in charge. She remembered the morning after a New Year's Eve party long ago when she and Anna found a pair of red-striped boxer shorts in the freezer. Not David's. Bart's, or maybe John Doe's? They were lodged between two bags of ice cubes.

Anna claimed she didn't recognize them. She had folded them up and put them in her shoulder bag. "At the very least they'll make a good dusting cloth," she told Maureen. Not that Anna was big on dusting, Maureen now thinks, and then feels uneasy, disloyal.

An hour later, Ronnie the Louisianan led the second shallow-water expedition, this time along a lovely sandbar abutting a coral reef that ran across the neck of an inlet. Abundant pale angelfish, filmy white ghosts with black fins and black markings like kohl around their eyes, drifted lazily past in little troops. Larger and more vivid spadefish merged with, then veered away from the gathering. It was possible, though not advisable, to put your feet down from time to time for anchor. The snorkelers were warned to be alert for fire coral and sea urchins.

Maureen wriggled closer in line to Ronnie. In case there were going to be any ugly surprises she wanted to receive an instant directive. But the viewing was leisurely and exotic. So leisurely that the woman in the red bathing cap and her male partner in whose waistband she seemed always to be rummaging almost didn't get back aboard in time. Ronnie had hauled anchor and Barnaby had already revved the engine as the two snorkelers rounded the reef.

By the time everyone had flippered out of the water after the second expedition, Laney was chilled.

"That's why these guys wear their partial wet suits," Anna said. "You have to realize, even though it's the tropics, there's about a twenty-degree difference between the water temp and your blood."

Laney pulled on her sweatshirt. She was tired. The flotation device had crept up around her shoulders and seemed to be tilting her downwards at an awkward angle, making it harder to keep up with the others. "God, my neck is stiff," she said to Maureen. "This sport is gorgeous, but fraught with peril."

"Considering how we've never done it before, I think we're making a terrific showing," Maureen told her. "Here. Let me try to loosen that up a little." Reaching over, she began to massage Laney's neck.

"At least we have this whole space to ourselves," Anna said. "Gives us a chance to spread out. Want to lie down here, Lane? Wouldn't that feel better?"

"Actually, this is heaven." Laney groaned with pleasure. "You go ahead, though."

Anna promptly stretched out on the deck between the benches of the little balcony and pillowed her head on a towel. "Wake me up when we get there."

Laney thinks, Anna's tired too, she just can't admit it. She's only two years younger than I am. She's going to out-last me just by pluck. Obscurely, Laney finds this comforting.

They ran due east for another thirty minutes. The wind had picked up and there was a considerable chop. Barnaby had less to say. Occasionally he called out a place name but the farther they went the less he seemed obliged to entertain the passengers. Although they were still in sight of land, the prospect seemed less hospitable, the distances greater. Here and there vast fortresses of rocks heaved their iron sides out of water. Some had collected enough earth to support scrub growth but most were barren piles of jagged-looking stony cliffs standing six feet or so above water. The boat headed toward a long, discontinuous collection of these, shaped like the gigantic vertebrae of a flexible dinosaur.

"Okay, dis here's our deep-water mooren," Barnaby announced. "You gonna see everythin' you came out to see, big en little. Dey was whale here last week. Jess don't go close dis side. We gonna tie up here, to dis ring the Coast Guard done cee-mented in. Reason dey done it, dey's lot of dope runnen round."

"They drop it from planes at night with light sticks attached," Anna said. "Ganja, they call it, marijuana. Then the partners come and get it at dawn with little speedboats."

Barnaby was still explaining. "Dere's bristleworm in dere, it kin sting you pretty good. Swim roun de odder side, dat's de bess place, some good caves go way in deep, and dey safe."

"What's so great about deep water?" Laney grumbled to

Maureen. She thought about sitting this one out but didn't want to be the wet blanket.

"Come on, Laney, we're gonna see us some whales," Maureen coaxed, and lowered herself into the sea.

The three women gave this side of Dinosaur Rock a broad berth. Once around the far side, true to Barnaby's prediction, there were myriad tropical fish, a football-field length of them, darting in and out of crevices, dodging staghorn coral and sea fans, even raining against their face masks and bumping blindly into their bodies. It was wildly beautiful and suffocating, all at once.

Laney looked back at the boat from time to time with a vague longing to be drying off on the little upper deck, to hear the motor chuffing its eggbeater sort of beat, and the soothing slow return journey under way. She could see Barnaby and his assistant eating their delayed lunch. Now they were drinking beer, that was it, *they* were dry and drinking beer, a whole six-pack of it while she gargled through her leaking mouthpiece, keeping up appearances. Anna and Maureen had ducked into a sort of alleyway that ran between two exposed hunks of spine. Anna was beckoning her frantically. Some incredible find, no doubt.

Laney had to paddle her way around an immense rock pillar to catch up with Anna and Maureen. Anna appeared to be sitting on a greenish plastic-covered hassock about the size of a small hay bale.

"It floats!"

"What is it?" Laney was baffled.

"Marijuana. Must have drifted in on the chop, then got wedged in here."

"What do you think we should do?"

"The first thing to do," Anna directed, "is to get it unstuck and float it out of here."

Maureen tugged, grunting. "If we just had a pry bar of some sort . . ."

Anna finally solved the problem. She took off her flotation device, dove down under the package, and on her third try managed to free it by butting with her head. The three of them stroked and shoved, finally working the bale out around the last rock onto the open sea.

The boat was gone. They could see it clearly steaming away from them, growing smaller as they watched it overtake the horizon. They could see the backs of people at rest against their cushions. Barnaby's back, too, was visible. He was at the helm, looking due west, heading home. The bill of his cap, tilted up on his head, formed a semi-halo against the sun.

Splashing furiously, Laney began to wave and call.

"Don't bother," Maureen said. "They can't hear us over the motor and no one's looking."

"I don't believe this is happening!"

"Look. Let's get out of the water, get up on the rocks, maybe we'll see a sailboat we can hail," Anna said.

Maureen paddled down the length of the spine, looking for a gentler slope. "This is about the best place."

"Not so easy." Laney struggled to haul herself up, slipped and fell back with a gasp.

"Oh Jesus, you're bleeding!" Maureen found a toehold and heaved herself up out of the water. "Here, grab this." She unclasped the flotation bib and held the tail of it out to Laney.

Anna boosted her from below and after a moment of blind flailing, Laney flopped onto the rock face, followed by a shaken Anna. The three of them perched on their pinnacle, taking stock. Laney's gashed knee continued to drip blood at a constant rate.

"It's not exactly spurting," she said. "But I think we need to stop the bleeding."

Maureen tugged and gnawed at the tube attached to her flotation vest; she was finally able to wrench it free. Under Laney's direction she twisted it around her thigh just above the cut.

"We have to loosen it every ten minutes," Laney directed. "But it's not such of a much, it should stop with this tourniquet."

"Always good to have a resident doctor when you're marooned on a rock pile," Maureen said.

"Somebody will come along soon," Anna soothed. "At the very worst, they'll figure out they forgot us and come barreling back in an hour."

"And if not them," Laney said, "the dope runners ought to come along after dark, wouldn't you think?"

"Where is that package anyway?" Maureen peered down to the cave where they had found it.

Anna pointed twenty yards out. "There it goes. Floating away on the chop."

"Too bad. We could use a little fix right about now."

"Oh? How would you suggest smoking it?"

"We could just chew some of it," Laney said. "That's what the kids do, after all, lots of times they bake it in brownies. Of course we don't know how pure this batch is or isn't." She shivered.

The sun was still glassy but a cloud bank had moved in from the west. Anna busied herself inflating the other two flotation devices. She spread one out on a relatively flat rock face for Laney to sit on, then propped her knee up on the other one.

"Thanks, love."

"Don't mention it."

"I wonder if one of us could swim for it," Maureen asked, eyeing the open water.

"It's got to be at least a mile across. And probably some current. Not easy, even with fins," Anna advised.

"I think we need to stay together. Try to stay warm. And alert. And calm." Laney loosened the tourniquet a twist. The bleeding had slowed but started up again. Wordlessly, Anna re-tightened the noose.

"We need to keep our circulation going," Maureen said. "There's no room to run in place, let's at least rub each other's arms and legs." And because it seemed intrusive to apply herself to Laney or Anna, she began briskly slapping her own biceps. She thinks, If they don't find us by dark we could all be in big trouble. A night in the open like this, all of us practically naked. She wonders how long a person can go without water before suffering dehydration. It doesn't seem appropriate to ask Laney this question.

Anna stood up. "I'm going back in."

"Are you crazy? What for?" Maureen asked.

"Going to get the marijuana. It's wrapped in plastic, we could use it to make a windbreak."

"Wait. I'll help."

"You stay with Laney. If I can get it close enough, then you can come down and help me haul it up."

Maureen squatted beside Laney and inspected the knee. "Does it hurt much?"

"No. I'm a little worried about hypothermia, though. I can't seem to get warm."

"Not in shock?" She took Laney's hand, then began kneading her shoulders and arms.

"Not so far as I can tell. Surprised but hardly shocked."

They watched Anna's inchworm advance, propelling the bale ahead of her, like a sea cow its calf. When she was close enough, Maureen worked her way down the rock face with both flotation devices and tied the waistbands to the strappings. She braced and hauled while Anna lifted and pushed. The bale was heavier out of water than they had expected. Maureen had to lean back and hold with all her strength while Anna found a way out of the water and clambered alongside.

"Finally!" Anna said, out of breath, as they brought it to the top. Laney meanwhile had gotten on all fours and crawled cautiously along the spiny ridge, scouting for an implement. There were plenty of loose rocks, but nothing with a sharp edge. Then she discovered a pile of jagged conch shells that had been shattered by birds and sorted through them for the best chunks.

"Great!" Anna and Maureen began sawing through the hemp strappings that held the plastic in place.

"This is like trying to butcher a side of beef with a butter knife," Anna said.

"Never mind. Keep it up, it's working!"

The square plastic wrapper, once they succeeded in opening it out, was just big enough for the three of them to huddle under. The redolent marijuana, still a luxuriant green, served as a mattress. They were under cover by the time the usual late-afternoon freshet struck, and lay together, flesh against flesh, stunned by the alternate growl of thunder and jabs of lightning visible on all sides.

"Animal warmth," Laney said. "This is how it is in the litter." A little light-headed now, she thinks in a detached way what an adventure they are having. How like Anna to prevail over the elements.

"This is how it was for Prometheus," Maureen said, as the sky savagely brightened and darkened around them. "Chained to his rock, baring his liver to the eagle."

"Gives you a little insight into the old myths," Anna agreed. She wonders if Barnaby has noticed yet that they are missing. Even so, she now knows they can hold out through the night, the three of them.

Laney realized she was holding her breath and exhaled slowly. "It's enough to make you a believer." Now she is warm enough to feel her knee throbbing. If they have to stay here all night she thinks it won't be terrible. Just uncomfortable. She is no stranger to discomfort.

Maureen finds herself almost dozing off, gently warmed by their combined body heat. A rock presses between her shoulder blades but it only causes a small gnawing ache. A smaller ache than grief, tinier than insomnia.

When the brief storm passed, a double rainbow appeared in the west. The sun hovering, just above the horizon, made a postcard appearance.

Something else materialized on that last thin sheet of light, grew larger and larger, and bore down on them, full throttle.

Barnaby was at the helm of a bright little powerboat. Beside him on the shelf, clearly visible through the windshield as he approached, stood three pairs of shoes.